THE BIBLICAL DOCTRINE OF RECONCILIATION

by

James Denney, D.D.

WIPF & STOCK · Eugene, Oregon

Wipf and Stock Publishers
199 W 8th Ave, Suite 3
Eugene, OR 97401

Biblical Doctrine of Reconciliation
By Denney, James
ISBN 13: 978-1-5326-4271-5
Publication date 11/3/2017
Previously published by Klock & Klock Christian Publishers, Inc., 1985

CONTENTS

CHAPTER I
THE EXPERIMENTAL BASIS OF THE DOCTRINE . . . . PAGE 1

CHAPTER II
RECONCILIATION IN THE CHRISTIAN THOUGHT OF THE PAST 26

CHAPTER III
THE NEW TESTAMENT DOCTRINE OF RECONCILIATION . . 121

CHAPTER IV
THE NEED OF RECONCILIATION 185

CHAPTER V
RECONCILIATION AS ACHIEVED BY CHRIST 233

CHAPTER VI
RECONCILIATION AS REALISED IN HUMAN LIFE 286

INDEX 333

CHAPTER I

THE EXPERIMENTAL BASIS OF THE DOCTRINE

RECONCILIATION is a term of wide scope and various application, and it is hardly possible to conceive a life or a religion which should dispense with it. There is always some kind of strain or tension between man and his environment, and man has always an interest in overcoming the strain, in resolving the discord in his situation into a harmony, in getting the environment to be his ally rather than his adversary. The process by which his end is attained may be described as one of reconciliation, but whether the reconciliation is adequate depends on whether his conception of the environment is equal to the truth. Men may be very dimly and imperfectly conscious of the nature of the strain which disquiets their life, and may seek to overcome it in blind and insufficient ways. They may interpret it as physical in its origin when it is really ethical, or as the misapprehension of a moral order when it is really antagonism to a personal God, and in either case the reconciliation they seek will fail to give the peace of which they are in quest. Nevertheless, reconciliation and nothing else is what they want, and its place in religion is central and vital.

It may be said that in the widest sense what men crave to be reconciled to is life, the conditions of existence in their sternness and transiency. Life is short and it is hard, and ever since men have thought and felt, they have been exercised

THE CHRISTIAN DOCTRINE OF RECONCILIATION

with the problem of how to adjust themselves to its laws and to find peace. They have a deep sense that life is lost when this adjustment is not made, and men live and die unreconciled to the very conditions of life.

> "Sed quia semper aves quod abest, praesentia temnis.
> Imperfecta tibi elapsa est ingrataque vita." [1]

Few men have been so profoundly conscious as the great poet who wrote these lines, of man's need of reconciliation to the very terms on which life is held. He did not seek to evade them by any light-hearted pursuit of enjoyment; his hope was in science, in the power of thought, in winning men to see and accept the inexorable necessities to which life is subject, and by accepting to overcome them. We may think that this is not much, and that as the necessities are inexorable it is all one whether we accept them or not, but this is really not true. It makes all the difference in the world whether a child accepts the order of the family in which he lives as an order not to be questioned, or is perpetually resenting it, and the greatest minds of our race have found a peace almost too deep for utterance in realising and accepting the inevitable order of the world. They are at once lost and uplifted in something unimaginably greater than themselves, and the words in which they utter their experience go deeper than ever plummet sounded.

> "Felix qui potuit rerum cognoscere causas,
> Atque metus omnes et inexorabile fatum
> Subjecit pedibus strepitumque Acherontis avari." [2]

---
[1] Lucretius, *De Rerum Natura*, iii. 957. See Ritschl's definition, iii. 189.
[2] Virgil, *Georgics*, ii. 490-2.

THE EXPERIMENTAL BASIS OF THE DOCTRINE

Here is a peace which passes understanding, a great reconciliation, coveted by the poet and promised to all who can master things in their sources, and, realising that they are what they are, can accept them as such. Whether they achieve it or not, there is an instinct for this peace in all human beings. As soon as we know anything we know that we are compassed about with necessity, and that to accept the necessities which nature lays upon us not only gives dignity to our own nature by making us partakers in the immensity of the universe, but brings rest and reconciliation to our minds.

If spirits so gifted as Lucretius and Virgil celebrated this reconciliation in the ancient world, it has had an even more illustrious prophet in modern times in Goethe. Goethe was not only a poet but a man of science, and he valued science not for its practical applications but for the sense it created and fostered of the ultimate oneness of man and the universe—in other words, for this peculiar reconciling virtue. In spite of frictions and tensions, it was one and the same power which revealed itself in the life, constitution, and course of nature, and in the being of man. The way to peace was not to resist nature, or to pervert it, or to triumph over it, but to realise our original and indefeasible unity with it. This is the cause, as much as the consequence, of Goethe's devotion to Spinoza. Nothing could be more congenial to him than a writer whose whole mind is summed up in the phrase, *Quicquid est in Deo est*. This was what he felt by instinct, and what he wished to see confirmed and illustrated by reflection, and therefore Spinoza was for him the prince of philosophers. On the other hand, he had a peculiar antipathy to Kant, because Kant was as profoundly conscious of the differences in the world as Spinoza of its ultimate unity. By emphasising these differences, and especially the ultimate difference between the physical and the ethical, and between right and wrong, with an implacable logical rigour, Kant gave the problem of reconciliation new aspects. It became far more difficult than when it was regarded merely as the problem of adapting oneself to the conditions of existence; perhaps in the form which it assumed in the hands of Kant, it became not merely difficult but impossible; the only philosophy Kant left open to himself was a philosophy of antinomies, all problem and no solution. But though the pantheistic reconciliation which merely assumes the unity of man and nature is less than Christian, it is not worthless or unreal. There are problems inevitable to the Christian which it has not raised, but on its own ground its value is not to be disputed. A truth which moved Lucretius and Virgil to the depths of their being, and which is pervasive and powerful in Spinoza, Goethe, and Wordsworth, is a truth which must have room made for it in every complete doctrine of reconciliation. We must have the peace which consists in being at one with the world and with the necessities in which it enfolds us, as well as the peace of reconciliation in the specifically Christian sense. And we must be able to bring the two into relation to each other, and to comprehend them as one.

In the ancient world the ideals known to the Greeks as ἀταραξία, and ἀπάθεια represent something akin to reconciliation. They represent a life that is untroubled either by circumstances, events, or emotions; and though they lend themselves easily to caricature because they easily degenerated into pedantry, they bear witness to some of the facts on which the need of reconciliation rests. The common life of men is restless, troubled, exposed to constant disturbance

THE EXPERIMENTAL BASIS OF THE DOCTRINE

both from without and within, and, different as their methods were of seeking to reconcile men to the conditions of existence, Stoics and Epicureans were far nearer than is often admitted in their conception of the end to be attained. Both wished to be delivered from what they saw made life painful and futile; both wished what might in a large sense be called redemption from a "vain conversation," and the reconciliation and peace which came in its train. The curious mixture of the Stoic and the Epicurean in Montaigne, whom a recent biographer describes as *Stoïcien par Epicuréisme*, and who alike in his Stoicism and Epicureanism was seeking to adjust his life wisely to the conditions of reality, shows the affinity of these different tempers. The solutions, however, of the problem of life embodied in terms like ἀταραξία and ἀπάθεια, and worked out by rules like ἀνέχου and ἀπέχου—endure and forbear—do not cover in its whole extent the need of reconciliation. They are moralising rather than ethical. Their interest is too exclusively in the individual, and they have too little sense of the original unity of man and nature so impressively represented by the great poets.

It is only when we come to the higher forms of religion that the problem of reconciliation becomes acute, and the experience connected with it well defined. The assumption—which is also the experience—of the highest form of religion, as we have it represented in the Christian Scriptures, is the existence of a personal God and of personal relations between that God and man. When these relations are interrupted or deranged by man's action, he finds himself alienated or estranged from God, and the need of reconciliation emerges. The personal God of the Bible is of course the Creator of the universe, and estrangement from Him means in a sense estrangement from everything that is, and demands a reconciliation of corresponding scope. Still, the heart of the reconciliation lies in the readjustment or restoration of the true personal relation between God and the creature which has lapsed by its own act into alienation from Him; in other words, it consists in the forgiveness of sins. Reconciliation to God comes through God's forgiveness of that by which we have been estranged from Him; and of all experiences in the religion of sinful men, it is the most deeply felt and far reaching. We do not need here to measure what is or is not within its power, but every one who knows what it is to be forgiven, knows also that forgiveness is the greatest regenerative force in the life of man.

Just because the experience of reconciliation is the central and fundamental experience of the Christian religion, the doctrine of reconciliation is not so much one doctrine as the inspiration and focus of all. Hence when any given doctrine of reconciliation is criticised, it is through an assumed system of Christian truth with which it is alleged to be inconsistent, or through some element of such a system. Such and such a view, it will be said, is unsound, because it does not enable us to do justice to admitted truths about God, or man, or the new life, or the Church, or perhaps the teaching or the spirit of Jesus. It is therefore not an abnormal but a natural and logically inevitable phenomenon that the third and constructive volume of Ritschl's great work *Rechtfertigung und Versöhnung* widens out into a fairly complete dogmatic system. The core of it, under the heading of *The Presuppositions*, contains the doctrines of God, of Sin, and of the Person and Work of Christ, which are essential as the basis of the Christian doctrine of justification and reconciliation; and a further proof is attempted both that the forgiveness of sins

THE EXPERIMENTAL BASIS OF THE DOCTRINE

is essential if God's ends with men are to be attained, and that this forgiveness is necessarily based on the work and passion of Christ. There is something surprising in the appearance of such speculative discussions as these last in the work of a writer who is ordinarily so much of a mere positivist in theology as Ritschl, but they indicate the vital importance of reconciliation both as an experience and a doctrine. Everything is essentially related to it, and the feeling is inevitable that a thing so vital could not be otherwise than as it is. The more wonderful and essential it is, the less do we feel at liberty to say that it might have come to us in some other way than that in which it actually has come. Rather are we convinced that there is a divine necessity in all that belongs to it; and though it may seem presumptuous to speak of necessity where God is in question, we must remember that the only alternative is to pronounce God *ex lex*—without law—which is as good as to abandon thinking altogether. It is not the intention of the writer to elaborate a system of theology, on the scale of Ritschl's, round the doctrine of reconciliation; the examination of what is presupposed in the doctrine will be confined as far as possible to a study of the nature of sin. But he would insist that in the experience of reconciliation to God through Christ is to be found the principle and the touch-stone of all genuine Christian doctrine: whatever can be derived from this experience and is consistent with it is true and necessary; whatever is incompatible with it lacks the essential Christian character.

It is a commonplace of modern theology that no doctrine has any value except as it is based on experience, and before proceeding to the Christian doctrine of reconciliation, it is indispensable to look at the experience or experiences which are covered by the term.[1] The *differentia* of Christian reconciliation is that it is inseparable from Christ: it is dependent on Him and mediated through Him. But Christ Himself and all the reconciling virtue associated with Him are themselves mediated to us in numberless ways. He works upon us in the way of reconciliation through all the institutions, customs, convictions, and characters which make up the Christian world in which we live. In what is called Christendom we have the benefit of an atmosphere ultimately due to Him, and impregnated with what are in the last resort powers of reconciliation originally embodied in Him. But though this is important it is not the main thing. The main thing—in the sense of that through which the reconciling power of Christ mainly enters with effect into the lives of sinful men—is the New Testament witness to Jesus. It is admitted, as has just been said, that this reaches us indirectly in ways which can never be fully traced, but it is most powerful when the mediation is most direct. An evangelist who has himself been reconciled to God through Christ, and who can make the New Testament witness to the reconciling power of Jesus his own, is a far more powerful minister of reconciliation than any institution or atmosphere can be. The sense of responsibility for reconciliation, the duty of being reconciled, do not become urgent except under a direct and personal appeal. A reconciled man, preaching Christ as the way of reconciliation, and preaching Him in the temper and spirit which the experience of reconciliation creates, is the most effective mediator of Christ's reconciling power. It is hardly another thing than this if we say that the reconciling power is most effectively mediated through the New

---

[1] "Es ist unmöglich das Object der Religion auf ausserreligiösem Wege zu erreichen." Tröltsch, *Zeitschrift für Theologie u. Kirche,* 1895, p. 432 f.

THE EXPERIMENTAL BASIS OF THE DOCTRINE

Testament. For when we read the New Testament with susceptible minds, we listen to the voice of those who were once themselves estranged from God, but have been reconciled to Him through Christ, and are letting us into the secret of their new life; it is the nearest approach we can make, and therefore the most vital, to the reconciling power which streamed from Christ Himself. It might be objected to this view that it connects reconciliation too closely with the historical Christ, who stands at an immense and ever increasing distance from us; His power, it might be feared, would grow continually less with time just as a light, though it may still burn as brightly, grows dim with increasing distance. But this is not the Christian view. There is certainly no reconciliation but through the historical Christ: there is no other Christ of whom we know anything whatever. But the historical Christ does not belong to the past. The living Spirit of God makes Him present and eternal; and it is not from Palestine, or from the first century of the Christian era, but here and now that His reconciling power is felt.

Personal relations are inexhaustible, and it would be idle to try to exhaust the ways in which Christ acts on a sinful man for reconciliation when they come face to face with each other through the New Testament or through the preaching of the gospel. But it is possible to indicate some of the lines along which impressions come.

When we see Jesus as He is presented to us in the gospels, we see a life which is at one with God. All the problems which distract and baffle us are solved here. There is no quarrel with the conditions of existence. There is no discontent, or querulousness, or rebellion. There is no radical inconsistency, no humbling division of the soul against itself. There is no distrust of God, no estrangement from

Him, no sense of sin. In one way it might seem incredible—it is so purely supernatural when compared with what we know as nature in ourselves and others; yet incredible as it might seem, it has never failed to impress men as absolutely real and at the same time as truly human. It is our life that we see in Jesus, but we see it in its truth and as it ought to be, a life in God, wholly at one with Him. This life is its own witness, and there is no human soul to which it does not appeal. Perhaps we do not need to distinguish too scrupulously the modes in which the appeal comes home to us. It may act like a spell or a charm on our whole nature at once, drawing us by an irresistible constraint to Jesus. We may be conscious in it of a grace which ensures our welcome when we approach, and of an authority which requires our implicit submission. We may have an unanalysed feeling that here "all's love and all's law," but through everything we are conscious that the very presence of such a Being in our world is a promise of reconciliation. He is not here for Himself, but for us. There is invitation in His presence as in His voice: it is as though He were saying all the time, "Come unto me all ye that labour and are heavy laden, and I will give you rest." When we really see Him, and virtue goes out of Him to heal us, we cry irrepressibly, "Thou, O Christ, art all I want; more than all in Thee I find." We do not stay to ask what He has done or what He can do for us; what He is—not according to a doctrine of His person, but in the rich and simple reality we see in the evangelists—is enough for us. *He* is our peace. The whole promise and power of reconciliation are in Him, and we know without proving that He can bring us to God and save to the uttermost.

But the whole experience of reconciliation may not be

THE EXPERIMENTAL BASIS OF THE DOCTRINE

made at once. There are probably many who are first impressed by the power of Jesus to reconcile men to the general conditions of existence. Their hearts have been set intently and passionately on things which some can only have if others want them—on wealth, on worldly honour, on present and visible success of various kinds; and it gradually dawns upon them in the presence of Jesus that here is the perfect life, and that with all these things it has no concern whatever. It is absolutely independent of them. It recognises in them difficulties and temptations, sometimes it might seem sheer impossibilities, in the path of those who would live the life which is life indeed; but at the same time it can deliver us from them. It reveals behind the world of pleasure, pride, and covetousness another world which is the true country of the soul, the world of the beatitudes; and when it wins men to dwell there, and to know what it is to be poor in spirit and meek and merciful and lovers of righteousness and of peace, it has reconciled them to much that was once irksome and intolerable in the order of the common world. When we learn, as the life of Jesus enables us to do, that a man's life does not consist in the abundance of the things which he possesses, that though lived on the plane of nature it is essentially a spiritual life, much that once estranged us from God and from the conditions of existence dies away. We can accept much with which we were once at war, because we are independent of it. This does not mean that we should have no economic ideals for ourselves or for society, or that no outward conditions have any meaning for the life of the soul. It means what we see when we look at Jesus: namely, that as far as true eternal life is concerned it can be enjoyed in all its fulness by one who takes no interest and has no part in the ordinary ambitions and conflicts of men. Something far finer than the ἀταραξία and ἀπάθεια of ancient moralists, something which reaches deeper and has a greater power to reconcile man to life, enters into all who absorb the beatitudes as they are illustrated and embodied in Jesus Himself.

Sometimes this aspect of reconciliation is not adequately recognised. The term is restricted too narrowly to a transaction in the sphere of conscience. But the end of reconciliation is to make saints, and no life impresses us as saintly unless it reflects, however obscurely, the glory of the beatitudes. We are not really reconciled to God through Jesus unless we are reconciled to this as the true life, and we are not reconciled to this as the true life unless we are reconciled to renouncing all the passion with which when we were ignorant of it we sought the chief ends of life elsewhere.

Important, however, as this aspect of reconciliation is, it must not distract us from what is central: the reconciling power of Jesus as exhibited in His attitude to sinners. It is sin which estranges us from God, and creates the problem of reconciliation. It is sin which hides God's face from us, and tempts us to shun His presence. It is sin which provokes His displeasure, and which makes us fear, distrust, and finally hate Him. In the gospels, indeed, we do not find any of this abstract language. They do not even speak of sin in the singular number, as an idea, but only of sins in the plural, as definite acts. It is not by any doctrine that we are reconciled to God; the reconciling power for sinful men lies in the attitude of Jesus to the sinful. This is happily one of the points in the gospel story about which there can be no dispute. There might be a question as to whether Jesus spoke any given word assigned to Him, or as to the circumstances in which it was spoken, or as to its proper

THE EXPERIMENTAL BASIS OF THE DOCTRINE

application; but it is quite inconceivable that the evangelists should misrepresent so new and wonderful a thing as the attitude of Jesus to the sinful, or the reconciling power which accompanied it. Jesus knew what sin was more truly than any man. He saw it in its roots and in its consequences. But He believed in forgiveness. He not only believed in it and proclaimed it, He embodied and bestowed it. The words of His enemies—"This man receiveth sinners and eateth with them"—though spoken malignantly, enshrine the ultimate truth of His life and work, and it is through this truth that His reconciling power is felt. The value of His teaching is not questioned. Parables like that of the prodigal son, whose father ran and fell on his neck and kissed him, or of the two debtors who had nothing to pay, and whose creditor freely forgave them both, can never lose their power to evoke penitence and faith, and through them to reconcile sinners to God. But far beyond the teaching of Jesus in reconciling power, inspired and divine as that teaching is, stands His actual intercourse with the sinful. Here He appears in act as the minister and mediator of reconciliation, and when we realise what He is doing, the possibility, the reality, and the nature of reconciliation are made plain to us. They are made plain at least if we realise through the power of God's Spirit that Jesus is the same yesterday, to-day, and for ever, and if He inspires in us that same penitence and faith which He won from the sinners He received on earth.

The evangelist who records the Pharisaic sneer—"This man receiveth sinners"—is rich in illustrations of it which enable us to see what reconciliation to God through Christ implies. One is the story in Luke vii. 36-50, of the woman who was a sinner. Apparently she was a sinner in the city, one of that unhappy class who walk the streets and live by sin. There are none in the world more friendless, none from whom the passers by more instinctively turn aside, none whom ordinary society would be so determined not to receive; in a word, none so hopeless. But one day this woman heard Jesus, and His holiness and love overcame her. She was drawn irresistibly to Him, and not long after, as He sat at meat in a Pharisee's house, she made her way in, and, standing behind Him, wet His feet with tears, wiped them with the hair of her head, kissed them over and over again, and anointed them with ointment. "What an extraordinary demonstration!" we are tempted to say. Was it hysterics, the weakness of a breaking wave? No, it was not hysterics, it was regeneration. It was the new birth of faith and hope and love, evoked and welcomed by Jesus: it was the passionate experience of a sinner's reconciliation to God. Such a thing is possible, for here we actually see it. Jesus did not shrink from the sinful woman: He received her. He took her part against the Pharisee. He spoke great and gracious words in her defence. "Her sins are forgiven, for she loved much." "Thy faith hath saved thee: go in peace." And as she went, she knew that friendless as she had been before she had now a friend with God; it is not too much to say, she knew that God Himself was her friend. We see from this incident what a profound, thrilling, and far reaching experience reconciliation is. It is something which moves nature in all its depths, which melts it and casts it into a new mould. It regenerates the soul which passes through it, and it is accompanied with the sense of an infinite debt to Jesus. How this last is to be explained we are not expressly told, but it was not for nothing that the sinful woman restored to God poured out her gratitude at Jesus' feet.

We have another instance of Jesus receiving sinners in

THE EXPERIMENTAL BASIS OF THE DOCTRINE

the story of Zacchæus (Luke xix. 1 ff.). Zacchæus was hated for his trade, and he was hated more for his success in it; he was rich, and he had made his money in what all his countrymen thought a disreputable way. He had not a friend in Jericho. But as Jesus passed under the tree into which Zacchæus had climbed to see Him, He looked up and said, "Zacchæus, make haste and come down; for to-day I must abide at thy house." Respectable people would not call on Zacchæus, but the Lord called on him. And that day salvation came to his house. It was the rising up of the new life in Zacchæus, the life inspired by the presence of Jesus under his roof, which declared itself as he exclaimed, "Behold, Lord, the half of my goods I give to the poor, and if I have taken anything from any man by false accusation I restore him fourfold." There is no boast in this, no resentful clearing of his character against the people who murmured that Jesus was gone to be guest with a man that was a sinner, no assertion that he had been unjustly accused. It is the new man who speaks here, and who reveals in this regenerate utterance what the coming of Jesus meant for him. Salvation came to his house when Jesus entered it. He brought with Him the power which reconciled Zacchæus to God, and in the very same act or process delivered him from his old sin of covetousness and made him a new creature. This experience is not separable from the sinner's reconciliation; it is part and parcel of it, and is the visible proof that it is real.

In both these cases, and one may say in all others that the gospel records, it is important not to forget that Jesus was present, and that it was His presence which made possible all the experiences which are included under reconciliation or regeneration. This is sometimes overlooked by those who are jealous for what they call free forgiveness.

Thus a recent writer on this subject says, "The free forgiveness of sins was the vital spark of Christ's teaching. 'Thy sins be forgiven thee.' Wherever He found repentance, there He scattered forgiveness; it was as water to the tender plant."[1] The simplest answer to this is to say that Jesus did not "find" repentance at all. It was not there ready made, waiting for forgiveness. He had to create or evoke repentance, and there was something in His character and in His attitude to the sinful which worked powerfully to this end. The sense of debt to Jesus on the part of Zacchæus and of the woman who was a sinner, would not have been what it evidently was if they had merely owed to Him an announcement or even an assurance that penitence like theirs could not but be forgiven. Their penitence itself was not an antecedent condition of reconciliation, made good on their part, without any obligation to Him; it was simply an element in the reconciliation, and they were His debtors for it as for everything else in that transforming experience. This, it may be said with confidence, is what is confirmed by experience still. We do not first repent of our sins and then come to Jesus; it is the visitation of our life by Jesus to which we owe first repentance and then all other spiritual blessings.

From this point of view we hardly need to raise the question whether there is any special relation between the death of Jesus and man's reconciliation to God. It is Jesus Himself who is our peace, and wherever we meet Him reconciling virtue goes out of Him. We may say indifferently that it is concentrated in His death, because there the spirit of His life is condensed and focussed; or that it is diffused throughout His life, because from every word or incident of His life there breathes forth on us the spirit in which He died.

[1] *Forgiveness and Suffering,* by Douglas White, M.D., p. 68.

THE EXPERIMENTAL BASIS OF THE DOCTRINE

But while we must guard against unreal distinctions, and especially against turning the death of Christ into a thing which can be looked at materially rather than personally, we must not ignore the fact that of all things which go to make up the life of Jesus His death is the most wonderful in reconciling power. To avoid the mistake just referred to, we may speak rather of Jesus in His death than of the death of Jesus. Jesus in His death has been the supreme power by which men have been reconciled to God. It is as the crucified that He has been able to create in sinners God's thoughts of sin, to evoke penitence, to inspire faith, to bring men back to the Father. It is not a doctrine, but a fact of human experience that this is so, and if we try to analyse the reconciling virtue which dwelt in Jesus we must do justice to this fact. Nothing forbids us to acknowledge the subduing power of love everywhere—and to be subdued by love is to be reconciled. Nothing forbids us to feel that there is something which at once overcomes and reconciles when we see Jesus at Jacob's well, and become conscious of the truth in *Quaerens me sedisti lassus*. But this cannot forbid us recognising the further truth—or, if it is not a further truth, the deeper sounding in the same truth—in *Redemisti crucem passus*. If the mistake has sometimes been made of speaking of Christ's death as a thing by itself which could be studied and appreciated, and even preached as gospel, apart either from Jesus or His life, we must not in avoiding it fall into the opposite error, and think that we can appreciate Jesus fully, even in His character of reconciler, though we do not think of Him in His cross and passion. The place given to the death of Christ in the New Testament peremptorily forbids this to the Christian reader.

When we think of the experience of reconciliation in its

THE CHRISTIAN DOCTRINE OF RECONCILIATION

dependence on the cross of Jesus there are two observations we cannot but make. The first is that it is never really separated in our minds from the whole story of the gospel, with all those moving words and incidents which are as much part of the life of Jesus as of His death. It is love which prevails against every form of evil in us—against pride, a hard heart, sensual passions, or whatever else; and the whole story is a demonstration of love. We see Jesus from beginning to end of it thinking of others, not of Himself. "If ye seek me, let these go" (John xviii. 8). "Daughters of Jerusalem, weep not for me, but weep for yourselves and for your children" (Luke xxiii. 28). "Father, forgive them, for they know not what they do" (Luke xxiii. 34). "Verily I say unto thee, To-day shalt thou be with me in Paradise" (Luke xxiii. 43). These words and their accompaniments get behind all the sinner's defences against God. We feel that in the very face of sin at its guiltiest, a love revealed and maintained itself against which sin was powerless. In the dreadful conflict the victory remained with love. Love proved itself in the Passion of Jesus to be the final reality, and no truth which takes possession of the heart of man can ever have power to subdue and reconcile like this. If we wish to experience or to preach reconciliation—which depends upon such love—we must not lose the revelation of it by reducing it to a symbol, like the cross, or a dogma, like that of satisfaction: we must keep before ourselves and others the concrete facts in which its reality first came home to men. Christ crucified must be "evidently set forth"—placarded (Gal. iii. 1) before men's eyes—that they may receive a due impression of all that there is in this wonderful sight.

The second observation is this. The story of the death of Christ never reaches us but through Christian tradition.

THE EXPERIMENTAL BASIS OF THE DOCTRINE

Christian parents and teachers introduce us to it, and when we are able to do so we go directly to the New Testament itself, the purest witness to the Christian tradition. The consequence is that we never see the death of Jesus as a mere spectacle, a purely objective or external event. We see it through eyes which have felt it, which have filled with tears as they gazed upon it. We see it through the emotions and experiences of those who have been subdued by it, and who cannot speak of it without telling us what it means, and how it works in surrendered souls. There is no proportion, it may be said, between what the disciples saw at the cross, and what they afterwards said about it; between the squalid horror of an ordinary military execution and the presence there of a power which should reconcile the world to God. We do not need to discuss at this point the soundness of their perception. The point is that as they looked at Jesus on His cross this actually was their experience: they became conscious through Him of a love which passes knowledge; it flashed out from His passion and overcame them; they were suddenly aware of a goodness which outweighed all the sin of the world and made it impotent; and through that goodness, or rather through Him in whose passion it was manifested to men, they were reconciled to God. Now when we say that the story of the death of Christ never reaches us but through Christian tradition, we mean that it never reaches us but in the atmosphere of this interpretation. From the first, when we learn that Jesus died, we learn that He died for us. As the children's hymn has it,

> "He died that we might be forgiven,
> He died to make us good,
> That we might go at last to heaven,
> Saved by His precious blood."

THE CHRISTIAN DOCTRINE OF RECONCILIATION

No person born and brought up in Christendom can so much as see the death of Christ except through an atmosphere permeated and impregnated with this interpretation of it. When the interpretation becomes formal, it may easily become inadequate, but what it rests on is the experience that in the death of Jesus the sinful soul has come face to face with a love which is stronger than sin. It is not sin which is the last reality in the world, nor any consequence of sin; it is not sin to which we have to reconcile ourselves, or sin's punishments, temporal or eternal. The last reality is beyond sin. It is a love which submits to all that sin can do, yet does not deny itself, but loves the sinful through it all. It is a love which in Scripture language bears sin, yet receives and regenerates sinners. All this is included in the reconciliation of sinners to God through Christ, and just because it has been from the beginning a matter of experience, not a dogma, it is quite legitimate that its influence should be felt in the simplest Christian teaching. We do not preach that Jesus died, but that He died for us, and in particular that He died for our sins. The love revealed in His death is revealed signally in relation to them, and there is no simpler way of describing the effect of His death than to say that it dispels the despairing conviction that for us sin is the last of all things, in which we must hopelessly acquiesce, and evokes the inspiring conviction that the last of all things is sin-bearing love through which the sinner may be reconciled to God.[1]

---

[1] One of the difficulties in writing about reconciliation, so far as it involves reference to the views of others, is that the worth of the common Christian interpretation of Christ's death as a reconciling death is admitted even by those who seem to repudiate every doctrinal statement of it which has ever been attempted from St. Paul down. It is not easy to make any criticism of a book on the atonement or on reconciliation which the author may not

THE EXPERIMENTAL BASIS OF THE DOCTRINE

There are two considerations further which should not be overlooked at this point. The reconciliation which is experienced through the sin-bearing love revealed in Christ has, like everything in the Christian religion, the character of absoluteness or finality. When we are constrained by this love we are irresistibly and completely constrained. We cannot and need not think of anything beyond it: that there should be anything beyond it is inconceivable. "Thou, O Christ, art all I want; more than all in Thee I find," is the spontaneous utterance of the reconciled sinner. The love he has met in Christ is wholly inexorable to sin, and wholly gracious to those who surrender to it, and it is in this twofold character that it is an absolutely reconciling love. The condemnation and repulsion of sin in it are just as unequivocal as the welcome given to the sinner. They are indeed part of it, and no one reconciled to God through Christ who died could ever imagine either that God ignored or condoned sin, or that he was called through reconciliation to anything but a life of unreserved obedience and holiness. Reconciliation as experienced has its outlook on a new life, and no doctrine of it is adequate in which this is not explicitly recognised.

From a very early time—perhaps from the time of St. Paul himself—the sense that reconciliation was a great achievement, involving effort or tension of some kind even on the part of God, has played a considerable part in theologising on this subject. In forgiving sins, it might be said, God takes sides with us against Himself; He has a right to exact something from us, and for our sakes forgoes that right.

plausibly represent as unjust. Naturally the New Testament writers have suffered most at the hands of theologians who believed that at heart they were at one with them, who wanted to have the New Testament on their side, but who could not find the apostolic way of expounding the reconciling death of Christ congenial.

THE CHRISTIAN DOCTRINE OF RECONCILIATION

His justice impels Him in one direction, and His mercy in another, and in this very act of pardoning men and reconciling them to Himself He must reconcile these divergent attributes. It is certainly part of the experience of reconciliation that God treats us better than we deserve. He does not deal with us after our sins, nor reward us according to our iniquities. It is also part of the experience of reconciliation to feel that such a display of God's mercy is miraculous; it is not something we could presume upon, but the most wonderful work of Him who alone does wonderful things. It is the characteristic of God in which He is incomparable. "Who is a God like unto Thee, that pardoneth iniquity?" But it is not a part of the experience to feel that there is a conflict between the divine attributes of justice and mercy, and that these attributes have to be reconciled to one another before man can be reconciled to God. A good deal of speculation deals with this idea, but it is speculative, not experimental. There is not in Christian experience any antagonism between justice and mercy: they are in active and immutable harmony with each other, and God always—not merely in forgiving sins—acts in unison with both. Mercy and justice do not need to be reconciled, for they are never at war. The true opposite of justice is not mercy, but injustice, with which God can have nothing to do either in reconciliation or in any other of His works.

The experience of reconciliation is bound up with other convictions which must not be overlooked, even though they only rise into consciousness casually, and cannot be reduced to any system. One of these convictions is that from beginning to end the work is carried on in the moral world. The power which Christ exercises in reconciling us to God is a moral power, not a physical or magical one, and in its operation it

THE EXPERIMENTAL BASIS OF THE DOCTRINE

is subject to the laws of a moral order. This not only means that there is no physical coercion in it, no denial of man's freedom, but that the power itself which reconciles is ethical in quality. But to say this is to say—when we speak of the man Christ Jesus—that it is power which has been ethically earned and accumulated. The moral personality in which it is lodged and out of which it proceeds, has been formed and developed, like other moral personalities, through the duties and trials of our common human life. It could not have been formed and developed in any other way. This is the truth underlying some rather equivocal expressions which have been used about the work of Christ in the reconciliation of man to God. One of the most embarrassing of these expressions is that which speaks of the merit or the merits of Christ. When we use it, we seem to think of some thing, detachable from the moral personality of Jesus and from its moral power, and capable of being attached or credited to some other person or persons. But in reality there is no such thing, and therefore it is an unreal question to ask whether Christ merited for Himself as well as for others, or for others only. It is an unreal question, because it can only be asked by leaving the moral world behind us, in which the whole being and power of Christ are realised. The only legitimate idea suggested by the term "merit"—and this holds when it is applied to sinners as well as to the Saviour—is that the whole business of salvation is transacted in the moral world. It is not a happy term to express this idea; it is a legal term for a moral value, and therefore inadequate and misleading; but this amount of truth it can be made to cover. All that Jesus did He did in fulfilment of His calling; He could not have done otherwise and been true to Himself. But while the experience of reconciliation as entirely ethical, alike in the power which produces it and in its fruits, compels us to say this, it may be questioned whether it is a fair equivalent of this when we are asked to say that Christ did nothing for others that He did not first do for Himself. Experience of reconciliation does not prompt or support a statement like this. On the contrary, Christ did something for us which He had not to do for Himself; He reconciled us to God. But in the whole work of reconciliation, in His obedience and in His passion, we may say, if we choose to employ legal terminology, that He "merited" *for Himself*; He did the will of His Father—fulfilled the calling with which the Father had called Him—and so merited His approval and reward. But outside of Christ's fulfilment of His calling, on which His moral power as reconciler depends, there are no quasi-material "merits" of Christ which are available for others because He does not need them Himself. Nowhere in the moral universe, and just as little in Christ as anywhere, is there room for the idea of supererogation.

There is much about reconciliation which experience does not demonstrate, because experience is never complete. A man may be assured that the reconciliation to God which He owes to Christ is final and absolute, yet have much to learn about the consequences of sin. All he knows about these consequences to begin with is that, be they what they may, they cannot and do not negate the reconciliation. But he has to learn by further experience how the healing power of reconciliation works in a sin-stricken nature, and, though he can never be reconciled to sin, whether there are not by the will of God painful and disabling consequences of sin to which in the meantime he must resign himself as patiently and unmurmuringly as he can. He has to learn what the

THE EXPERIMENTAL BASIS OF THE DOCTRINE

standing temper of the reconciled life will be in his own case. It may be determined in part by his natural temperament, in part by his past life, in part by the completeness with which he has received the reconciliation; it may be more triumphant or more subdued, more akin to joy in the Holy Spirit or to *"getröstetes Sündenelend"*; but it does not affect the reconciliation itself. Most men after they receive the gospel have much to learn of the scope of reconciliation. They do not realise how much God covers, and that reconciliation to Him has not had its perfect work until we are reconciled also to our fellows, to the order of providence, and to the inexorable laws of the spiritual world.

Of one thing, however, there is never any question: the place of Jesus is the reconciliation. *He* is our Peace.

CHAPTER II

RECONCILIATION IN THE CHRISTIAN THOUGHT OF THE PAST

ALL sound and legitimate doctrinal construction must be based on experience, and it is to such experiences as have been described in the previous chapter that we must refer all attempts at dogmatic definition. It has been recognised in that chapter that the reconciling power of Jesus is mediated to us in the last resort by the primitive testimony to Him in the New Testament, and it can hardly be questioned that in the New Testament there is not merely a testimony to Jesus, and a record of experiences due to Him, but a great deal of reflection upon Him. Accordingly it has become almost a convention with theological writers to start with a discussion of the New Testament doctrine, or of the New Testament types or suggestions of doctrine, whatever be the subject in hand. But there are reasons for adopting a different course. We should not indeed count among these that advanced by an American theologian, that to regard Scripture as the sole source and norm for Christian theology "is incompatible with the idea, now gaining considerable acceptance, that later types of Christianity have a significance in some degree comparable with New Testament types, and so it is not the truest way to maintain the value of the Scriptures themselves."[1] Primitive historical Christianity must

[1] Lyman, *American Journal of Theology*, Oct. 1915, p. 608.

IN THE CHRISTIAN THOUGHT OF THE PAST

always be essentially normative, and if later types of religion so diverge from the primitive type as to find the New Testament rather an embarrassment than an inspiration, the question they raise is whether they can any longer be recognised as Christian. But apart from such radical and questionable ideas there are good grounds for looking at the course of Christian thought in general before specially investigating the thought of the New Testament. One is that Christians had begun to think and to express themselves on the subject before the New Testament as we know it had been canonised and established in its present authority in the Church. Another is that it was long before Christians thinking on reconciliation had any idea of the wealth of New Testament reflection on the subject. The New Testament contains in a great variety of forms testimony to Jesus as the reconciler, and to His gospel as the word of reconciliation—we can apply to it, as the writer to the Hebrews applies to the Old Testament, the terms πολυμερῶς καὶ πολυτρόπως; and as this testimony came to men in one form or another, along one channel or another, it evoked faith and other Christian experiences, including Christian reflections, which last can hardly be said to be dependent on what we mean when we speak of the New Testament. It is well worth while, holding the latter in reserve, to survey the course of Christian thought independently.

It is beyond the scope of these lectures, however, to do this in minute detail. At a comparatively early date the Christian Church hammered out, for better or worse, dogmas of the Trinity and the Incarnation, and the history of these dogmas has an almost official character and can with comparative ease be made plain. But the Church has never had in the same sense a dogma of reconciliation. There is

THE CHRISTIAN DOCTRINE OF RECONCILIATION

nothing in the history of Christian thought on this subject analogous to the definition of the ὁμοούσιον at Nicæa. It was not till after the Reformation, when dogma in the old sense had become impossible, that the various branches of the Church began to frame explicit official statements about the way in which Christ reconciled man to God, and especially about the meaning of His sufferings and death. But this does not mean that there was no Christian thinking on the subject. There was a great deal, at first independent and casual, but afterwards starting from and controlled by the orthodox doctrine of the Person of Christ. What is intended in this chapter is not to give an account of everything that theologians have incidentally or expressly said upon the subject, but only to indicate the main types of interpretation which have emerged in the course of Christian history.[1]

[1] Besides the histories of doctrine generally, like those of Thomasius, Harnack, and Seeberg, in which, of course, it finds a place, important books have been written expressly upon the subject. One is Baur's *Christian Doctrine of Reconciliation in its historical development from the earliest times to the most recent* (1838). Another is the first volume of Ritschl's *Justification and Reconciliation*, the first edition of which appeared in 1870. These books are typical of their authors. Baur operates a great deal with the categories of the Hegelian philosophy, and subdues the movement of Christian thought to them with astonishing skill and occasional violence. He devotes the first section of his work to the period from the earliest days to the beginning of the twelfth century (Anselm); Ritschl refers to this period in his introduction, but virtually starts with Anselm as the first writer who raised questions on the subject in such a form that the answers yielded material for doctrine. Both aim at tracing a natural sequence or genealogical connection in the ideas which emerge in history, and both, it may be said without offence, tend, as they approach their own time, to disappear in the sand. Instead of a genealogy of ideas we get *précis* of books, and even of controversial pamphlets, in which the writers are so earnestly engaged in clearing up their relations to one another that the interest of reconciliation to God is lost. Besides these reference may be made to Oxenham's *Catholic Doctrine of the Atonement* (1st ed. 1865), and to the learned work of the Abbé J. Rivière, *Le Dogme de la Rédemption: Essai d'Etude Historique* (2nd ed. 1905), completed by *Le Dogme de la Rédemption: Etude Théologique* (1914). In attempting

IN THE CHRISTIAN THOUGHT OF THE PAST

In primitive Christianity two ideas are universally connected with the death of Christ, and employed in its interpretation. It is spoken of as a sacrifice and as a ransom. The first of these finds its application more readily if our main thought is that of man's reconciliation to God through Christ and His Passion; the second, if our main thought is that man owes to Christ and His Passion emancipation from some evil or hostile power. But it is necessary to look at both more closely.

Sacrifice in the forms in which it was familiar to ancient religion is quite unknown to us, and it is therefore hard for us to understand. Pious people in ancient times took it for granted; it was assumed to have some meaning or power, and no questions were asked about it. For us, it is merely a subject for questions, and the literature in which it has been investigated is of vast extent. Much of this literature and of its conclusions is irrelevant to our present study. When it is pointed out, for example, that in an ancient religion sacrifice was merely the normal mode of worship, and that it had no particular relation to sin or its removal, it is enough to reply that when the death of Christ is spoken of as a sacrifice, it always has precisely this relation. It is a sacrifice for sin, and not a sacrifice in any vaguer sense. Its value is that somehow or other it neutralises sin as a power estranging man and God, and that in virtue of it God and man are reconciled. In all probability, by the first century of the Christian era, all sacrifices among the Jews had this character of being expiatory or propitiatory sacrifices; whatever the *modus*, the effect was that they purged or put away sin.[1] It is quite

to indicate in outline the course of Christian thought on the subject of these lectures, the writer ventures to assure his readers that he gives no account at second hand of books which he has not read.

Holtzmann, *N. T. Theologie* (first ed.), 64 ff. 302.

obvious that immoral ideas might easily gather round the practice of sacrifice. Dull consciences might regard the sacrifice as a bribe by which God was won over to disregard what justice would have required Him to punish. Protests against the misunderstanding and abuse of sacrifice, as if it implied that the sinner could buy himself out of the due consequences of his sin, are as universal in ancient religions as sacrifice itself. Here Isaiah and Plato, the Psalter and Seneca are at one. In sacrifice, we are warned, it is not the mere thing which is looked at, but the mind of the offerer. *"Ne in victimis quidem,"* says Seneca, *"licet opimæ sint auroque praefulgeant, Deorum est honos, sed pia ac recta voluntate venerantium."* Grotius, in making this quotation, reminds us that Scripture itself in treating of the death of Christ makes mention now of His love and again of His obedience. It is not the sacrifice as such, the *res sola*, which avails: its virtue is dependent on something in the offerer. But while this is not to be questioned—in other words, while the moral conditions under which sacrifice had its value are, of course, to be allowed for—the main matter remains. All sacrifice was sacrifice offered *to God*, and, whatever its value, it had that value *for Him*. No man ever thought of offering sacrifice for the sake of a moral effect it was to produce on himself. If we say that the death of Christ was an atoning sacrifice, then the atonement must be an objective atonement. It is to God it is offered, and it is to God it makes a difference. Whatever objections may present themselves to it on reflection, this point of view was universal in the ancient Church. The death of Christ was an atoning sacrifice through which sin was annulled and God and man reconciled. The most radical objection, of course, is that Christ is God's gift to man, and therefore cannot be a sacrifice offered by or for men to God; but, in point of fact, this objection never had weight. The sense that Christ is the Father's gift to the world never deterred Christians from thinking of Him instinctively as a sacrifice to God for the putting away of sin. They accepted both ideas fully, and were never arrested by the sense of any antagonism between them.

The other conception of Christ's death, which is equally universal in primitive times, is the conception of it as a ransom. Whatever be the power which holds him, man is held in bondage somehow: it may be bondage to sin, or to death, or to demons, or to the devil, but he is indubitably a slave. The result of Christ's work, and especially of His Passion and death, is that man is set free, and he realises, as he looks at the cross, what his emancipation has cost. It has cost the death of the Son of God, who on the cross gave Himself a ransom for him. The truth of this, in the appeal it makes to our feeling and experience, is unquestionable, and it is as easy to apprehend as everything involving the notion of sacrifice is difficult. But when the primitive Christian mind, in dealing with this idea of ransom, passes from the domain of feeling into that of speculation, it becomes involved in conceptions which are curiously impossible for us. When the question is asked, By whom or by what is man enslaved? the answer ordinarily given is that he is enslaved by Satan, through his sin. By his sin, man has given Satan a just hold upon him. The Enemy has rights in him. The sinner is justly enslaved, and justice must be recognised in the process by which he is set free. This requirement is met in the death of Jesus. Here is the ransom which is paid to Satan, and which makes the liberation of man a just act. We have been bought with this great price into Christian freedom, and are not in bondage to sin or Satan any more.

THE CHRISTIAN DOCTRINE OF RECONCILIATION

The mythological expansion of these ideas has often been exhibited and derided. When it was pointed out that Satan, after all, did not get keeping Christ, and that therefore the ransom was not really but only apparently paid, the theory was expanded so as to include a deception of Satan, and the justification of that deception. Perhaps the fullest illustration of this is given in such as passage as cc. xxiv.-xxvi. of the *Catechetical Oration* of Gregory of Nyssa. It is frankly admitted, in a figure found also in Gregory the Great (*Mor.* xxxiii. 7) and John of Damascus (*de Fid. Orthod.* iii. 27), that the Devil, taken in by the bait of Christ's humanity, was caught on the hook of His divinity which lay hidden beneath it. It was a case of the biter bitten. But Gregory of Nyssa argues that the justice of God was shown in this, that the enemy who had deceived man was in turn himself deceived. And further, he urges that the deception had also in view the ultimate good of Satan. The divine cannot come into contact with evil without prevailing against it, and Christ both liberates man from wickedness and heals the inventor of wickedness himself (*Or. Catech.* xxvi. *ad fin.*). This to our minds has lost contact with reality altogether, yet it was in contact with reality when it started. It is true to experience to say that man's emancipation from evil has cost Christ dear. It is true to the most elementary forms of Christian experience to say that He gave Himself a ransom for us. It is also true to say that He had to do it. In the work of man's deliverance from sin and reconciliation to God, we are in contact with moral necessities which cannot be ignored and which make the task of our deliverer costly and severe. The sense of this was universal in the Church, and though the mythological form in which it often found expression is grotesque and incredible—how could the demands of righteousness be satisfied by a fraud?—it is nevertheless a witness to an ineradicable Christian feeling which can never be ignored. We were not bought for nothing, we were bought with a price. Our redemption was conditioned by the recognition of moral necessities which had to be recognised, and the recognition of which involved the death of Jesus on the cross.

We may say of ransom, as has been said of sacrifice, that it has its meaning and value in relation to God. The ransom is not paid to us. Its virtue does not lie in what we think about it. It has infinite worth in itself and to God, and if it has any significance which we can call atoning, it must be that of an objective atonement. It is important to realise that this is involved in both the ideas which were universally employed in the early Church to interpret the death of Jesus. Both of them imply that Christ did with God for men something which they could not do for themselves, and which made them infinitely His debtors.

In the thought as in the life of the ancient Church it soon became possible to distinguish characteristic tendencies in the East and the West. Perhaps they have sometimes been too broadly distinguished, and the fact that from the close of the second century all Christian teachers had practically the same New Testament in their hands, and regarded it with the same reverence as an inspired authority, in many respects assimilated their language even when the fundamental tendencies of their thought were by no means the same. Writers of the school of Ritschl—Harnack, for example, in his *Dogmengeschichte*—emphasise the speculative character of Greek Christology and soteriology. It is a Logos Christology, determined fundamentally by the idea that the eternal Logos takes human nature into union with

Himself in the womb of the Virgin, and by doing so achieves the redemption of the race. In Christ's person humanity is actually redeemed and made one with the divine. The logic of this conception would entitle us to say that the incarnation—not in an ethical sense, as including the whole manifestation of the divine in the human throughout the life and death of Jesus, but in a physical or sacramental sense—was everything, and that the work of man's salvation was accomplished when the Word assumed flesh. It is this logic which historians like Harnack tend to stress, perhaps unduly, though no one with any considerable acquaintance with the literature will question that the Logos Christology does carry into Christian thinking the taint of the Logos philosophy—a comparative indifference to fact and to history, a tendency to assume that the eternal truth of Christianity remains in our hands, with an *a priori* certainty as it were, though we have never been or have ceased to be interested in the story of Jesus. So far the reading of the Greek theologians by Ritschl and Harnack is justified. On the other hand, it must be remembered that people who read the New Testament every day and regarded it as divine, could not easily cease to be interested in the story of Jesus. It may have been inconsistent, but happily there is nothing of which the human mind is more capable than inconsistency. A recent historian of our subject, M. Rivière, distinguishes in the Greek fathers, besides the speculative strain criticised by Ritschl and his disciples, what he calls a realistic line of thought on the atonement. As typical of the speculative he takes Irenaeus, and of the realistic Origen. The choice is surprising, for if there is any father in whom the speculative genius of Greece is incarnate it is Origen; Irenaeus, in spite of his daring idea of a *recapitulatio* of all things in Christ, is by comparison a sober and pedestrian mind. It seems fairer to say that what M. Rivière describes as realistic ought rather to be called Biblical, and that the extent to which it prevails depends upon the extent to which a theologian was preoccupied with the Bible. A man who wrote commentaries, like Origen, no matter how speculative his bent was, would inevitably use Scripture language and speech with Scripture ideas more than a mere writer of philosophical theology. The same holds still more strongly of a preacher like Chrysostom. The question remains, however, as to the relation between the Scripture language or the Scripture ideas such writers employ and the general trend of their thoughts. It is not easy to avoid the impression that as far as their minds had unity—as far as they really aimed at self-consistency—the Greek fathers were as a whole under the ban of their Logos philosophy. That was the vital thing for them when their minds moved spontaneously; the Biblical or realistic element in their thinking does not represent anything as spontaneous or vital. It was not a realistic strain balancing the speculative one; it was incidental and casual; it came up when they had their Bibles in their hands, or in their memories, but it had not the native root in their minds which the other had; it was not properly adjusted to the other, and it never had the determining influence over it which in a historical religion was its due. The speculative strain, in short, belongs to the structure or constitution of their minds, which is by comparison constant; the realistic strain, to the content of their minds, which is by comparison inconstant; and, taking Greek Christian thought on reconciliation as a whole, it is unquestionably the former which preponderates.

To illustrate this, it will be sufficient to give an account of one typical work, the well-known treatise of Athanasius on the Incarnation of the Word. The very designation of the treatise, which is taken from its first chapter—Τὰ περὶ τῆς ἐνανθρωπήσεως τοῦ λόγου διηγησώμεθα implies the speculative point of view and its centrality. The writer does not start from any ethical experience which he owes to Christ, or from any incident in the life of Christ—though, as we shall see, references to these, at subsequent stages of his argument, are not wanting—but from a dogmatic conception of Christ's person of a highly speculative character. This is confirmed by the appeal which he makes at c. 41 to the Greek philosophers who laughed at the idea of incarnation. It is inconsistent, he argues, for men who admit that the Logos pervades the whole universe to question that it can unite itself to man. "The philosophers of the Greeks say that the universe is a great body; and rightly so. For we see it and its parts as objects of our senses. If, then, the Word of God is in the universe, which is a body, and has united Himself with the whole and with all its parts, what is there surprising or absurd if we say that He has united Himself with men also?"[1] The very fact that this appeal is made, and that an analogy is assumed between the presence of the Word in the universe and the incarnation of God in Christ, shows how speculatively Athanasius thought of the incarnation. If we keep our minds closer to the facts, what we really mean by the incarnation is that the life which Jesus lived in the flesh—that moral and spiritual life in the concrete fulness and wealth which the evangelists display—was divine; whether there is any analogy between the presence of God in it and that presence of God in the universe

[1] Translation from *A Select Library of Nicene and Post-Nicene Fathers*, Second Series, vol. iv. p. 58 (Oxford, 1892).

which is recognised by philosophy in the fact that the reign of law is co-extensive with the world, is a matter about which most Christians do not think, and about which few of those who do think would agree with Athanasius. Nevertheless, this speculative conception of the incarnation is the determining principle of all Athanasius' systematic Christian thinking. It is uppermost in his mind, and it depresses and thrusts into the background much that to men free from this speculative obsession must seem far more important. The incarnation means for him that the eternal Word assumed flesh in the womb of the Virgin; in doing so, He united the human nature to the divine; and in principle the atonement, or the reconciliation of humanity to God, was accomplished. As it has been expressed by more modern writers, the incarnation is the atonement or the reconciliation. "Since man alone (43. 3) of the creatures had departed from the order of his creation, it was man's nature that the Word united to Himself, thus repairing the breach between the creature and the Creator at the very point where it had occurred."[1] Repairing the breach, it must be added, by an incarnation which is consummated when the human nature is united to the divine in the miraculous conception—an incarnation which, whatever its motive on the part of the Word, can only be called metaphysical rather than moral.

Now, be the speculative fascination as great as it may, this is not a position in which a Christian mind can rest content. We know that we are not reconciled to God in the assumption of flesh by the Word in the Virgin's womb, but by the man Christ Jesus. We must get something at least of what is meant by the name of Jesus into this speculative incarnation if it is to have any value for us at all.

[1] Robertson in *Select Library,* ut supra, p. 32.

THE CHRISTIAN DOCTRINE OF RECONCILIATION

We must get this quasi-philosophical dogma charged with history, the history unfolded to us by the evangelists, if it is to hold any place in our minds. It may be that the more the history counts with us, the less interest we shall have in the dogma; but the history—in other words, that which we know of Jesus, and through which His reconciling power is exerted upon us—is the one thing we cannot do without. Dominated though he was by his speculative conception of the incarnation, Athanasius himself was conscious of this, and the great interest of his treatise to a modern reader is to see how much he has to make room for which has no essential relation to his principle.

At the very beginning he makes it plain that the incarnation of the Word has an ethical motive. It did not take place in the order of nature (φύσεως ἀκολουθίᾳ), but in accordance with the φιλανθρωπία and ἀγαθότης of His Father, and for our salvation (1. 3). But though it is ethical in motive, it is not specifically ethical in aim or result. Athanasius does no doubt at a later stage point to the triumphant history of Christianity in the moral world as illustrating the power of Christ and proving that He was the Son of God, the incarnate Word; the overthrow of idolatry, the reign of peace, the birth of continence, the scorn of death in His followers, all prove that Christ is what the Church declares Him to be. But this does not give the incarnation an inner relation to these things from the first; we do not see how it has produced them, nor is there any indication given that it was adapted or intended to produce them. The one thing which bulks in the mind of Athanasius from first to last is not the sin of man, nor the estrangement between man and God, nor the need of effecting a change in man's relation to God in the sphere of conscience, but the fact that man's sin made him liable to death, and that therefore to abolish death must be the supreme achievement of the Saviour. God had attached to sin the penalty of death, and He was bound to keep His word. But if He merely kept His word, then man, the creature He had made in His own image, would perish for ever: a conclusion not to be contemplated, because unbecoming and unworthy of the goodness of God (6. 10). Here was a difficulty God could not get over by a mere *fiat*: He could not simply take back His word, and annul the connection between death and sin. The liability to death was now inherent in human nature, and had to be dealt with in another way. Athanasius never wearies of expounding the way; he apologises for saying the same things so often, even about the same (20. 3). The opening sections of c. 9 are typical. "The Word, perceiving that no otherwise could the corruption of men be undone save by death as a necessary condition, while it was impossible for the Word to suffer death, being immortal and Son of the Father; to this end He takes to Himself a body capable of death, that it by partaking of the Word who is above all might be worthy (ἱκανὸν) to die in the stead of all, and might, because of the Word which was come to dwell in it, remain incorruptible, and that thenceforth corruption might be stayed from all by the grace of the resurrection. Whence, by offering unto death the body He Himself had taken, as an offering and sacrifice free from any stain, straightway He put away death from all His peers by the offering of an equivalent."[1] Although the terms "offering and sacrifice" naturally suggest to a New Testament reader some reference to sin, there is no express or interpreted reference of this kind in the treatise of Athanasius.

---

[1] Translation from *A Select Library of Nicene and Post-Nicene Fathers*, ut supra, p. 40 f.

THE CHRISTIAN DOCTRINE OF RECONCILIATION

The "corruption" mentioned in this passage is purely physical: it is φθορά as opposed to ἀφθαρσία, mortality as opposed to immortal life. This is conspicuous in what immediately follows. "And thus He, the incorruptible Son of God, being conjoined with all by a like nature, naturally clothed all with incorruption, by the promise of the resurrection. For the actual corruption in death has no longer holding ground against man, by reason of the Word, which by His own body has come to dwell among them." The fruit of the cross, he tells us emphatically at the close (56. 3), is resurrection and incorruption, and this is bestowed on men when the Nord returns in His glory.

In spite, however, of the concentration of thought on the incarnation, as the necessary preliminary to the abolition of death—in spite of the familiar formula αὐτὸς γὰρ ἐνηνθρώπησεν ἵνα ἡμεῖς θεοποιηθῶμεν, where the "deification" of man means no more than "that he is made incorruptible and immortal (54. 3)—room has to be made, consciously or unconsciously, under the pressure of the New Testament, for ideas more capable of verification in spiritual experience. The sense of this is curiously betrayed by Athanasius himself. As far as his conception of the incarnation is concerned, there is no reason in the nature of the case why the incarnate Word should not have died the moment He came to be. Athanasius has actually to find a reason why He did not do so. "He did not immediately upon His coming accomplish His sacrifice on behalf of all, by offering His body to death and raising it again, for by this means He would have made Himself invisible" (16. 4). On the theory of Athanasius, there was no reason why He should not have made Himself invisible in this way; but if He had done so, there would have been no man Christ Jesus, no gospel story, and no Christian relig-

[40]

ion. What this curious question—Why did not the Logos die when He became incarnate?—ought to have suggested to Athanasius, was that in his conception of the incarnation there was something radically unreal. Apart from the whole life depicted in the gospels there is no incarnation at all; the assumption of flesh by the Word is a phrase. What has value to God and reconciling power with man is not the incarnation conceived as the taking up of human nature into union with the divine; it is the personality of Jesus, fashioned, as every personality is fashioned, through the temptations and conflicts, the fidelities and sacrifices of life and death; the self which is offered to God as a ransom is the self which has acquired in these human experiences its being, its value, and its power; apart from these experiences and what He earned and achieved in them Jesus is nothing to us and has nothing to offer to God. But the speculative conception of the incarnation had become so organic to Greek theology that Athanasius could not transcend it, and when he made room beside it for things which Christianity could not do without it was inevitably in a somewhat casual way.

Sometimes a promising ray of light from the moral world breaks into his metaphysics, yet is not able to assert itself sufficiently. An interesting illustration occurs in 10. 5. Athanasius is referring to the fact that for the Christian death has lost its old character; it no longer has the curse in it of the primal sentence on sin (Gen. iii.). He knows as well as every Christian that the heart of Christianity is here.[1] But he never comes to deal expressly with the question how the

[1] Cf. 9. 4. "Our next step would be to narrate the end of his bodily life and conversation, and to tell also the nature of his bodily death (ὁποῖος γέγονεν ὁ τοῦ σώματος θάνατος); especially because this is the sum of our faith (τὸ κεφάλαιον τῆς πίστεως ἡμῶν), and all men are full of it."

character of death has been changed; or, in other words, how Christ has so dealt with sin—to which death owes its dreadful character—as that men may die reconciled to God, instead of dying under a curse. The formal references to the cross as curse in 25. 1. 2 do not supply the blank. When we come upon an expression like ἡ αὐτοδικαιοσύνη καὶ ὁ λυτρούμενος τὰς πάντων ἁμαρτίας (40. 2), our hopes are raised only to be dashed. When Athanasius recapitulates or summarises, as he is so fond of doing, sin and reconciliation fade from view. The moral world as good as vanishes, and we are left with nothing but physical categories, like corruption and incorruption, to interpret the work of Christ. "Now that the common Saviour of all has died on our behalf, we, the faithful in Christ, no longer die the death as before, agreeably to the warning of the law; for this condemnation has ceased; but"—here comes in his interpretation of words which surely demand a more ethical rendering—"corruption ceasing and being put away by the grace of the resurrection, henceforth we are only dissolved, agreeably to our bodies' mortal nature, at the time God has fixed for each, that we may be able to gain a better resurrection" (21. 1). It is not too much to say that the metaphysical incarnation which was the vital centre of Athanasius' thought—his sacramental union of the divine and the human in the incarnate Word—had dulled his sense of an ethical union and communion of man with God, and of the powers by which such a union and communion can be impaired and destroyed, or restored and perfected.[1] The same holds of Greek theology generally, and of the type of piety akin to it. It is too much out of

---

[1] It is significant that he only mentions the forgiveness of sins once, and then only in connection with Christ's work as seeking and saving the lost during His life on earth (14. 2).

relation to the world in which moral creatures, conscious of their estrangement from God, and needing and longing for reconciliation to Him, live and move and have their being. It asks and answers questions which are not theirs, and their questions it is apt to disregard. Though it is the theology of men who had the New Testament in their hands, and who could not but speak to a large extent in its language, it is at the same time the theology of men whose philosophy of the incarnation rendered them at times almost incredibly insensible to the facts of the life of Jesus, and to the way in which His death told on the sinful as a reconciling power. Possibly it is true that in modern theology Christ's victory over death has been too much overlooked. This corruptible must put on incorruption and this mortal must put on immortality: so St. Paul teaches, and so Athanasius may remind us. But the victory over death is conditioned by the victory over sin, and of this, unfortunately, Athanasius has little to say. The death of Christ makes us ἀνυπευθύνους καὶ ἐλευθέρους τῆς ἀρχαίας παραβάσεως (20. 2): it delivers us from the death in which Adam's sin involved mankind—that is all. And the benefit of this also comes to us in ways which are hardly ways of the ethical world—the ways of orthodox doctrine and of sacramental grace. It is true that Athanasius once uses the expression οἱ ἐν Χριστῷ πιστοί (21. 1); but no one would say that faith (πίστις) was in him, as in St. Paul for example, the element of all Christian experience. Experience, in short, has contributed too little to the doctrine of Athanasius on what Christ does for men; it has not sufficiently either inspired or controlled his thoughts; and great as are the patristic names which represent the same type of teaching from Irenaeus and Origen, through Athanasius and the Gregories, to Cyril of Alexandria and

THE CHRISTIAN DOCTRINE OF RECONCILIATION

John of Damascus, it is not here we can hope to find the true key to the doctrine of reconciliation.[1]

That there is a broad contrast between Greek and Latin, or more generally between Eastern and Western Christianity, is a familiar fact, and the general character of the contrast is also familiar. It has been put in a variety of ways which all mean the same thing. Western Christianity has been described as more realistic, more Biblical, more practical, more ecclesiastical, less speculative than Eastern. Its theology is less metaphysical and more psychological. In one word, it is more experimental. Nothing gives a better idea of the difference than to consider that in all the literature of the Greek Church there is no book which offers even a remote resemblance to Augustine's *Confessions*. Now reconciliation is pre-eminently a subject to be treated on the basis of experience. What it means and how it is accomplished can be known only to the reconciled, and we naturally expect the most vital contributions to the doctrine from men whose Christian personality and experience enters freely into their writings. It is in the world of ethics, not of metaphysics, that the real problems are raised; and even if, for this very reason, there is a greater possibility of fatal errors emerging, there is a greater hope of fundamental truths being reached.

Augustine's is undoubtedly the greatest name in the West, but it is impossible to ignore Tertullian, to whom Latin Christianity owes more, both of its ideas and its vocabulary, than to any other. Tertullian's interests were intensely practical, and his writings give us a more vivid idea than any others

[1] A very high estimate of the work of Athanasius, and a readiness to find in him both greater nearness to the New Testament and greater nearness to modern theology, may be seen in Thomasius, *Christi Person und Werk,* ii. 131 ff.; and also in Moberly's *Atonement and Personality,* 349 ff.

which survive, of what Christianity meant in the everyday life of men in his time. He was supremely interested in it as a law and a discipline, and he was especially concerned with the method in which that discipline was to be exercised so as to secure for it its proper place and power in the lives of the Church's adherents. He was a lawyer, and it was natural for him not only to make large use of the vocabulary of his profession—which he could do in the way of allusion or illustration—but to be largely influenced by its ruling categories. It is more owing to him than to any one that the relations of God and man came to be regarded as legal relations, and sin, for example, as a kind of legal liability, which might be dealt with in ways analogous to those with which his profession had made him familiar. This may be an inadequate way of conceiving sin, but it has the advantage of being definite and specific. The problem sin presents is not one which can be escaped by a flight into metaphysics or mysticism; it is much more intractable than the kind of problem faced by Athanasius in the *De Incarnatione Verbi*, and it demands a more palpable answer.

In meeting the docetic opinions of Marcion, Tertullian puts Christ's death with decisive emphasis into its true place. If Marcion was right, he says, "God's entire work is subverted. Christ's death, wherein lies the whole weight and fruit of the Christian name, is denied, though the apostle asserts it so expressly as undoubtedly real, making it the very foundation of the gospel, of our salvation, and of his own preaching."[1] In spite of this, however, Tertullian has no full interpretation of the death of Christ. The grace of God comes to man in or through it, but he does not directly explain how Even in connection with baptism, in which all the previous

---

[1] *Adv. Marcionem*, iii. 8.

sins of the baptized are cancelled, he does not lay stress on grace, but on the penitence by which the bestowal of grace is conditioned. The forgiveness of sins, in fact, is bought from the very beginning by a penitence which sincerely renounces the past, and as sincerely accepts the life of renunciations to which Christianity calls.[1]

But it is in connection with what is known as the second repentance—which for Tertullian is the last—that is, in connection with the reconciliation to the Church of those who have fallen into certain kinds of sin after baptism, that Tertullian develops ideas which came to have great influence on the Western theology of reconciliation. In the reconciliation of such penitents to the Church, and their restoration to fellowship with the body of Christ, we have to deal with an experience in the moral world, and with what it was every one's concern should be a profound, passionate, and determining experience; and the interest of this is that the penitential system of the Church, as it was conceived thus early by Tertullian, yielded the categories which were afterwards applied to interpret the reconciling work of Christ. All the elements in the later Roman Catholic sacrament of penance can clearly be distinguished in Tertullian; contrition, confession—it is of course public confession, and on this he lays immense stress [2]—and satisfaction. For the future, the last is the most significant. Satisfaction, in the strictly legal sense of the term, is identical with punishment.

---

[1] *De Paenitentia*, vi.: "Hoc enim pretio Dominus veniam addicere instituit, hac paenitentiae compensatione redimendam proponit impunitatem."

[2] *De Paenitentia*, x. f.: "Most men either shun this work, as being a public exposure of themselves, or else defer it from day to day. . . . They dread likewise the bodily inconveniences they must suffer: in that unwashen, sordidly attired, estranged from gladness, they must spend their time in the roughness of sackcloth, and in the horridness of ashes, and the sunkenness of face caused by fasting."

IN THE CHRISTIAN THOUGHT OF THE PAST

The man who has broken a law makes satisfaction by enduring the penalty which is attached by the law to his offence. But the "satisfaction" which is made by a Christian when after post-baptismal sin he is reconciled to the Church is not the acceptance of his sin's penalty. Even if the sorrow and tears of the Church which accompany his own are added to it, they do not raise it to this height. At the most the satisfaction is quasi-penal: it is something which is taken by God as a ground for annulling the real penalty: in Tertullian's own words, the penitent sinner, who makes satisfaction for his sin, *"temporali afflictatione aeterna supplicia non dicam frustratur sed expungit."* [1] The important point is that in order to be forgiven sin had to be taken seriously both by the sinner and by all who wished to help him and to whom he was to be reconciled, and that the seriousness of forgiveness was condensed into the term satisfaction.

This term is not applied in Tertullian to the work of Christ in relation to sin;[2] *He* is not conceived as making satisfaction to God, in whatever sense; to make satisfaction is the work of the sinner himself. But Tertullian speaks of the Church as sympathising with the penitent and co-operating with him in the quest for reconciliation, and in the very connection in which he does so, he identifies the Church with Christ. "Non potest corpus de unius membri vexatione laetum agere; condoleat universum et ad remedium con laboret, necesse est. In uno et altero ecclesia est, ecclesia vero Christus. Ergo cum te ad fratrum genua protendis, Christum contrectas, Christum exoras. Aeque illi cum super te lacrimas agunt, *Christus patitur, Christus patrem deprecatur.*

---

[1] *De Paenitentia*, ix.

[2] Cyprian applies the "satisfacere Deo" to Christ: *v.* Harnack, *Dogmengeschichte*, 1. 482, *note.*

THE CHRISTIAN DOCTRINE OF RECONCILIATION

Facile impetratur semper quod Filius postulat."[1] Here the way is not obscurely indicated to the use which was afterwards so largely made of the penitential system of the Church and of its ruling ideas, as giving a key to the interpretation of the work of Christ in connection with the reconciliation of sinners to God. The formula was bound to come, and for better or worse it did come, that Christ by His death—in which is concentrated "the whole weight and fruit of the Christian name"—made satisfaction for sins. But the original ambiguity of *satisfactio* and *satisfacere* clung to the term. Some rendered it rigorously in the legal sense, and then to make satisfaction was the same thing as to pay the penalty, which in this case was eternal death. Others, in accordance with the facts involved in the sinner's satisfaction for his own sin, could only regard the satisfaction of Christ as improperly or quasi penal. It was far more adequate than anything the sinner could offer to God—it was adequate to satisfy God for the sin of the whole world; but it was not, as the assumption just referred to would have made it, something to which the human satisfactions performed by penitents bore no analogy at all. There had to be pain or sacrifice in it as in all satisfactions made by men, but it was not precisely penal pain. It was pain by which the penal pain due to sin was avoided. It was pain which in a way was a substitute for punishment: "*In quantum non peperceris tibi, in tantum tibi Deus, credo, parcet*" (*De Paen.* ix.). If we do not find in Tertullian the Anselmic formula that every sin must be followed by *either* satisfaction *or* punishment,[2] we find ideas which remarkably approximate to it.

Few things in the history of Christian thinking are more extraordinary than the progeny of this ambiguous idea of

---
[1] *De Paenitentia,* x.   [2] Anselm, *Cur Deus Homo,* i. xv.

satisfaction. Many theologians in applying it to Christ took it in the strict legal sense. He made satisfaction for sin by enduring the penalty which was due for it to man. But this penalty was eternal death, or the pains of hell. Could any one say that Christ had endured this? Luther said so. "In His innocent, tender heart He was obliged to taste for us eternal death and damnation, and, in short, to suffer everything that a condemned sinner has merited and must suffer for ever." And again: "*Sensit poenam infernalem.*"[1] Calvin, with all his constitutional caution, is almost equally emphatic. He makes much of the *Descensus ad inferos*, "that invisible and incomprehensible judgment which He underwent at the bar of God; that we might know that not only was the body of Christ given up as the price of our redemption, but that there was another greater and more excellent price—namely, that He endured in His soul the dreadful torments of a condemned and lost man."[2] One might conceive a man driven to this by the logic of legal satisfaction, and contemplating it with awe, but there is no trace of such emotions in the statement of it by John Owen, which cannot be read without a shudder. "The punishment due to our sin and the chastisement of our peace was upon Him; which that it was the pains of hell, in their nature and being, in their weight and pressure, though not in tendence and continuance (it being impossible that He should be detained by death), who can deny and not be injurious to the justice of God, which will inevitably inflict those pains to eternity upon sinners?" M. Rivière[3] thinks that this terrible idea of Christ's satisfaction for sin originated in Protestantism, but, as we

---

[1] See the abundant collection of passages in Köstlin, *Luthers Theologie*, II. 411 f.

[2] Calvin, *Institutio*, II. xvi. 10.   [3] *Etude Théologique*, 248 f.

shall see later, he can illustrate it copiously from Catholic preachers, and it is really given in the very conception of satisfaction when the term is taken in the strictly legal sense.

Another strange branch from the same root developed in the Middle Ages. The satisfaction rendered by the sinner came to be looked at materially, as a thing or *quantum* which was what it was and had its own value unconditionally, provided only it was there. It was quite possible in the mediæval Church for a rich man to hire a poor man to do for him the satisfaction which the penitential discipline of the Church imposed on him for his sins—say, to recite the Psalter a certain number of times, or to fast a certain number of days. The Church naturally objected to this as immoral, but it was too much in keeping with a purely legal conception of sin to be easily overcome. The very formula in which it was condemned—He who takes the sins of others on himself is not worthy to be called a Christian [1]—shows that this was a case in which the worst had come to be through the corruption of the best. For surely there is a high sense in which to take the sins of others on oneself is the very badge of the true Christian. Tertullian represents the Church as shedding tears with the penitents, entering with sympathy into the whole ethical process through which their sin is overcome and their reconciliation achieved—joining with them, in fact, in making satisfaction; and it is in this sympathetic entrance into the experience of the penitents, in this taking the sins of others on itself, that he identifies the Church with Christ. This is the other line, the spiritual as opposed to the legal or material one, on which the penitential system with its satisfactions yielded ideas for the interpretation of Christ's work. It was the parent not only

---

[1] Cremer in *Studien und Kritiken*, 1893.

of the crude and immoral *redemptiones* of the Middle Ages, when the satisfaction for sin was a *thing* which any one could render mechanically for any one else, but also of what many have regarded as the loftiest and most spiritual interpretation of the reconciling work of Christ, that which makes it with Macleod Campbell and Moberly a vicarious penitence. We do not need to make Tertullian responsible for either of these developments, or to say which can best legitimate itself in his thought. The real interest is that the work of Christ is henceforth going to be interpreted on the analogy of human experiences in the moral world, experiences in which sin and satisfaction and reconciliation may be poignantly real. They may not enable us completely to interpret the cross, but, at all events, the light they throw on it will be the light by which men actually live.

While much both of the thought and the language of Western Christianity is owing to Tertullian, its supreme representative is Augustine. Augustine was a great nature, and what Bagehot called an experiencing nature. All that befell him, and especially all that he had responsibility for, struck deep roots into deep soil. He had a unique power of self-observation and of self-expression. He had lived in sin, and had been delivered from it, and in the estimation of the Catholic Church he ranks as a great saint. If any one can give us real help to the truth about Christian reconciliation, it ought to be such a man. It is true that Augustine in his pre-Christian days had been not only a sinner but a philosopher, and that when he became a Christian he found it even harder to get rid of his philosophical bias than of his sensuality. The strain of Neo-platonism, not to speak of Manichaeism, came out in his mind to the very end, and, as an infra-Christian mode of thinking, it sometimes curiously flawed what was otherwise pure Christian truth.

Sin has admittedly the double character of involving responsibility and of bringing with it moral disablement. It is something we have to answer for, and it is also something which enslaves us and keeps us from doing what we would and what we ought to do. No sinner can help being conscious of his sin in both modes, but in Augustine the latter immensely preponderated. It was not responsibility, or the bad conscience attending on sin, which mainly troubled him; it was the bondage of the will, intensified, as he came to believe, into a corruption of the whole nature. It is not necessary for our present purpose to raise any of the questions involved in the Pelagian controversy; but it is obvious that the more distressing the experience of sin, the more serious must be the problem of redemption and reconciliation. Augustine was perfectly sure that he could not save himself from his sins; without divine help he was a lost man. But the point is that the divine help, if it was to bring salvation from sin, must come in the form of a power annulling his inability to good, renewing his corrupt nature, restoring energy and freedom for good to his will. Although it is fair to say that in the West as contrasted with the East, Christian thought deals with sin and forgiveness rather than with death and immortality, in Augustine it is not guilt and pardon that are in the foreground, but moral impotence and renewing grace. And grace is not an attitude or a disposition on the part of God to the sinner; it is infused grace; it is a holy divine power actually lodged in the heart of man and enabling him to overcome his old sins. This is the grace which justifies the sinful, and it justifies him progressively by making him more and more righteous.

IN THE CHRISTIAN THOUGHT OF THE PAST

This is in keeping with the Neo-platonic philosophy, in which good is identical with being, and evil is conceived negatively as the mere defect or absence of good. Man's moral inability can be regarded as just such a defect, which is made good by the coming to the sinner of the strong grace of God.

But how does God's grace come to man for his salvation? This is by no means an idle question. The philosopher—who is ideally a god-intoxicated man—is apt to assume unconsciously that it comes directly, without any mediation. No philosophy has ever been more independent of history, or more indifferent to it, than Neo-platonism, and a philosophy which ignores history can, of course, have no essential place for Christ. As we shall see, there are traces even in Augustine of this radically non-Christian mental attitude, but in the main he gives the only Christian answer to all questions about grace: "No man can be reconciled to God and come to God except through Christ." [1] "The whole Church holds that every man is separated from God but he who is reconciled to him through Christ the mediator, and that no one is separated from God except by the sins which cut him off. Hence there is no reconciliation except by remission of sins, and that only through the grace of the compassionate Saviour." [2] The great thing in salvation is no doubt renewal, or *renovatio*; but, as Augustine himself says, *"renovatio in-*

---

[1] *De Peccatorum Mer. et Rem.,* 1. lxii.: "Non alienentur parvuli a gratia remissionis peccatorum. Non aliter transitur ad Christum; nemo aliter potest Deo reconciliari et ad Deum venire nisi per Christum."

[2] *Ibid.,* 1. lvi.: "Universa ecclesia tenet . . . omnem hominem separari a Deo nisi qui per mediatorem Christum reconciliatur Deo, nec separari quemquam nisi peccatis intercludentibus posse. Non ergo reconciliari nisi peccatorum remissione, per unam gratiam misericordissimi salvatoris, per unam victimam verissimi sacerdotis."

cipit a remissione,"[1] and remission is everywhere connected with Christ. Though grace is the grace of God, and is ultimately indistinguishable from the presence of God in the heart—it is *He* who says to the soul, "I am thy salvation" —it is not for the Christian a thing of which he has either idea or experience apart from Christ.

Sometimes this is recognised in Augustine with a breadth which admits of no definition or limitation. This is especially the case where reference is made to the name of Christ. Thus, is a well-known passage of the *Confessions*,[2] speaking of the enthusiasm for philosophy awakened in him by reading Cicero's *Hortensius*, he says: "To the great ardour which this book kindled there was only one drawback, that the name of Christ was not there. For this name, according to Thy mercy, O Lord, this name of my Saviour, Thy Son, my tender heart drank in even with my mother's milk and kept hidden in its depths (*pie biberat et alte retinebat*); and no book, be it ever so learned, polished, or true, where that name was not found, could wholly take possession of me." There is more of the secret of Christ's reconciling and renewing power revealed in a sentence like this than can easily be reduced to a formula, but Augustine does not shrink from definite thoughts on the subject. His great word for the interpretation of Christ in His saving work is Mediator. In view of the sin of man—his original sin, aggravated by all kinds of actual transgressions, and exposing him to the wrath of God—"a mediator was necessary, that is, a reconciler (*reconciliator*), who by the offering of a unique sacrifice, of which all the sacrifices of the law and the prophets were shadows, should

---

[1] Notebook, p. 211, foot (Gottschick).
[2] Lib. iii. c. iv.

appease this wrath."[1] There is nothing metaphysical in this conception of Christ as mediator. He does not, like the Logos in some philosophies, mediate between God and the universe, or even between God and man; He mediates specifically between God and sinners. Augustine's favourite text in this connection is 1 Tim. ii. 5: "There is one God, one mediator also between God and man, himself man, Christ Jesus, who gave himself a ransom for all." Augustine believed that Christ Jesus was both God and man, but it was as man He did His mediating and reconciling work.[2] This is important, because it leaves it open to him, or rather obliges him, to interpret that work by human analogies. In the passage just quoted from the *Enchiridion*, Augustine has used the figure of a sacrifice—*sacrificium singulare*, he calls it—which was universally current in the Church. He does it without explanation, as was usual; but he assumes, as was also usual, that the sacrifice dealt with sin for its removal, and so annulled the wrath of God. In another passage, where the power of demons is that which has to be overcome, he writes: "It is overcome then in His name who assumed man and lived without sin, that in Himself, *priest and sacrifice*, there might be made remission of sins, that is, through the mediator between God and men, the man Christ Jesus: through Him, when He had made purgation of sins, we are reconciled to God."[3] The uniqueness of Christ's sac-

---

[1] *Enchiridion de Fide, Spe et Charitate*, 10.

[2] Sermo ccxciii. 7: The apostle, he says, quoting Rom. ix. 5, knew Christ to be God, and God over all; yet when it came to the point of commending Him as mediator he did not call Him God, but the man Christ Jesus. "Non enim per hoc mediator est, quod Deus est; sed per hoc mediator, quia factus est homo."

[3] *De Civitate Dei*, x. 22.

THE CHRISTIAN DOCTRINE OF RECONCILIATION

rifice is condensed in the fact that He is at once priest and victim; it is this which makes His sacrifice the reality to which all the sacrifices of the Old Testament are but shadows. But it remains to be discovered how we are to attach any rational and ethical ideas to the designation of Christ as at the same time sacrifice and priest. A real clue is put into our hand in *De Civitate Dei* (x. 6), where Augustine discusses the true conception of sacrifice, apart (in the first instance) from any relation to Christ. The true sacrifice must have as its object man's attachment to God in a holy fellowship (*ut sancti societate inhaereamus Deo*). It must be related to the supreme good, in the possession of which we may be truly blessed. "A man himself, who is consecrated in the name of God and vowed to God, in so far as he dies to the world that he may live to God, is a sacrifice." May we not say that it is in this sense that Christ is a sacrifice, and that it is because He leads from beginning to end the kind of life here described, and is able to draw sinful men into fellowship with Himself in it, that He is acceptable in God's sight, and that God for His sake puts away His wrath against the sinful, and admits them to His peace? When we say this, at all events, we are saying what we can understand. We are speaking of the man Christ Jesus, and of an ethical achievement of that man, which is intelligible to us, and not alien. We are dealing with something which is transacted in the moral world and makes a moral appeal to us. The sacrifices which Augustine assumes to be required from the Christian when he seeks reconciliation after sin, furnish an analogy by which we can interpret the sacrifice of Christ. "You are a sinner," he says; "take vengeance on yourself, descend into your conscience, exact the penalty from yourself, torture yourself; for thus you offer sacrifice." And again: "It is not enough to change your manners for the better, and to give up evil deeds, unless satisfaction also be made to God for what has been done, by the pain of penitence, by the sighing of humility, by the sacrifice of the contrite heart and the co-operation of alms." [1] Of course Christ could not offer such sacrifice for His own sins, for He knew no sin; but was it impossible for Him, when moved by compassion for sinners, to be affected in relation to God and their sins in a way which such language may not inappropriately describe? Augustine says expressly that He made our sins His own that He might make His righteousness ours.[2] But if He made our sins His own, must not His experience, and especially His emotions, in regard to them, have been in *reality* what ours *ought* to have been? He would really feel the sorrow we should have felt; He would really acknowledge the wrong in them all as we should have acknowledged it, but for deadness of conscience could not; He would really submit, as our pride and fear prevented us from submitting, to the consequences attached to sin by God. Augustine does not believe that sin is ever unattended by such consequences. Pardon involves the acceptance of them, and hence he does not shrink from using words like *punishment* even in connection with Christ. "By taking on Him punishment (*poenam*) and not taking on Him guilt (*culpam*) He destroyed both guilt and punishment." [3] But we have to remember here what has already been said about interpreting Christ's reconciling work on the analogy of the penitential system. Though an ancient writer could derive *poenitere* from *poenam tenere*, it was only in an improper

---

[1] Gottschick, 138 f.
[2] Gottschick, 168.
[3] Compare Gottschick, 181 f.: "Suscepit Christus sine reatu supplicium nostrum, ut inde solveret reatum nostrum et finiret etiam supplicium nostrum."

sense that the sufferings, or renunciations, or sacrifices demanded from sinners under this system, by way of satisfaction, could be called penal. Strictly speaking, they were not punishments, but the means by which punishment was averted. Hence, just as Tertullian can say of the penitent sinner, that *afflictatione temporali aeterna supplicia expungit*, so Augustine can say of Christ, *Mortem tuam aeternam occidit mors temporalis Domini.*" When Christ died as He did die on the cross, He was not punished, but He accepted the last consequence of sin in a spirit with which God was well pleased; He made a satisfaction to God—though Augustine does not use the term *satisfactio* to describe what He did—on the ground of which God can turn His anger and punishment away from all who come to be one with Christ.

This last point is of the highest importance in Augustine. Christ is the head of a body which is one with Him, and it is His body only for which His work avails. *"Non justificat nisi corpus suum, quod est ecclesia."* [1] The Word became flesh, he says, that He might become head of the Church. Often when Christ speaks, it is *ex persona ecclesiae*. He suffered in the Church and the Church in Him.[2] When He cried, "My God, my God, why hast thou forsaken me!" He spoke *ex persona membrorum*. He was completely identified with His members in all their interests and fortunes. But this identification is not metaphysical, it is ethical. It is not one with the assumption of flesh by the Word, it is the supreme achievement of the love of Christ for sinners. It is the *ne plus ultra* of love, the utmost reach of its moral passion. And it is by something correspondingly intense

[1] Gottschick, 166 f.
[2] Epist. cxl. (Gaume's Ed., II. 638 A.C.).

and ethical that we become one with Him, and share in the benefits of His passion. He not only unites Himself to us, but He unites us to Himself, and it is as we are caught up into this union that all the experiences of reconciliation—its blessings and its cost—come home to us together. In this connection the language of Augustine is nothing less than astounding. Christ and His members are one Christ, he writes. And a little further on, "We have been made not only Christians, but Christ." [1] Christ includes us in one body with Himself (*concorporans nos sibi*), making us His members, that in Him we also might be Christ. It is through this in the long run that we are reconciled and renewed.

Augustine has apparently little interest in the question, that had been raised even in this time, whether this way of reconciling men to God was necessary. They are fools, he says bluntly, who declare that the wisdom of God could not otherwise set man free than by assuming man, being born of a woman, and suffering at the hands of sinners.[2] Yet this purpose of redemption was the cause of the incarnation. Christ had no reason for coming into the world but to save sinners.[3] This is the true experimental and Biblical ground on which to stand. Attractive as it may appear to speculative minds, the idea that Christ would have come apart from this redemptive purpose—to complete creation, or give humanity a Head—departs from the line of religious and especially of Christian interest. It finds the motive of the incarnation in some speculative or metaphysical fitness, and not where Scripture and experience put it, in love. It

[1] In *Joan. Evgm. Tractatus*, xii. 8; xxi. 8.
[2] *De Agone Christiano*, 12 (xi.).
[3] Sermo clxxv. 1: "Christi nulla fuit causa veniendi nisi peccatores salvos facere."

THE CHRISTIAN DOCTRINE OF RECONCILIATION

is the supreme distinction of Augustine among the representatives of the ancient Church that he conceived Christ fundamentally as the mediator of the love of God to sinful men, and that when he spoke of that love he charged it with all the meaning that can be drawn from the gospel story. None of the fathers is steeped as he was in the synoptic gospels; none had learned so profoundly as he, from the whole life and passion of Jesus, what the love of God to sinners means. In spite of the Neo-platonic taint in his conception of renewing grace, when he comes to the point it is the love of God as exhibited in the man Christ Jesus which is everything to him. This is what makes him the most living of all the fathers. For nothing but love wins and reconciles.[1]

Augustine is very conscious of the difficulties involved in the idea that the love of the eternal God should only be revealed at a particular time, and especially in the idea that the love which came from God Himself in Christ should make a difference in God's attitude to men, but he simply states the difficulties in the most vivid form; he does not solve them. "Far be it from God to love any one in time with, as it were, a new love which was not in Him before."[2] Yet there must be some way in which justice is done both to God's eternal love to men, which is the source of salvation, and to His wrath against sinners, which constitutes the need of salvation. Using the term "hatred" to express the latter, Augustine says that in a wondrous and divine way even when God hated us He loved us. He knew how, at one and the

---
[1] *De Fide et Symbolo*, 18: "Non enim reconciliamur illi nisi per dilectionem qua etiam filii appellamur."
[2] Gottschick, 121, *note* 211.

same time, in every one of us, both to hate what was our work and to love what was His own. He loved all His saints before the foundation of the world, *sicut praedestinavit*; but when they are converted and find Him, then they are *said*—it is only a *façon de parler*—*to begin to be loved by him*. The truer truth is *diligenti reconciliati sumus*.[1] He already loves us when we are reconciled; or, as Calvin put it afterwards, wrestling with the same problem, *"Quia prius diligit, postea nos sibi reconciliat."*[2] It ought to be acknowledged, in spite of his profound sense of the corruption of human nature, that Augustine recognises in man the capacity for redemption. There is still in the sinner something which is of God and which is dear to God; he even uses the startling expression "Christ loved nothing in us but God"—or the divine.[3] It recalls Ritschl's definition of Christian love as the identification of oneself with God's interest in others, or with that which is of God in them, and by bringing the love of Christ once more within the range of a human analogy, it helps us to understand it more fully.

But there is one aspect of Christ's love, or one mode of its manifestation, to which Augustine ascribes supreme power in the work of subduing sinners, winning them, and reconciling them to God—namely, His humility. This it was which exercised an overpowering influence upon Augustine himself. Nothing could show more conclusively that his conception of the mediator and His love comes from the gospel story and from it alone. We may seek in vain in the Epicureans and Stoics, in the Manichaeans and Platonists,

[1] Gottschick, 113.
[2] *Institutio*, 11. xvi. 3.
[3] In *Joan. Evgm. Tractatus*, lxv. 2: "Quid enim nisi Deum dilexit in nobis? Non quod habebamus sed ut haberemus."

THE CHRISTIAN DOCTRINE OF RECONCILIATION

for the one thing which is most characteristic of the gospel. Whatever else we find in them, we do not find humility. *"Via humilitatis hujus aliunde manet: a Christo venit. Haec via ab illo est qui cum esset altus, humilis venit."* It is the sum of Christ's teaching. *"Quid enim aliud docuit humiliendo se, factus obediens usque ad mortem, mortem autem crucis? Quid aliud docuit solvendo quod non debebat, ut nos a debito liberaret? Quid aliud docuit baptizatus qui peccatum non fecit, crucifixus qui reatum non habebat? Quid aliud docuit nisi hanc humanitatem?"*[1] It is so great a thing to be a little one that unless Christ, who is so great, condescended to teach us we could never learn the lesson.[2] The primal sin and the root of all sins is pride, the desire and determination to be independent of God; and we cannot be reconciled to God but in the humility which is willing to be absolutely dependent on Him, and which appeals to us irresistibly in the lowly life of Jesus. It is impossible to exaggerate the place of such thoughts in the mind and heart of Augustine, and they passed from the gospels through him into the life of the Western Church as the most vital and valuable element in its piety. Christianity may be said to be summed up in this one word, *humilitas*. *"Est paene una disciplina Christiana."*[3] And again, *"Doctrina Christiana, humilitatis praeceptum."* This is the ethical side of the matter, but what is most relevant to the subject of these lectures is that the humility of Christ, as it is revealed in His life and death, is the most moving form in which the reconciling love of God appeals to the great soul of Augustine. It is his last word in the gospel of reconciliation: *"Jam humilis Deus et adhuc superbus homo?"*[4]

The philosophical strain in Augustine—the strain, in other

---
[1] *Enarratio in Psalmum*, xxxi. 18.
[2] *De Sancta Virginitate*, 35.
[3] Sermo cccli. 4.
[4] Sermo clx. 5.

words, which was apt to be indifferent to history, and therefore eventually to the historical importance of Christ—betrays its survival, in spite of all that has just been said of his debt to the gospels, in one or two singular passages which must not be ignored. They are passages in which the idea of grace—which, when it has reconciling and renewing power, must be identified with the life of lowly love in which it is revealed—is treated as if it were independent of Christ and His life and death in the flesh, and related to God alone. Instead of being the mediator of grace, Christ stands as the supreme illustration or example of it. The grace by which Christ is good from the beginning is the same by which others, His members, are changed from bad to good.[1] Every man from the beginning of his faith is made a Christian by the same grace by which that man, the son of Mary, is made the Christ. He is not only an *exemplum vitae*, that by imitating Him we may live righteously; He is also *exemplum gratiae*, that by believing on Him we may hope to owe righteousness of our own to the same source to which He owed His.[2] The most striking form in which Augustine puts his view, is that which makes Christ the most illustrious example of predestination. In his book on the predestination of the saints, he says in effect, "Look at the Saviour Himself, the mediator between God and man, the man Christ Jesus. Will any one say that by antecedent merits of its own, whether of works or of faith, the human nature which is in Him acquired this position, or came to be what it is?" "Respondeatur quæso: ille homo, ut a Verbo Patri coaeterno in unitatem

---

[1] *Op. imperf. contra Julianum,* I. cxxxviii. and cxl.

[2] The doubtful reading in this sentence (*Operis imperf. contra Julianum,* I. cxl.)—*per ipsum* or *per spiritum*—I have omitted in translating. If *per ipsum* is read, it is an attempt to combine the experimental with the philosophical view of grace, which is at least formally inconsistent with itself.

personæ assumptus, Filius Dei unigenitus esset, *unde hoc meruit?*" If this is offered as any suggestion of how men are saved by the grace of God—the reconciliation of sinners to God being brought into some kind of parallelism to the predestination of the Son of Mary to be the Christ—the true answer is that absolute predestination is not the explanation of anything in the moral world. The man who asserts predestination thus, without mitigation or remorse, has cancelled the world of history and experience, and cannot say anything to the purpose whether about the Saviour or the saved. It is a wonderful proof of the tenacity of what is bred in the bone, that a man who could say what Augustine has said of the reconciling power of God's love as exhibited in the humility of Jesus should still be haunted by a conception of God and his salvation which really dates from his pre-Christian days and is completely irrelevant to the gospel.

It is hardly an exaggeration to say that in Augustine may be found, latent or patent, all the ideas on which the Western Church lived for a thousand years. His own experience as a Christian was so profound, intense, and varied, that it could not soon be systematised; there is no trace of system in his own self-expression, and just as little—though there is more formalism—in even the greatest of his successors, like Pope Gregory I. Hence we do not lose anything for our purpose if we pass directly from Augustine to Anselm, from the fifth century to the eleventh. Anselm, the first and perhaps the greatest of the scholastic theologians, made a truly heroic effort to present the truth of the Christian doctrine of reconciliation in a scientific and systematic form. For him, as for all Christians in his time, there was only one dogma, that of the incarnation of the God-man; this was the one truth on which the Church as a whole had declared its mind. The title of his famous work, *Cur Deus Homo?*—Why did God become man?—intimates that what he is in quest of is the rationale of Christianity itself. If he can answer his question, he has rationalised the Christian religion and raised to the level of science the dogma which was accepted by faith on the authority of the Church. Anselm emphasises in his preface this character of his work. The argument that he is going to conduct, though it is all about Christ, does not owe anything to Christ. It is to be as convincing to Jews and pagans as to Christians, to those who are stating objections to the truth as to those who acknowledge the truth, to those who are seeking reasons *for* faith as to those who are seeking the reasons *of* faith. This is not attractive or convincing to the modern reader. We are not interested in what can be said in defence of Christianity *remoto Christo* or *quasi nihil sciatur de Christo*; we do not believe that Christ and all that the Church believes about Him—including the contents of the gospels—can be deduced by a necessary process of reasoning from any premises whatsoever, just as we do not believe that history is a subject for deductive reasoning at all. History is a datum, and even in Christ it has to be taken as it is given, not deduced. Nevertheless, Anselm was a great Christian, and in answering the question *Cur Deus Homo?* he wrote a great book. Put briefly, the answer to the question is that God became man because only thus could sin be dealt with for man's salvation, and God's end in the creation of man secured. In other words, the rationale of the incarnation is in the atonement. It is through the atonement that the incarnation is seen to be rationally necessary and therefore credible. All Christians accept it as a fact, but those who follow Anselm's arguments, and are convinced by them, accept it also as a necessity of reason. It has its place not only in faith but in science.

It would be possible to give a fair account of Anselm, centring on two of his famous sentences: *Nondum considerasti quanti ponderis sit peccatum* (1. xxi.), and *Deum non decet aliquid in suo regno inordinatum dimittere* (1. xii.). It is safer, however, to follow the order of his own thoughts.

Even in the eleventh century, Anselm met people who made the objections to the Christian faith which are current to-day. If God had to redeem men, why could He not redeem them *sola voluntate*, by the mere exercise of His will? Why speak of redemption at all? Whose slaves are we from whom God cannot deliver us merely by putting forth His almighty power? If you speak of being redeemed from His anger, is not His anger simply His will to punish, and can He not change His will without more ado? Then, going past these preliminary yet far reaching objections, the atonement as it was currently presented is directly assailed. "Who, if he were to condemn the innocent that he might set free the guilty, would not himself be judged worthy of condemnation?" (1. viii.). It is because he writes with these objections present to his mind—objections to the very idea of an atonement, and objections to the atonement as it was believed to have been in point of fact accomplished—that Anselm has made one of the great contributions to this doctrine.

His fundamental assumption, which is often overlooked, ought to be put in the foreground. It is that God's end in the creation of man must be attained. This is an agreed point before the discussion opens. God created man for blessedness in fellowship with Himself, and therefore man must attain to such blessedness. If he did not, God's intention would be finally defeated, which is for Anselm an impossible supposition. Here he is at one with Athanasius (see p. 39 *supra*). We might ask whether the natural and inevitable inference from this rational necessity, as Anselm calls it, is not universal salvation, but this is a question he does not raise. He proceeds to point out that all men by their sin have forfeited the blessedness of communion with God, and can therefore only attain to their chief end through the remission of sins (1. x.). Hence the question arises, What is sin?

This is a question which had not before been asked with sufficient precision, yet it is one on the answer to which all ideas of the nature and necessity of atonement are dependent. Sin, according to Anselm, consists in the creature's withholding from God the honour which is His due. "He who does not render to God the honour which is due to Him takes away from God what is His; he robs God of His honour (*Deum exhonorat*), and this is sin" (1. xi.). There has been much discussion of Anselm's introduction into theology of the honour of God. What does it really mean? It may be that it carries with it some flavour of ideas of personal rank or dignity, such as lay at the root of the feudal system. But this is certainly not the main thing, and it is absurd to say that Anselm, or those to whom his thoughts appealed, conceived of God as a feudal baron, and not as the Father of our Lord Jesus Christ. When Anselm speaks of sin as robbing God of honour, it is his way of saying that when we sin we wrong a person, and an infinitely great person, not merely a law or a principle; and it is not very bold to say that no conception of sin which ignores this is adequate to the truth about sin as it is revealed in the Christian conscience. Anselm himself is only too apt to conceive of sin quantitatively, as if it were a thing, which could be quite well comprehended without any personal reference at all; but when he presents it as the withholding of honour from God, or as the dishonouring of God, the personal reference, which is indispensable, is brought into view.

We now have man in his sin on the one hand; and on the other, unattainable because of sin, yet destined, as truly as God is God, to be attained, we have the blessedness of man in communion with his Maker. What is to be done? If God is not to suffer a final defeat, sin must be annulled or overcome somehow. It is the highest merit of Anselm that he sees it to be impossible for God to ignore sin, or to treat it as less real or less awful than it is. To forgive sins by a mere arbitrary exercise of will would be to treat sin as if it were not, and so to bring confusion into God's kingdom. It would not be the annulling of sin, but the annulling of the moral order through which God expresses Himself in the world; go to the bottom, and it would mean not that sin had ceased to be sin, but that God had ceased to be God (I. xii.). It does not become God, as Anselm puts it, *aliquid in suo regno inordinatum dimittere*. Nothing, he says, is less to be endured in the moral world (*in ordine rerum*) than that the creature should take away the honour due to the Creator, and not pay or make good what it takes away. We can see now that there are present to Anselm's mind two modes or aspects of sin with which the atoning work of Christ has to do. On the one hand, we must think of it as the violation of a universal moral order, a violation carrying consequences in its train which cannot be treated as if they were not. On the other, we must think of it as an infringement of the honour due to a very great person, an honour which is defined by Anselm as the submission of the will of the rational creature to the will of his Creator. These two ways of conceiving sin blend to some extent in Anselm's mind, and if we would be just to him we must remember both; but the form of his thoughts—it would not be as true to say their substance—is mainly determined by the latter. It is with sin as the taking away by man of the honour due to God that he is expressly concerned.

Now here there are only two possibilities, and Anselm simply announces them. God's honour must be restored, and it can be restored—here he argues from human analogies—either by satisfaction being done for the offence, or by punishment for it being endured. In the case of satisfaction the offender makes good his offence, in the case of punishment it is made good upon him by the act of the offended.

Of these two ways of dealing with sin, punishment, it might be said, is the simpler, and raises no problems. If God punished sin He would merely make good His own honour upon the sinner, without the sinner's will, and the sinner would perish under the infliction. It is putting the case too strongly to say that this raises no problems; it raises no special problems, but it brings up the all inclusive problem of man's creation. Why did God create rational beings at all if they were to perish thus? Why did He begin to do something which He was not able to finish? According to Anselm, it is inconceivable that God's purpose in creating man should be finally frustrated in this fashion; and as this is an assumption of reason, it is rationally necessary that not the easy way of punishment, but the hard way of satisfaction, should be followed in dealing with human sin. Anselm is profoundly impressed with its hardness, and this also is to be set down to his credit. It is not enough, he argues, to restore what one has taken away; there is something (so it might seem) of insult as well as injury in depriving God of His honour; and the sinner *pro contumelia illata*, for the contempt he has put upon God, must give back more than he has taken away. If we take this too pedantically, it may be made to introduce analogies which are quite foreign to the divine nature and to the relations of God and man; it has been interpreted to mean that God to Anselm was a Norman baron, and sinners creatures to be treated as unmannerly vassals. But there is nothing like this in the *Cur Deus Homo*. What is suggested in the passage quoted (I. xi.) is that in sin a person has been wantonly wronged as well as a law broken, and that the situation thus created is not one which can be formally or easily adjusted. It is rather one of tragic intensity. Sin creates an enormous liability. We ought not, Anselm argues, to commit the slightest sin for worlds; not to gain worlds, not even to save worlds from ruin, should we permit ourselves a single glance contrary to the will of God. Hence to make satisfaction for sin not even the world would be enough to offer to God; no, not whole series of worlds. Something must be offered greater than all worlds, greater than everything which is less than God Himself.

A satisfaction like this, manifestly, is out of man's power; he cannot render it. But it does not need to be urged that *this* satisfaction is impossible for the sinner; *all* satisfaction is equally so. Whatever good a man does or can do is already due to God on other grounds, and cannot be brought into account as satisfaction for sin. If, however, satisfaction is to be rendered at all, it must be by a human being, one of the same stock with the sinner. The emphasis laid by Anselm on this point is not to be ignored. It may be due to a peculiarity of Germanic law, according to which only the fellow tribesmen of an offender were allowed to make satisfaction for him; the act of satisfying proceeding on the basis of a natural unity existing between the performer and him for whom the performance was done. But it may also be due—though Anselm is supposed to be arguing on grounds of pure reason, and with no debt to revelation—to the unconscious influence of the New Testament idea that the Saviour and the saved are all of one (Heb. ii. 11). At all events, Anselm is so convinced of its importance that he argues that it was necessary that the redeemer, who makes satisfaction, should not be a new man made out of nothing like the first, but one taken by a virgin birth from the original stock of humanity (II. vi.-viii.). He must be man that He may be entitled to act for the sinful race, and He must be God that He may be able to offer to God the immeasurable satisfaction which shall be equal to the necessities of the case. Hence the need for the incarnation or the God-man. It is the necessity of making satisfaction for sin, in order that men who have sinned may nevertheless attain the destiny of blessedness in eternal life with God, which explains the one dogma of the Christian faith—namely, the incarnation. As it has already been expressed, the rationale of the incarnation lies in the atonement. Were it not for the atonement, no one could say that the incarnation had any necessity in it which appealed to reason.

This no doubt contains many Christian thoughts, but for the modern mind it is artificial in form. When Anselm proceeds to ask what the satisfaction is which the God-man actually renders, he becomes still more artificial. The God-man must do something for the honour of God to which He is not obliged upon other grounds. The obedient fulfilment of God's will, as that will stands for all reasonable creatures, cannot be the satisfaction; for as a reasonable creature the God-man is already obliged to this on His own account. But He is not obliged to die—for death is the wages of sin, and He has not sinned—and hence His death, the surrender of His infinitely precious life, may be offered to God by way of satisfaction. According to Scripture teaching, this is the satisfaction which He does offer—He died for our sins—and it is so precious that it more than countervails the sin of the whole world. This connection of ideas enables Anselm to say that the incarnation and passion of the God-man are to reason demonstrably necessary in order to man's forgiveness and blessedness. When he comes, however, at the end of his treatise (II. xix.), to show how man gets the benefit of Christ's satisfaction for sin, he is not very happy. Christ's death was an immense gift, freely given to God, without any obligation on Christ's part to give it, and as such it is entitled to a reward from God. God cannot, however, give Christ anything, for He needs nothing, all that is the Father's being already His; and consequently the reward due to Christ for the stupendous work of supererogation in His death—a reward which God must bestow somewhere—comes to those for whose salvation the Son of God became man. The rational necessity seems to lapse here, and all Anselm can say is "Quibus *convenientius* fructum et retributionem suae mortis attribueret, quam illis propter quos salvandos (sicut ratio veritatis nos docuit) hominem se fecit, et quibus (ut diximus) moriendo exemplum moriendi propter justitiam dedit? frustra quippe imitatores ejus erunt, si meriti ejus participes non erunt." The idea in the last clause here, in which Christ's death is represented as a death for righteousness, in which we are bound to imitate Him, is quite disparate from that in which it is represented as a work of supererogation to which

IN THE CHRISTIAN THOUGHT OF THE PAST

Christ was not bound, and which for that very reason can be offered to God as a satisfaction for man's sin. But if the argument fails to satisfy us at this point, it is not so with Anselm and his interlocutor. The saint seems to have contemplated his conclusion with a fair degree of complacency. *"Nihil rationabilius, nihil dulcius, nihil desiderabilius mundus audire potest."*

Anselm is so important in the history of Christian thought on our subject, that it is worth while to state explicitly what seem to be the merits and demerits of his doctrine. By its merits are meant its points of agreement with Scripture and with Christian experience, and by its demerits its failure to do justice to these authorities.

Its final merit is that it has a profound sense of the seriousness of sin. It may no doubt be held that Anselm considers sin too much as the doing of dishonour to a great person, and too little as a corruption or perversion of nature, or as the violation of a universal moral order (though this last, as we have seen, is not excluded); but he is right in emphasising the gravity of the act, and the desperateness of the situation it produces. He is right in saying that we ought not to commit the slightest sin for worlds, which is only another way of saying that even the slightest sin involves a responsibility for which there is no material measure. In his time men thought they could make satisfaction for it themselves, without too much trouble; they even thought that in some cases they could hire others to make satisfaction for them. In our time the tendency is to think satisfaction superfluous. A generation trained upon natural science is apt to extenuate sin, to ascribe it to heredity, to environment, to irresistible natural impulses which will be outgrown and had best be forgotten; it is not thought of in any serious way as creating a responsibility which must be faced as all it is before the weight of it can be lifted from the conscience. As against all such dispositions the New Testament and the Christian conscience support Anselm when he says: *"Nondum considerasti quanti ponderis sit peccatum."*

It is a further merit of Anselm that he shows a strong sense that the necessity for satisfaction—whatever be said of the nature of it—lies in God Himself. It is a divine demand which is satisfied by it: it does not become God *aliquid in suo regno inordinatum dimittere*. It is a divine interest which is safe-guarded by it, the honour of God. Anselm may conceivably have been quite wrong in his idea of what the divine demand in the case of sin is, or as to what is required to do justice to it; but he is not wrong in thinking that where sin is in question the supreme interests at stake are divine, and that it is God to whom all dealings with it must have reference.

Finally, it is a merit of Anselm that he treats the forgiveness of sins as the result of Christ's redemptive work. Even in Augustine we found indications of a grace of God—a redeeming grace—of which Christ is rather the most illustrious example than the only source or channel. There is nothing of this in Anselm. As far as sinners are concerned, God's grace and Christ's work are for him the same thing. It will hardly be questioned that in this he is truer to the New Testament point of view as well as to common Christian experience.

The demerits of Anselm's theory are as obvious and in some ways as important as its merits. Partly they lie in inner imperfections and inconsistencies, partly in failure to embrace particular aspects of the truth as they are reflected in the New Testament and in Christian experience. Perhaps the most conspicuous is that Anselm gives no prominence to the love of God as the source of the satisfaction for sin, or to the appeal which that love makes to the heart of sinful men. Starting as he does with the abstract proposition that God's end in creating man *must* be attained, he almost succeeds, no doubt involuntarily, in banishing from his dialectical deduction of the truth the motive of love either on one side or the other. It is not by the spontaneous grace of God; it is not by a free movement of mercy, the wonderfulness of which comes upon us again and again; it is not by the love which shines into our hearts as we look at the "friend of sinners" in the pages of the gospels, that the satisfaction for sin is explained; it is deduced by what Anselm calls a rational necessity, and belongs to the world of metaphysics, not of spiritual experience. This is what comes of constructing arguments about Christianity *remoto Christo*, arguments which will appeal equally to Jews and pagans as to Christians.

A kindred demerit of Anselm is that in the *Cur Deus Homo* the death of Christ is treated merely as a thing, a *quantum* of some kind. It is not interpreted in connection with His life; in fact the possibility of so interpreting it is almost explicitly denied. The relation of the life and of the death to God is quite different. Christ owed God His life, just such as we know it to have been, but He did not in the same sense owe Him His death. His death is something valuable, we can hardly tell why; He has no definite use for it, and therefore He can freely offer it to God as a satisfaction for the sins of men; but it is not filled with the moral value of love to man or obedience to the Father's will. *Ex hypothesi* it is outside of the world of moral obligation, and is therefore not susceptible of moral construction.

It is in some respects another way of putting the same

truth if we say that no *real* connection is established by Anselm between the death of Christ and the sin of the world, which sin, nevertheless, can only be remitted on the ground of that death. This is due to the entire arbitrariness of the idea of satisfaction. It seems fairly certain that the word *satisfactio*—though commonly enough applied, in connection with the penitential system of the Church, to the acts or sacrifices by which the Christian who had fallen into sin made good his fault, and was reconciled to God and His people—was never before Anselm expressly applied to the work of Christ. This gave plausibility to the attempt of Cremer to derive the idea in Anselm—and especially to derive the idea that *satisfactio* and *poena* were alternatives which excluded each other—not from the penitential system, but from a peculiarity in German tribal law.[1] Here the satisfaction was not the punishment, nor anything akin to it, but the *Wehrgelt* or payment, by which liability was covered and punishment averted. But though this provided an easy explanation of some degenerations of "satisfaction" in the mediæval Church,[2] it has hardly succeeded in standing criticism. The idea of satisfaction in Anselm has too much that is analogous to it in the penitential system, and ideas analogous to his are too widely diffused in quarters not open to Germanic influence, for Cremer's suggestion to hold. From the very beginning, as we have seen in connection with Tertullian, a kind of ambiguity attached to the term satisfaction, even when the satisfaction was rendered by men. In law, satisfaction was penal; it was rendered to the law

---

[1] Cremer, *Studien und Kritiken,* 1880 (pp. 7 f.), *"Die Wurzeln des Anselmischen Satisfaktionsbegriffes";* and 1893 (pp. 316 f.), *"Der germanische Satisfaktionsbegriff in der Versöhnungslehre."*

[2] See what is said above of the *redemptiones* on p. 50.

by paying its penalty. In the discipline of the Church it was not strictly speaking penal; it was a means of averting the penalty. But it was painful, it was due to sin, and in that sense it was *quasi*-penal. Anselm, by defining Christ's death merely as an *alternative* to the punishment of sin (*necesse est ut omne peccatum satisfactio* AUT *poena sequatur*), and by refusing to define it in relation to His life, as something which He owed to God, and which therefore entered into His vocation and could be morally understood, has practically made it meaningless. When the Bible says Christ died for sins, it assumes a real connection of death and sin which makes the proposition intelligible; but though Anselm would not have questioned such a connection, he does not have it in his mind when he speaks of Christ offering His death to God as a satisfaction for men's sins. The absence at this point of a link in the chain of Anselm's "rational necessities" is one of the worst flaws in his argument.

To conclude the estimate of his demerits, Anselm gives no clear account of the way in which the work of Christ comes to benefit men. Christ is left standing, so to speak, with the merit of His death in His hand, and looking round to see what He can do with it. What is more suitable or becoming (*convenientius*) than that He should give it to those who in virtue of the incarnation are His kindred? Nothing could be less like than this to all we know about how the work of Christ takes effect in human lives. In not tracing "satisfaction" originally to the love of God, in not exhibiting it as an integral element in the life of the man Christ Jesus, and as therefore possessed of moral value, and in not relating it vitally to the new redeemed life in man, Anselm left great blanks in his doctrine of reconciliation. Only a work of signal merit on other grounds could have asserted its influence as the *Cur Deus Homo* has done, in spite of such drawbacks.

In discussing Anselm's doctrine attention has been confined to his own explicit exposition of it. It has often been pointed out that in his other writings, especially those of a devotional character, utterances are to be found to which his doctrine, deduced by rational necessity, fails to do justice. The boldest expressions of Scripture are cited and perhaps exaggerated, and in particular the distinction between satisfaction and punishment is ignored. "Behold," he cries to God, "the punishment (*poenam*) of the God-man, and relieve the misery of created man. See the *supplicium* of the redeemer,[1] and forgive the sin of the redeemed." "The unrighteous sins and the righteous is punished (*punitur*); the guilty is in fault and the innocent is beaten; the ungodly offends and the godly is condemned."[2] These expressions may indicate that Anselm had more in his soul than he was able to bring into his system, or they may represent intense emotions which, when it came to the point of construing Christ's passion intellectually, he deliberately declined to rationalise: in any case they do not affect the interpretation of the *Cur Deus Homo*, nor its value as an authoritative exhibition of his mind.

The most striking defect in Anselm's doctrine—its failure to relate the work of Christ to its source in the love of God—was apparently made good by his younger contemporary Abälard. In Anselm a primacy seemed to be given

---

[1] *Supplicium* is the public punishment inflicted on a criminal as distinct from *poena*, the penalty attached to any kind of offence.

[2] Bernard of Clairvaux represents God as saying: "Mihi incumbit sustinere poenam, poenitentiam agere pro homine quem creavi." On the impossibility of regarding *satisfactio* as a legal, and *meritum* as an ethical, term in Anselm, see Loofs' *Leitfaden* (4th ed.), pp. 508 f.

in God to something else than love—at all events where sin was concerned. Sin created an infinite liability which had to be dealt with by an infinite satisfaction: that is the one necessity in the divine nature which Anselm emphasises. Abälard refuses to recognise it. Christ's whole work is for him a manifestation of love, and love does not need any explanation. It is the universal language which every one understands without an interpreter. Christ's death reconciles us to God, because it is a demonstration of love which awakes in us an answer of love, and exactly in proportion as it does so justifies the sinful and annuls the punishment of their sins. "Our redemption is that supreme love awakened in us by the passion of Christ, a love which not only frees us from bondage to sin, but wins for us the true liberty of the children of God, so that we fulfil all things not so much from fear as from love of Him who showed grace to us so great that, as He himself tells us (John xv. 13), greater cannot be found."[1] There is an experimental truth in this, but it leaves an ultimate question unanswered, or rather unasked. The death of Christ can only be regarded as a demonstration of love to sinners, if it can be defined or interpreted as having some necessary relation to their sins. At the very beginning of the *Cur Deus Homo* (I. vi.), Anselm's interlocutor makes it plain that there is no proof of love in man's redemption through the death of Christ—unless there was no other way in which he could be redeemed; in other words, unless this painful way was inevitable, and was freely accepted by Christ in spite of all its pain. The whole aim of Anselm is to show that there was no other way; that there were necessities in the divine nature which, if man was to be saved, required a satisfaction which they could only have through the incarna-

[1] See Baur, *Die Christliche Lehre von der Versöhnung*, p. 194.

tion and passion of the Son of God. He may or may not have been felicitous in the exposition of these necessities, but it must be admitted that he was dealing with a real question; it is not too much to say, with *the* real question involved in the relation of God to sinful man. The traditional language of the Church recognised the question, and it was impossible for Abälard not to use expressions which implied that it had been asked and that an answer of a certain kind commanded general acceptance. No one can speak the language of Christianity and completely elude or escape its ideas, and though, when Abälard speaks of the love of God or of Christ as the key to reconciliation, he is usually taken as the representative of subjective theories of atonement—theories which find the whole meaning of the work of Christ in its influence upon man—he often uses expressions which imply that it has also significance in relation to God. He wrote a commentary on Romans, and the commentator on Romans, who does not write with the object of showing his superiority to his text, must be a virtuoso in exegetic evasion if he does not come on irreducible things in which Paul is rather Anselmic than Abälardian. Hence it is not astonishing to find Abälard saying that ours was the guilt for which He had to die, and that we committed the sin whose penalty He endured;[1] though these are manifestly forms of speech which belong to another order of thought than that which is conscious and predominant in him. So also, while he gives predominance to the love of Christ, as the stimulus of love in men, he admits that it never does everything in sinners that they need to have done; their justification or righteousness is always imperfect, and what is wanting in this respect has to be supplemented by the righteousness of Christ, and especially

[1] Rivière, 58 ff.

IN THE CHRISTIAN THOUGHT OF THE PAST

by His intercession for them. Here the divine and objective necessities, which are ignored in the initial emphasis laid on love, get a subordinate recognition; in the salvation of sinners, the righteousness and the intercession of Christ—which have no value but Godward—turn out to have an indispensable place. But no stress is laid on this, and Abälard may be said to represent subjective doctrines of atonement as fairly as Anselm to represent objective ones. At one point in Abälard we find a curious assumption of what has been referred to above as a non-Christian element in Augustine. The vital thing in Anselm is the necessity of satisfaction, its absolute divine necessity, which implies the corresponding necessity of Christ to make it and so to ensure the forgiveness of sins. But Abälard can treat Christ not as the necessary mediator of God's grace to the sinful, but—as Augustine sometimes did—as merely an example or illustration of that grace. "By what merits did this man win His sinless conception, birth, and life from beginning to end? (By none), but through the grace of the Lord who assumed Him." The logic of this is that the grace of which Christ was the most signal illustration, and not Christ Himself, is the main thing to think about. Abälard expressly argues so in the passage quoted.[1] "He then who showed to man so great a grace as to take him into personal union with Himself, how should He be unable to bestow the lesser grace of forgiving him his sins?" What this means is that the forgiveness of sins is not necessarily connected with Christ and His work; as far as reconciliation is concerned, Christ has no assured place in the Christian religion. But neither the New Testament, nor the common tradition of Christianity, nor any formal pronouncement of any body of Christians, could be alleged in support of such a

[1] Baur, *op. cit.*, 192 *n*.

view. Abälard undoubtedly did great service in emphasising the love of Christ and the appeal it makes for love, and in bringing the discussion back again from the metaphysical to the moral world. But he had not entered deeply enough into the moral world himself; passionate and tragic as was his career, he had not comprehended, as Anselm had, how much sin meant to God, nor what a problem it created for the Creator. It is not countered simply by saying "grace" —that may be the *sola voluntas* of Anselm in which the problem is not solved but ignored; and if it is answered, as it may rightly be, by saying, "Christ," then Christ must be defined by relation to the problem created for God by sin; and this Abälard never attempted to do. In particular the death of Christ has for him no specific significance.

Abälard and Anselm might not unfairly be taken to represent the collective mind of the mediæval Church on redemption and reconciliation. We do not find in their successors any new ideas, but only varying degrees of responsiveness to ideas already to be found in one or the other. The nearest approaches to comprehensiveness—it would be going too far to say, to system—are to be found in Peter the Lombard and Thomas Aquinas. On the whole, Peter has greater sympathy with Abälard. "The death of Christ justifies us," he writes, "as love is called forth by it in our hearts." [1] He quotes with approval the Augustinian saying in which the initial love of God is emphasised as in Abälard: *"Jam nos diligenti Deo reconciliati sumus."* [2] He does not agree with Anselm about the absolute necessity of the satisfaction made by Christ. God could have saved us otherwise if He had so

[1] *Petrus Lombardus*, Antwerp edition (1757), p. 373.
[2] *Ibid.*, p. 375.

willed, but of the method actually adopted we can say that it was better suited (*convenientior*) to our wretchedness, and that in it the devil was overcome not by the power but by the justice of God. It is strange to find this notion of redemption from the devil, who is regarded as having rights against men which cannot be overridden—a notion so emphatically rejected both by Abälard and Anselm—reappearing in the Lombard. He even puts it in an offensively aggravated form. The cross is a mouse trap, and the blood of Christ is the bait with which it is set to tempt the devil.[1] But it is stranger still to find side by side with this grotesque mythology a fragment of Neo-platonic philosophy of which Peter also makes use in dealing with the embarrassing problem of Satan. He is conscious of its difficulty, and only says with regard to it "*explicabo ut potero*"—I will do my best to unravel it. He does not feel at liberty to put the devil absolutely in the right by giving him a claim over man which could neutralise the final claim of God. God, he says, did not lose man from the law of His power when He allowed him to fall into the power of the devil: the devil himself is not beyond the scope of God's power, no, nor of His goodness. For, whatever be the life of man or devil, it could not subsist but through Him who gives life to all things.[2] Here good and being are identical, and we are once more in a world in which moral experience loses its meaning and real moral questions cannot be asked. This is the world in which the devil must be saved, because nothing which is can be lost. The questions which after-

---

[1] *Petrus Lombardus*, Antwerp edition (1757), p. 373: "Et quid fecit Redemptor captivatori nostro? Tetendit ei muscipulam crucem suam; posuit ibi quasi escam sanguinem suum."

[2] *Ibid.*, p. 377. "Quia nec diabolus a potestate Dei est alienus, sicut nec bonitate. Nam qualicunque vita diabolus vel homo, non subsisteret nisi per eum qui vivificat omnia."

wards vexed some quarters of the Church about the extent of Christ's work are distinctly present to Peter's mind and clearly answered. Christ offered Himself for all, as far as the sufficiency of the price is concerned; but for the elect alone, as far as its efficacy goes; for He effected salvation only for those predestined to it. But side by side with this he sets the moral conditions through which salvation is realised. "Christ by His death reconciled all believers to God, inasmuch as all are healed from ungodliness who by believing have loved the humility of Christ, and by loving have become imitators of it."[1]

Thomas Aquinas absorbed into himself more completely than any mediæval theologian all the thoughts of his predecessors, and he kept his independence in relation to them; but though he was extraordinarily powerful, it is difficult to think of him as an original mind. His *Summa Theologica* is a lake into which many streams have flowed, and from which many have drawn, but it is not a spring. To indicate the main points of his doctrine in relation to what has been already said, is really to give the results of his criticism, not the gains of his experience or insight.

Thomas differs from Anselm in denying the absolute necessity of satisfaction. "If God had willed to free man from sin without any satisfaction whatever, He would not have violated justice." There is no one *over* God to be injured by His acting in this way, and therefore this way was open to Him. It is difficult to argue about the possibility of applying the category of necessity to God, or the senses in which it may or may not be applied. Thomas starts with the idea that it is inapplicable to God in any sense, as inconsistent with His omnipotence, and so the question is fore-

[1] *Petrus Lombardus*, Antwerp edition (1757), p. 376.

closed.[1] But omnipotence, which is (so to speak) a natural attribute of God, is not so clear a conception that we can make use of it to bar questions about what is necessary or not necessary for God in the moral world. Thomas himself points out that though it was not necessary for Christ to suffer *necessitate coactionis*—by a necessity of outward compulsion—it was necessary *necessitate finis*—by the inward compulsion of the end He wished to attain. Perhaps this is not very far from what Anselm meant. Satisfaction is necessary, on Anselm's view, if men are to be saved; that is, it is necessary *necessitate finis*. Whether the end itself is necessary is probably a question on which Thomas and Anselm would have agreed: God cannot deny Himself, and though we cannot make claims as of right upon Him, it is truer to say that all that He does is necessary than that the category of necessity does not apply to Him at all. It would not apply if necessity were the opposite of freedom, but God is the Being in whom freedom and necessity are one. Thomas formally puts in the place of necessity *convenientia*. It was *convenientius*, more to the purpose, that man should be set free by the passion of Christ than by the mere will of God. We attain in this way greater and better blessings. Thus it reveals the love of God, it gives us the example of Christ's humility and obedience, it merits for us not only liberation from sin but justifying grace and heavenly glory, it is a powerful motive to sanctification, and it contributes to the dignity of man that in man sin and death should be overthrown.[2] All this sum of advantages is of course related to man; it does not touch upon, and therefore it cannot pre-

[1] *Summa*, vi. p. 378. "In Deum autem non cadit aliqua necessitas quia hoc repugnaret omnipotentiae ipsius."
[2] *Ibid.*, III. Quaest. xlvi. Art. iii.

judice, the question whether there is or is not a necessity in God for dealing with sin by way of satisfaction if man is to be delivered from it.

When Thomas speaks of the mode in which Christ's Passion effects its purpose, he makes scrupulous use of all the categories which have ever been applied in this connection. When we relate it to the divine nature, the Passion of Christ acts *per modum efficientiae*; when we relate it to the will of Christ's soul, it acts *per modum meriti*; when it is considered as in the very flesh of Christ, it acts *per modum satisfactionis*, inasmuch as we are freed by it from liability to penalty (*a reatu poenae*); *per modum redemptionis*, inasmuch as we are freed by it from bondage to sin (*a servitute culpae*); *per modum sacrificii*, inasmuch as through it we are reconciled to God. Of all these "modes" there are only two of which Thomas has anything new to say, the *modus meriti* and the *modus satisfactionis*, and it is necessary to look at them more closely.

The notion of *meritum* appears in Anselm only in connection with Christ's death. Christ's death has "merit" as a work of supererogation, standing on a different footing in relation to God from His life, the obedience in which, as already due to God, constituted no merit. In Thomas *meritum* has a different and a far larger place. Christ, he says, from the beginning of His conception merited eternal salvation for us.[1] The "merit" in the passion is due to its not being imposed from without, but voluntarily endured (*secundum quod aliquis eam voluntarie sustinet*): in other words, accepted in the way of obedience to the will of God. Obedience is preferred to all sacrifices, and therefore it was *conveniens* that the sacrifice of the passion and death of Christ should proceed from obedience.[2] This brings merit,

[1] *Summa*, III. xlvii. Art. i.   [2] *Ibid.*, III. xlvii. Art. ii.

which in Anselm was a precarious *plus* added to the moral world, into the moral world itself, and it also brings Christ's death into the same moral whole as His life. Thomas admits that the passion had an effect which the *praecedentia merita* had not, but this was due not to its exhibiting greater love, but to its being the kind of work which was proper to produce that effect.[1] Merit is often an equivocal term, but what it seems to imply in Thomas is that the whole work of Christ, including His death, must be capable of being morally interpreted. Such an interpretation gives it moral significance for the Saviour Himself, and presents it as something not alien to those who are to be saved, but capable of a moral appropriation by them. The emphasis laid on this in Thomas marks a distinct advance on Anselm's theology, if not on his piety.

The idea of satisfaction also assumes a somewhat different complexion in Thomas. There are no doubt passages in which it seems to bear the same arbitrary character as in the *Cur Deus Homo*. For example, Thomas writes that any one makes satisfaction for an offence, in the strict sense of the term, who renders to the offended person something his love for which is equal to or greater than his hatred of the offence.[2] This is in keeping with the idea which makes punishment and satisfaction alternatives. But there are also passages in which Thomas approaches the view that punishment and satisfaction are akin—that punishment makes satisfaction, and that satisfaction is penal. Thus he says that in the giving up of Christ to die there is shown both the severity of God, who would not let sin go unpunished

---

[1] This seems to be the meaning of a rather difficult passage in *Summa*, Tertia Pars, Quaest. xlviii. Art. i.

[2] *Summa*, III. xlviii. Art. ii.

(*sine poena*), and the goodness of God, who when man could not make a sufficient satisfaction by any penalty he might suffer, gave him One to make satisfaction for him.[1] Similarly in another passage he writes: "It is an appropriate mode of making satisfaction for another, when one subjects himself to the penalty which another has deserved."[2] This indicates the line on which, rightly or wrongly, much theological speculation proceeded in the future. Instead of being an alternative to punishment, satisfaction was regarded as the endurance by one of the punishment due to another.

But the main peculiarity in Thomas is the prominence he gives to the idea of the union of Christ and His people—of the head and the members. It is in virtue of this unity that Christ is able to do anything for His people, and that they are able to appropriate and profit by what He does. Anselm had indeed insisted on the necessity that the redeemer should be of the human stock, but it is with quite another emphasis Thomas teaches that He who sacrifices and they who are sanctified are all of one. "The head and the members are as it were one mystical person, and therefore the satisfaction of Christ extends to all believers as to His members." "Since grace was given to Christ as to the head of the Church, that from Him it might overflow upon His members, it is manifest that Christ earned eternal salvation not only for Himself, but also for all His members."[3] There is always the possibility here of lapsing from the level of the new humanity to that of the old, and treating as members of Christ all the children of Adam instead of those who are united to Christ in some free and spiritual fashion. Thomas does not lapse in this way. "When a sufficient satisfaction has been ren-

[1] *Summa*, III. xlvii. Art. iii.   [2] *Ibid.*, III. l. Art. i.
[3] *Ibid.*, III. xlviii. Art. i.

dered," he says, "liability to punishment is removed; but the satisfaction of Christ takes effect in us only in so far as we become one body with Him as members with their head. And the members ought to be conformed to the head." [1] Strictly speaking, this should mean that there must be a community of experiences between Christ and those who are redeemed by Him. His life and death are a life and death fulfilling moral demands which are binding upon *them*, and the experiences of love, obedience, humility, suffering, through which He merits salvation for them as for Himself must become theirs, in union with Him, if they are to have the benefit of His satisfaction. But even where this union is insisted on, there is the consciousness of a limit of some kind on both sides. After all, it is Christ who makes the satisfaction of which we avail ourselves in this way—Christ, not we; and there is something which, though it may be inspired in us by that union, it is still for us to do, not for Him. "*Non est similis ratio de confessione et contritione, quia satisfactio consistit in actu exteriori, ad quen assumi possunt instrumenta inter quae computantur etiam amici.*" This sentence shows vividly both how consciously the penitential system of the Church was being used to interpret the work of Christ, and what difficulties the interpretation encountered. Penitence consisted of three parts, contrition, confession, and satisfaction. It is the last alone which Thomas uses to interpret the Passion. He cannot bring into his interpretation the contrition and the confession. Yet in ordinary human penitence it is the contrition and confession which give the satisfaction its value, and the "outward act," in which Thomas says satis-

[1] *Summa*, III. xlix. Art. iii. "Exhibita satisfactione sufficienti, tollitur reatus poenae . . . satisfactio Christi habet effectum in nobis in quantum incorporamur ei ut membra suo capiti . . . membra autem *opertet* capiti conformari."

faction consists, must surely have some moral soul to give it worth to God. If we as members of His body have to enter somehow into the satisfaction of Christ and to make it our own, must not He somehow enter, as head of the body, into the experience of His members, as with contrite hearts they confess their sins to God.[1] It is impossible to read the passage just quoted without thinking of Macleod Campbell, and if Thomas criticises by anticipation the idea of vicarious (or sympathetic) contrition or confession, the impulse to do so shows how closely that idea is connected with the conception that Christ and His members are one mystical body.

The mediæval Church in its thoughts on Christ's work did not get beyond this point. Satisfaction remained its one interpretative category. It might be more or less rationalised, as in Thomas, or more or less de-rationalised, as in Duns Scotus, who makes it merely arbitrary, but it was the one idea with which theologians operated in explaining the death of Christ. And it must again be noticed that if the atoning work of Christ is to be understood through this category, it must be a work of objective atonement. The satisfaction is meant for God, not for the sinner. Christ represents the sinner in making it, but it is made to God who is offended by sin. It neutralises or averts His anger, so that henceforth He is not against the sinner but on his side. Apart from the satisfaction, the sinner has no hope toward God, and yet he knows that in the last resort it is the love of God from which the satisfaction itself has come. All mediæval theologians would have subscribed to Augustine and Peter the Lombard: *"Jam diligenti reconciliati sumus"*—He

[1] "Tantum valuit Christi meritum quantum voluit et potuit ipsum Trinitas acceptare." (Quoted in Thomasius, *Christi Person und Werk* [3rd ed.], ii. 158.)

loved us already when we were reconciled to Him. But all would also have maintained that our sins are forgiven only for Christ's sake—*propter Christum*.

The Reformation undoubtedly marks the greatest crisis in the history of Christianity, but it is difficult to tell exactly the difference it made to the central doctrine of the gospel. What it did in principle was to expel *things* from religion, and exhibit all its realities as persons and the relations of persons. Grace, for example, ceased to be a thing, or *quantum*, which could be "infused" in man, or administered in appropriate quantities or qualities through the sacraments;[1] it became the attitude of God to sinners as exhibited in Christ. Correspondingly, in principle, faith became the attitude of the sinner who gave himself up unconditionally to the God who was manifested in Christ as a gracious sin-bearing, sin-forgiving God: it was the whole life of such a man, with all its promise and potency, and it was as incapable of being supplemented as of being broken up. A consistent hold of the truth

[1] It is impossible to put too strongly the fact that the grace of the gospel in the mediæval Church was a *thing*, doled out through the sacramental system, not the attitude of God in Christ to sinners. It is the same in the modern Church of Rome. To complete the doctrine of justification, the Council of Trent says (sess. vii. proem) "*consentaneum visum est de sanctissimis ecclesiae sacramentis agere, per quae omnis vera justitia vel incipit, vel coepta augetur, vel amissa reparatur.*" The Lutheran branch of the Reformation Church lapsed far in this direction, but it was against its own principle, and in contradiction of the earliest statement of its own faith. "*Non justificant signa,*" says Melanchthon in the first edition of the *Loci* (ed. Kolde S. 235). "Apostolus ait: Circumcisio nihil est; *ita baptismus nihil est, participatio mensae Domini nihil est, sed testes sunt* καὶ σφραγῖδες *divinae voluntatis erga te,* quibus conscientia tua certa reddatur, si de gratia, de benevolentia Dei erga se dubitet . . . *Ita sine signo justificari potes, modo credas.*" To emphasize the necessity of the sacrament for justification is to magnify the thing at the expense of the person, to subject the higher category to the lower; to make justification independent of the sacraments is to give the personal its true place in religion, and is alone consistent with the principle of the Reformation.

that Christianity means the interaction, in the world of personal relations, of the sin-bearing, sin-forgiving God and the sinner unconditionally abandoning himself to that God in Christ, would have required a wholly new theology to match it, but to the production of such a theology the Protestant Church was for the time unequal. To a large extent it put its new wine into old bottles, and it was haunted by the sense of a radical inconsistency which it knew not how to overcome. A singular illustration of this is given in the second part of the Augsburg Confession, in which the first Protestants presented their conception of Christianity to Charles v. It begins with the words: "Inasmuch as the Churches among us"—that is, those which had followed Luther—"dissent in no article of faith from the Catholic Church, but only omit some few abuses," etc.[1] In a sense this was true, too true; but it ignores the main point that, for the evangelical Christian, faith is no longer a maker of "articles"; it is one whole and indivisible thing, the attitude of his sinful soul to God in Christ, his new life as a Christian. For better or worse, however, Protestantism took over from the earlier and inferior type of Christianity, under the heading of "articles of faith," certain doctrines or explanations of the Christian life and its presuppositions, and among other things it took over the doctrine of Christ's satisfaction for human sin.

Luther, it must be allowed, had no enthusiasm for the term. It used to be said that there was no reference to Anselm in all his works, and that probably he had never read him; but even if this is doubtful,[2] Anselm's direct influence on him can have been but small. The idea of satisfaction, too, was

---

[1] Conf. Augs., Part II. *init.* "Cum ecclesiae apud nos de nullo articulo fidei dissentiant ab ecclesiae catholica," etc.

[2] Loofs, *Leitfaden zum Dogmengeschichte* [3rd ed.], p. 346, *note.*

bound up with the penitential system of the mediæval Church, which more than anything roused the indignation of Luther as concealing, disguising, and corrupting the gospel. But in spite of this, both the term and the idea survived, and if they did not come to more prominence in the Reformation Churches, they certainly did not fall into the background. It is interesting to notice the extent to which authoritative utterances coincide in the Roman and the Reformation branches of the Church. Thus the fourth article of the Augsburg Confession teaches that men cannot be justified—obtain forgiveness of sins and righteousness—before God by their own powers, merits, or works; but are justified freely for Christ's sake (*propter Christum*) through faith, when they believe that they are received into favour (*in gratiam*) and their sins forgiven for Christ's sake, who by His death satisfied for our sins (*propter Christum qui sua morte pro nostris peccatis satisfecit*). In quite similar words, and with the same religious interest in view, the Council of Trent (sess. vi. c. 7) declares that the *official cause* of justification is a merciful God who freely washes and sanctifies, sealing and anointing with the Holy Spirit of promise, who is the earnest of our inheritance; while the *meritorious cause* is His most beloved and only begotten, our Lord Jesus Christ, who when we were enemies, because of the great love with which He loved us, by His most holy Passion on the tree of the cross, earned for us justification, and made satisfaction for us to God the Father (*sua sanctissima passione in ligno crucis nobis justificationem meruit, et pro nobis Deo Patri satisfecit*). It would be impossible to find a more exact correspondence both of thought and expression. The Roman Church and the Reformation Church agree in holding (1) that sin is freely forgiven; (2) that it is forgiven for Christ's sake, *propter Christum*; and

(3) that we may fairly interpret the last idea—"for Christ's sake"—through the idea of a "satisfaction" for sin made by Christ.

In Protestant theology the equivocal character of the idea of satisfaction, which has been sufficiently explained, tends to disappear. The satisfaction of which the theologians think is not the Anselmic one, which has no relation to punishment, nor that of the penitential system, which is only *quasi*-penal, but that of Roman law, which is identical with punishment. What comes more and more steadily into view is the idea that Christ made satisfaction for our sins, by bearing the penalty of them in our stead. Even in the Roman Church the satisfactions imposed under the penitential system and discharged by sinners are called *satisfactriae poenae*."[1] Melanchthon is as explicit as words can be: "*Deus justitiae suae puniendo satisfecit; justitia servatur in recipienda poena.*"

But in proportion as men rose above the conception of sin and satisfaction, as mere things or abstract ideas, and had their faith and attention concentrated on the personal Saviour by whom they were reconciled to God, this position became intolerable. It left no significance for salvation to anything in Jesus except His death. It almost prompts us to ask again, as Athanasius did, why He did not die whenever He was born, and make the satisfaction in the most direct way. The Christian soul felt instinctively that the life of Jesus must come into His work somehow as well as His death; wherever we see Jesus, in whatever attitude, however engaged, reconciling virtue goes out of Him. This was recognised when the life of Christ was dragged in, so to speak, side by side with His death, and, though it had not the significance of satisfaction for sin assigned to it, was nevertheless invested with

---

[1] Conc. Trid. sess. xiv. 8.

another significance equally necessary to salvation. The life was the active obedience and the death the passive obedience, and though they were alike in respect that both were obedience, each fulfilled its separate and independent function. Thus the Westminster Confession, in c. xi., repeatedly distinguishes in this way the "obedience *and* satisfaction" of Christ, or His "obedience *and* death," the satisfaction or death being the ground on which we are cleared from sin, while the obedience constitutes a righteousness of Christ which is imputed to believers. The utmost refinements or discriminations in this mode of thought were probably to be found in the Puritan theologians of America. "Though the Redeemer obeyed in suffering and suffered in obeying, and His highest and most meritorious obedience was acted out in His voluntary suffering unto death, and in this greatest instance of His suffering the atonement which He made chiefly consisted; yet His obedience and suffering are two perfectly distinct things, and answered different ends, and must be considered so, and the distinction and difference carefully and with clearness kept up in the mind, in order to have a proper understanding of this very important subject. The sufferings of Christ, as such, made atonement for sin, as He suffered the penalty of the law or the curse of it, the evil threatened to transgression, and which is the desert of it, in the sinner's stead, by which He opened the way for sinners being delivered from the curse, and laid the foundation for reconciliation between God and the transgressors, by His not imputing but pardoning their sins who believe in the Redeemer and approve of His character and conduct. By the obedience of Christ, all the positive good, all those favours and blessings are united and obtained, which sinners need in order to enjoy complete and eternal redemption or everlasting life in the kingdom of God."[1] More important, however, than any such refinements was the persistence of the idea that the whole work of Christ, His active and passive obedience, constituted in some sense a merit or merits, in virtue of which men could be reconciled to God. It is to God, in the first instance, that the life and death of Christ have value; and it is out of regard to their value, jointly or separately—in other words, it is *propter Christum*—that God admits men to His peace, or that men are justified or reconciled to God. Theologians, from the greatest to the least, are at one here. Luther says expressly that the forgiveness of sins is *"abverdient"* from God; it is won from Him by the merits of Christ.[2] In speaking of Christ's intercession, Calvin represents the same view with equal explicitness. Christ, he says, turns God's eyes to His own righteousness, in such wise that He turns them from our sins; He so reconciles God's mind to us as to pave a way of approach for us to His throne; nay, He fills God Himself with grace and clemency, who would otherwise for wretched sinners have been full of horror.[3] It is the same fundamental strain of thought which is represented when the Council of Trent says: *"nobis justificationem meruit"*—He earned grace for us.[4]

It is evident that a doctrine of atonement—as the basis of the reconciliation of God and man—which can be summarily exhibited thus, is open to a great deal of criticism. In point of fact, it was subjected to a good deal, and it might almost be said that the history of Christian thinking on the subject throughout a long period, down even to the present

[1] Hopkins's *Works*, vol. i. 347 f., quoted in Park's collection of *Discourses and Treatises on the Atonement* (Boston, 1859).
[2] See Köstlin, *Luthers Theologie*, ii. 425.
[3] *Institutio*, II. xvi. 16.   [4] *V. supra*, p. 93.

day, turned on the destruction or the defence, the supplementing or the transmuting, of the system of ideas just outlined; instead of following the course of this criticism, which is full of eddies and cross currents, it will be sufficient to indicate in a systematic rather than a chronological way the main points on which it fastened.

It was early alleged that this doctrine of justification and reconciliation, in many essential points a doctrine common to the Roman and the Reformation Church, contained an insoluble contradiction. This contradiction can be put in various ways, but principally it was put in these three.

(1) There is a fatal inconsistency, it was asserted, in trying to combine the grace of God and the merits of Christ as the ground of forgiveness and reconciliation. You may say that God forgives freely (*gratuito*), or that He forgives for Christ's sake (*propter Christum*), but you cannot say both, for they are mutually exclusive. This is the burden of all Socinian criticism of the atonement, and it is urged with desolating iteration in the work of Socinus *De Jesu Christo Servatore*. If God forgives freely, He does not forgive on the basis of a satisfaction made for sins; and if He forgives on the basis of a satisfaction, He does not forgive freely. His forgiveness, indeed, in the latter case is superfluous, for the satisfaction has cleared the score, and there is nothing left to forgive.

Formally and dialectically the Socinian criticism was irrefragable, but its difficulties began when it had to explain what it meant by *gratuito*, and what place Christ filled in its doctrine of man's salvation. Socinus never wearies of telling us that God determined to forgive sin out of His mere and pure benignity: there is nothing in forgiveness but this. But is this true? Or is it not rather the indubitable fact that in Christian forgiveness, in Christian reconciliation, there is something besides this? There is Christ. What is the Socinian, who lays all the emphasis on *gratuito*, to do with Him? Is it possible to prevent anything as Christianity in which Christ is not represented as the Saviour? and if He is represented as the Saviour, does not the problem rise again for Socinianism which was supposed to have been got rid of when the *propter Christum* of the satisfaction theories was dismissed by appeal to the *gratuito*? Socinus, who utterly repudiates satisfaction, tells us why he still calls Jesus Saviour. He is our Saviour "because He announced to us the way of eternal life, and in His own person, not only by the example of His life, but by rising from the dead, clearly showed it, and will give eternal life to us who believe Him (*nobis ei fidem habentibus*).[1] There is nothing in this that distinctly refers to sin, forgiveness, reconciliation, or the Passion of Jesus, and what is wanting in the opening sentences of Socinus' great work is not made good in the course of it. It is the simple truth that he has no rationale of Christ at all in relation to forgiveness. In spite of his laborious exegetical effort, New Testament experiences and ideas are not the inspiration but the stumbling-block of his thoughts. His task is not to absorb and assimilate the New Testament construction of Christianity, but to explain it away. He often speaks of Christ "intervening" between God's decree to forgive out of pure mercy, and the taking effect of that decree in the actual experience of pardon; but why any one should "intervene," why in particular there should be an intervention so tragic, which has asserted such a reconciling power in Christian hearts, he has no idea whatever. It is this which explains the curiously non-Christian impression left on the

[1] F. Socinus, *De Jesu Christo Servatore: ad init.*

mind by the *De Jesu Christo Servatore*. There is no suggestion in it of a personal relation to Jesus, of an infinite debt to Him, of an inspiration of which He is the immediate source. At the best He is an argument for something else, and even if He gets a place in the mind He has no home in the heart. If Socinianism were true, no one could ever have written, even in a mood of morbid and crazy exaltation, "I am crucified with Christ, and it is no longer I who live, but Christ who lives in me." Even the expression "faith in Christ" is extremely rare; it is usually *fidem ei habere*, or even more disinterestedly, *ejus verbis fidem habentes*. That this is not an unfair estimate may be shown by the following characteristic passage from the *De Jesu Christo Servatore* (Pars Secunda, c. xiii.). "The death of Christ is said to have expiated our sins, not because it either moved God to condone our sins, or patched up or made good the guilt of our faults; but because the expiation of our sins, which depended wholly on the mercy of God alone, *followed immediately on the accomplishment of Christ's suffering* (*Christi supplicio peracto*). For *as soon as Christ had suffered the death of the cross*, He obtained by God's decree (*ex Dei decreto*) not only to be Himself endowed with immortal and eternal life, but to have the power of endowing with the same us who believe Him (*qui illi fidem habemus*) and are His. And in reality the expiation of our sins is nothing but our full and permanent liberation from the death of sin." There could not be a clearer indication both that Socinus felt that there was something in the whole Biblical and historical estimate of Christ's place in redemption, with which he could not but deal, and that his attempt to deal with it is quite unreal. *Non propter hoc*, he seems to say—thinking of forgiveness and of the death of Christ; *non propter hoc—sed tamen post hoc*, and that *ex Dei*

THE CHRISTIAN DOCTRINE OF RECONCILIATION

decreto! It is not respectful to the decree of God to deny it, in this fashion, anything but a purely arbitrary character.

Theologians who felt the formal logic of Socinus unimpeachable were not so much affected by it, just because they felt at the same time that he evaded the problem to which their logical perplexities were due. Those perplexities did not emerge into consciousness for the first time when the Reformation doctrine of Christ's satisfaction for sin was defined. They were present to the mind of Augustine when he wrote *"et quando nos oderat diligebat."* They are present to the mind of everybody who feels, as Christians have felt from the beginning, that *in Christ God somehow takes part with sinners against Himself*. He *is* estranged and offended by sin—this is not an imagination but an experience of the sinner; and the sinner finds Him a gracious God—and this also is not imagination but experience—not in a way to which Christ does not matter, but only in Christ. In point of fact, the *gratuito* and the *propter Christum* are experimentally quite consistent, and the only difficulty is to find a statement which will do justice to this experienced fact. To play off the one expression against the other, as Socinianism does, however logical it may be in form, is in fact a mere irrelevance.

Of those who maintained the truth of the *propter Christum* side by side with that of the *gratuito* none shows a more candid appreciation of the Socinian difficulties than Calvin (though the *Institutio Christianae Religionis* is more than forty years earlier than the *De Jesu Christo Servatore*). Calvin formally raises the question how it is consistent to say that God, who comes to meet us with His mercy, is our enemy until He is reconciled to us through Christ. He seems to argue that this, which is the ordinary way of putting it, is rather designed to make sinners feel how wretched and disastrous is

IN THE CHRISTIAN THOUGHT OF THE PAST

their lot apart from Christ, than to give adequate expression to the truth: it is speaking, as Paul says, "after the manner of men," and is not to be pressed. But though the weakness of our faculties is allowed for in this mode of speech, it is not false.[1] It conveys the true impression that it is only through Christ that sinners have a standing with God. The ultimate truth, that which is covered by *gratuito*, is stated by Calvin with all the distinctness which could be desired. "*Sua dilectione praevenit et antevertit Deus Pater nostram in Christo reconciliationem.*" It was because He *first* (*prius*) loved, that He afterwards (*postea*) reconciled us to Himself. When Calvin tries formally to conciliate this first love of God—this absolutely free grace—with the doctrine that Christ merited for us forgiveness of sins, what he does is to make the merit of Christ depend on the grace of God. "*Christus nonnisi ex Dei beneplacito quidquam mereri potuit . . . ex sola Dei gratia (quae hunc nobis constituit salutis modum) dependet meritum Christi.*" The same way of meeting—or evading—the same difficulty is taken in the Westminster Confession (c. xi. 3), where, after a declaration of the "proper, real, and full satisfaction" made by Christ to the Father's justice on behalf of sinners, we are told with equal emphasis that "inasmuch as He was given by the Father for them, and His obedience and satisfaction accepted in their stead, and both freely, not for anything in them, their justification is only of free grace." Whether this was or was not the right way to define the relation of the *gratuito* to the *propter Christum*—of free grace to the merits of Christ—the truth, it was felt, lay *in* the antinomy, and was lost when one element of it was used merely to reject the other.

[1] *Inst. Chr. Relig.*, II. xvi. 3: "Atqui hoc tametsi pro captus nostri infirmitate dicitur, non tamen falso."

THE CHRISTIAN DOCTRINE OF RECONCILIATION

It is a remarkable fact that in wrestling with this problem Calvin falls back on Augustine's idea that Christ Himself is the most shining illustration of free grace. It was not by merits either of faith or works that He attained the dignity of Saviour. On the contrary, the grace by which any man, from the beginning of his faith, is made a Christian is the very same grace by which this man, from His beginning, is made the Christ.[1] Of all ways of subsuming the merits of Christ under the grace of God this, for the unsophisticated Christian mind, is probably the least attractive or convincing, and it strikes one oddly, after following Calvin into an atmosphere so rare, to find him snubbing Peter the Lombard and other scholastics for *stulta curiositas* and *temeraria definitio*.

(2) A second way in which the contradiction between the *gratuito* and the *propter Christum* was brought out was this. If, it was said, Christ is God's free gift to men, and makes satisfaction to God for men's sins, clearly God is supposed to make satisfaction to Himself. To the Socinian criticism this was the *ne plus ultra* of absurdity. But again it was felt that an attack upon the form might leave the substance unaffected. Formally it might seem a flat contradiction that God should make satisfaction to Himself; or if not a flat contradiction, the work of making satisfaction would have the same kind of unreality as a game of draughts in which a man plays his right hand against his left. But really this was not the case. The question at issue is not so much whether God forgives, but how; not even whether He forgives freely, but whether His free forgiveness is easy or difficult, costly or cheap, an unspeakable gift or a trivial one. It was a sound instinct that made the Church as a whole

---

[1] *Institutio Christianae Religionis*, ii. 17. See p. 81, *supra*.

IN THE CHRISTIAN THOUGHT OF THE PAST

cling to the idea of a difficult, costly, and overpowering forgiveness, and reject and even resent a criticism of the idea of satisfaction—and of God as making satisfaction to Himself—by which the character of forgiveness was imperilled. There are divine necessities which must be asserted in the very act of pardoning and reconciling—there are principles or realities to which justice must be done—if forgiveness is to be the unspeakable and inspiring gift it ought to be, and in genuine Christianity is: and this vital truth is covered, it may be inadequately or infelicitously, but still effectively enough for the ordinary Christian mind, when we say that in the very process by which He forgives, God makes satisfaction to Himself in Christ. The fact that Christ, to put it so, is not only, as in Socinianism, the preacher of a forgiveness which exists in entire independence of Him, but the incarnation or embodiment of all that is meant by forgiveness in the gospel, secures for forgiveness its passionate and tragic character. However we ought to express it, there is a satisfaction to God at the heart of it without which it could not be bestowed.

(3) The third way of exhibiting the contradictions involved in the common doctrine of reconciliation was to point out that it rested on the assumption of an internal contradiction in God Himself. All doctrines of satisfaction—so it was argued—implied an inner schism in God's nature. The divine attributes were at war, and it was in reality they which had to be reconciled. God's mercy pulled Him in one direction, and His justice in another. His mercy urged Him to forgive the sinner freely, but His justice was inexorable, on the other side, and, till its demands were satisfied, God's pardoning love could not have free course. In this way a division was made in God Himself—which was inconceiv-

able; and a primacy was given to justice as against love—which was contradictory to Scripture.

The doctrine of the divine attributes is as difficult as any in theology, but some things in it are fairly plain. The Socinian criticism was quite right in asserting that there could be no schism in God. Justice is in no sense at war with mercy. The opposite of justice is not mercy, but injustice, and God is never either unmerciful or unjust. He is just when He exercises His mercy, and He is merciful when He exercises justice. This is quite sound, and quite generally admitted. But the criticism which pointed it out was regarded with suspicion because it was believed to be only another mode of that same criticism which by sinking the *propter Christum* in the *gratuito*, or the *merits of Christ* in the absolute *grace of God*, offered in the long run a Christianity in which Christ had no essential place. Instead of finding in Christ the proof of a love in which justice is done to the whole and indivisible character of God, the tendency of this criticism was to assert a love in God so unconditional, so akin to a physical force, that any definite relation of it to righteousness disappeared, and the very presence of Christ in the world, to say nothing of His Passion, had no vital connection with reconciliation. In principle, Christ and His Passion were superfluous; or, if they had a certain value for impressing men, they were quite unessential to God. As this, for the common Christian consciousness, is an impossible conclusion, the tension (so to speak) between the divine attributes was endured, to avoid worse. The mockery of Strauss, for whom the tension of justice and mercy is resolved, in Christ's satisfaction, just as in the parallelogram of forces the tension of two opposing pulls is resolved along a diagonal line, was as little able as the Socinian dialectic to dislodge from the

Christian mind something which at this point it felt to be involved in its faith and experience. It does get in Christ and His passion, what it gets nowhere else, the assurance that forgiveness is something in which all the divine attributes—the justice of God as well as His mercy, His severity as well as His goodness—get their due. And as such an assurance is indispensable, it clings to it for its life in spite of formal logical difficulties.

Besides this line of criticism, which dwelt in such various forms on the essential contradiction of the grace of God and the merits of Christ, there was another largely represented in the Church. It had its motive in the feeling that the doctrine of reconciliation had become, so to speak, too objective; it was being regarded too exclusively as the doctrine of a work of Christ which had value for God, but which had no security for taking effect in man. It was outside of us, and there only. It had reference, it might seem, only to the past; it achieved for men the forgiveness of sins, but even when forgiveness was appropriated by faith and the believer justified, there was no security for the new life. The work of Christ had not been defined in such a way as to guarantee this. It even became a point of orthodoxy to distinguish sharply between justification, or the righteousness of Christ imputed to faith, and sanctification, or the new character wrought in the justified by the Holy Spirit. It was in the former alone that the sinner had standing in the sight of God; the latter was rather the moral vindication of the gospel than an essential element in it. The former, justification, had the completeness of the work of Christ; the latter, sanctification, had the imperfection of everything in which man is participant. But though imperfect it was real, and a sound instinct taught men, in spite of orthodoxy,

THE CHRISTIAN DOCTRINE OF RECONCILIATION

that it is much more important that justification and sanctification should be inseparable, than that they should be distinguished. Hooker, in his famous sermon on *Justification*, strongly urges the distinction. "St. Paul," he writes, "doth plainly sever these two parts of Christ's righteousness from one another," [1] and he thinks it important to insist on this understanding of St. Paul. Chalmers, out of a wide experience of the effects of distinguishing justification and sanctification—in other words, of a too exclusively objective view of the work of Christ—betrays a different concern: "I think that holiness is looked upon by some evangelical writers in rather a lame and inadequate point of view. They value it chiefly as an evidence of justifying faith. They are right in saying that it gives no title to God's favour,[2] but they are wrong in saying that its chief use is to ascertain that title, or to make that title clear to him who possesses it. It is in fact chiefly valuable *on its own account. It forms a part and an effective part of salvation.*" [3] No simple mind could ever be insensible to this, and the doctrine of an objective satisfaction, a finished work of Christ, outside of us, had no sooner taken definite shape, than a consciousness arose that it was not related as it ought to be to the new life of the believer, and that if it were not open to criticism upon other grounds, it at least required more adequate statement.

The earliest protest in this sense was made by the Reformation theologian Osiander. He taught justification by faith, but interpreted it "mystically," not legally. It did not consist in the imputation of Christ's righteousness, but in

[1] Hooker, *Works*, ii. 607 (Oxford, 1865).
[2] Cf. Hooker, *ut supra*, p. 609. "The best things we do have somewhat in them to be pardoned."
[3] *Life*, by Hanna, ii. 184.

IN THE CHRISTIAN THOUGHT OF THE PAST

the essential indwelling of God in the soul, mediated through faith. His favourite text was Jer. xxiii. 6, "The Lord is our righteousness." Justification is not a moral opiate, which the mere imputation of another's righteousness might be alleged to be; it is the promise and potency, or rather it is the very presence, of a new righteousness in the heart, identical with Christ's inhabiting there. There is no justification in which sanctification is not at the same time involved. The ceaseless controversies in which Osiander lived make it difficult to give any representation of his views which will not be contested, but the motive of his thoughts is unquestionable. He seems to have held that when Christ came to earth from heaven, He brought with Him His divine and eternal righteousness; it was this which He maintained all through His career, and this also—not any righteousness achieved in His life on earth—which becomes the possession of those in whose hearts He dwells by faith. Yet he believed that Christ on the cross made satisfaction for sin to the righteousness of God, and that the merit of Christ is the ground on which the essential divine righteousness becomes ours. Newman was conscious of an affinity to Osiander,[1] and the motive of his *Lectures on Justification* is much the same as that of the sixteenth century theologian. "There really must be . . . in every one who is justified, some such token or substance of his justification";[2] there must be something real and not merely imputed. So again, if we except the first clause, it is quite in the line of Osiander when Newman writes:[3] "Justification comes *through* the sacraments; is received *by* faith; *consists* in God's inward presence, and *lives* in obedience." Upholders of the orthodox

[1] *Lectures on Justification*, p. 387 f.
[2] *Ibid.*, p. 131.   [3] *Ibid.*, p. 275.

doctrine would not all have admitted that it was open to the kind of criticism here in view,[1] but the evidence of observers so unlike as Chalmers and Newman is conclusive as to the direction in which it tended to degenerate. A finished work of Christ, outside of us, and not directly related to a new life—a justification not organically related to sanctification—was undoubtedly a moral peril. Romanists might pretend to guard against it by the doctrine that justification comes through the sacraments—initially through baptism, and afterwards through penance—conferring as they do grace *ex opere operato*; and predestinarians, Calvinist or other, might evade all such difficulties by teaching that the work of Christ avails for the elect alone, and takes effect in them as an irresistible grace, by which all God's ends are infallibly secured; but those to whom sacramental grace and predestination are not solutions of any problem, but counsels of moral and intellectual despair, are undoubtedly in a difficulty. They must admit that a doctrine of Christ's work is wanted in which the new life is not an addendum, or a

---

[1] The charge that the doctrine of satisfaction, or of an objective atonement, is inevitably immoral in effect is strongly urged by Socinus, *De Jesu Christo Servatore,* Pars III. c. xi. But it was familiar much earlier. The *Augsburg Confession* c. xx. presupposes it when it writes: *"Falso accusantur nostri quod bona opera prohibeant,"* etc. It may indeed be traced back to the apostolic age ("Let us do evil, that good may come," Rom. iii. 8; "Let us continue in sin that grace may abound," Rom. vi. 1); and the very fact that the Pauline gospel and the orthodox satisfaction theory were open to the same accusation or perversion was used as an argument for their identity. There is an odd kind of composure, not to say complacency, in the way in which Hopkins (quoted in Park, *ut supra,* pp. 95-6) limits the effect of the atonement to the past. "The atonement, therefore, only delivers from the curse of the law, and procures the remission of their sins who believe in Him, but does not procure for them any positive good; it leaves them under the power of sin, and without any title to eternal life, or any positive favour or actual fitness or capacity to enjoy positive happiness." This is the style of a schoolman perhaps, but not of an evangelist or an apostle.

casual consequence merely, but the end which that work has in view from the beginning, and which it is divinely adapted to secure. To use words which are useful, though apt to be misunderstood: the work of reconciliation must have justice done to its subjective as well as its objective reference; the doctrine must recognise its ultimate effect in man as well as its value for God.

In addition to these more or less articulate criticisms (1) of the inconsistency between satisfaction and free forgiveness, an inconsistency coming into consciousness in various forms, and (2) of the inadequacy with which the work of Christ was related to the new life in man, there was a further ground of dissatisfaction with the doctrine in a growing sense of its artificiality. Somehow or other, it had lost contact with experience. Its purpose was to explain how men are reconciled to God, to give an intelligible rationale of the process; but reconciled men failed to find in it a convincing reflection of the manner in which the reconciling power of God in Christ had taken effect in their souls. There was too much apparatus in it, and too little personality. In particular, men came to feel that there was something about it inconsistent with the nature of saving faith. Unconsciously, faith in a person was being displaced in favour of faith in articles. A *lex credendi*, including human definitions of satisfaction and merit, of active and passive obedience, of imputation and of divine indwelling, arose, if it was not erected, between the soul and the reconciling love of God in Christ. Access to God as Saviour, which the gospel makes free to all, or which it conditions only by entire surrender to Him, was virtually blocked by a preliminary demand for orthodoxy. "Clear views of truth," as they used to be called approvingly, were the way of salvation; and these clear views of truth were given in definitions made by men. The gospel was intellectualised, not only in the good sense that saved men applied their minds to it, as they had proved it in experience, but in the bad sense that it was presented in a form which might or might not satisfy the wise and prudent, but was certainly of no use to babes. It is this criticism by life which really discredits imperfect doctrines, and it can hardly be questioned that under it the traditional doctrine of reconciliation suffered severely.

In the century following the Reformation there was only one outstanding attempt made to rehabilitate the doctrine of satisfaction as against the Socinian criticism. This was the once celebrated *Defensio fidei catholicae de satisfactione Christi* by Grotius. It was published in 1617, but though it affected to be a defence of the Catholic faith about the satisfaction of Christ, and used the language of the established doctrine with the utmost freedom, it in effect put something quite different in its place. The orthodox doctrine made Christ's satisfaction penal; Christ made satisfaction by bearing the punishment of sin. To begin with, Grotius seems frankly to accept this view. With every kind of emphasis he reiterates the penal character of Christ's sufferings. The whole of his first chapter is occupied with the exegetical vindication of this "catholic" conception against the exegetical caprices of Socinus. "God," he writes, "moved by His goodness to do us a signal benefit, but hindered by our sins which deserved punishment, determined that Christ voluntarily out of His love towards men should pay the penalty of our sins (*poenas penderet pro peccatis nostris*) by enduring the sorest torments and a bloody and shameful death, that we, subject to the demonstration of God's justice (*salva divinae justitiae demonstratione*), should on condition of true faith be freed from the penalty of eternal death (*a poena mortis aeternae*)." So again he says, "to bear sins by suffering, and that in such wise that others are thereby set free, can indicate nothing else than the taking upon one of another's punishment" (*poenae alienae susceptionem*). He explicitly applies this to the case in hand. "The exaction of penalty and the affliction of Christ are of one piece (*cohaerent*)." We are justified or freed from the divine penalty, and that this might be, Christ was made sin—that is, *poenam divinam tulit*. The cross of Christ, therefore, he concludes, "*poenae rationem habuit*." If it is too strong to render this, "was of the nature of punishment," it at least implies that it cannot be understood unless we can interpret it by relation to punishment. And as if to leave no opening for ambiguity, he writes boldly, "*Est ergo punitio in Deo activé, in Christo passivé.*" Yet when he comes to the point, this is not what he establishes as the real character of Christ's sufferings. Penal suffering would be determined simply by sin, it would be what the sinner deserved according to the law; it would be his sin finding him out and returning on his own head. It would be inflicted by a judge according to the terms of a statute; it would be an exercise of retributive and distributive justice. But when Grotius thinks, not through the orthodox doctrine which he set out to defend, but spontaneously, this is not what he finds in the Christian religion. God, to Grotius, is not a private person, as He is to Socinian criticism. Grotius points out the inapplicability to God of the categories so frequent in Socinus—*pars offensa*, *creditor*, *dominus*, etc. Neither, however, as on the orthodox theory of penal satisfaction, is God a judge, formally administering criminal law. He is not *Judex*, but *Rector* or Ruler, and when we think of Him in this character our conception of what we call punishment changes. It is not the inexorable reaction of sin against the sinner; it is not the self-vindication of the law; from the ruler's point of view it has an ulterior object which determines its character. The right of punishing does not exist for the sake of Him who punishes, but for the sake of some common interest (*causa alicujus communitatis*). For every punishment has as its aim the common good (*bonum commune*); in the hands of the *Rector* it has in view the interest of the *regnum*. Every positive penal law—that is, every law attaching a certain punishment to a certain offence —is, without qualification, *relaxabilis*; a dispensation can be granted from it as long as the *bonum commune* is secured. What God does as ruler, in the case of Christ's satisfaction, is to grant a dispensation from the penal law on a condition which secures that the common interest shall not be prejudiced. The common interest is that reverence for God and His law should be maintained, and this is secured when forgiveness comes in such an awful and impressive way as through Christ's sufferings. Looked at strictly, we cannot say that Christ's sufferings are determined by the actual sins of men; they have no proper relation to anything men have actually done; they have in view rather possible and prospective sins, and their purpose is by arresting these to give God's love room to operate. Christ does not suffer the penalty of sin, in spite of the language which Grotius uses so freely in his opening chapter; He suffers something which may be said to be equivalent to that penalty, because in the government of the world it serves the same purpose—the maintenance of order and of reverence for the law as safeguarding the common good. But what it is Christ suffers, or what it is in His sufferings which gives Him this virtue, Grotius does not tell. There is something arbitrary in the death of Christ—something which reminds us irresistibly of Scotus and Socinus, and which takes us out of the region of rational and moral necessities where alone the mind can breathe. Notwithstanding these inconsistencies and drawbacks, the short treatise of Grotius had enormous influence. It introduced a new conception of God, which, whether or not it was adequate to the Christian truth, acted as a powerful stimulus to thought. It provoked more searching study of such ideas as law and punishment. It directed attention to the effect of Christ's work on men as well as on God—to the new life, as well as to the maintenance of God's honour or the satisfaction of His law. It helped to remove the ban of individualism, and to revive the idea of the Kingdom of God by its emphasis on the idea of a common good. Holland and New England were profoundly affected by it, and its very confusions were in its favour. It insinuated new ideas while professing merely to defend the old, and men through it got the benefit of all the truth there was both in old and new.

With the disintegration of the satisfaction theory, the natural tendency was to regard forgiveness as easy and cheap. Towards the end of the eighteenth century, when Rationalism was in vogue, sin was not thought very serious, nor forgiveness very hard. The one was apt to be discounted, and the other as nearly as possible taken for granted. Only men who had felt the sinfulness of sin, and their own inability to vanquish it without divine help, would have in their minds the motives which gave birth to the theory; consequently they only would have a natural sympathy with it. Curiously enough, the two greatest intellectual forces of the period on the Continent stood here on opposite sides. Kant, with his austere morality, taught the presence in man of a radical evil, an intimate and constitutional badness, which

THE CHRISTIAN DOCTRINE OF RECONCILIATION

in itself presents us with an insoluble problem.[1] This is the negative premiss of Christianity as a doctrine of redemption and reconciliation, and whether Kant did or did not personally accept the Christian way of handling the problem, he was so far on the Christian side as to recognise that it was there. He reduced the satisfaction of Christ to the idea that always the new man must bear the sins of the old; when the bad man becomes good, it is by accepting the punishment of his iniquities, and as a new creature expiating through sorrow and suffering the sins of his past. Kant's younger contemporary Goethe stood at the opposite pole. He had no difficulty about admitting the hereditary and other defects of human nature; among the multitudinous experiences of his all-experiencing life he had at one time breathed the atmosphere of the Moravian Brotherhood, and apparently thought himself entitled to be at home in it. But the Brethren would not regard him as a Christian; not even his own and his mother's friend, Fraülein von Klattenberg would do so. It was only by accident that he discovered why. He had no adequate sense of evil, and therefore no adequate sense of the total dependence of man on grace. As his friends pointed out to him, when he unfolded his view of human nature, he was a genuine Pelagian, and could have no unity with those who thought as they did of sin and redemption. But to have this pointed out did not make him penitent. On the contrary, he gloried in the very thing they censured. Kant's doctrine revolted him. He reproached the philosopher with sinning against himself, and charged him with "impiously beslobbering his philosopher's gown with the stain of radical evil." If the Goethean conception of human nature, working like a leaven in men's minds,

[1] *Die Religion innerhalb der Grenzen der blossen Vernunft: Erstes Stück.*

tended to destroy interest in a divine work of redemption and reconciliation, the Kantian one had the opposite effect. Just in proportion as men felt the enormous power of the evil which was in them to disable and defeat them morally, they were prepared to listen to a gospel which met this evil not with a mere proclamation of pardon, but with a demonstration of redeeming love definitely related to the evil itself. Granting that the doctrine of satisfaction did not do justice to what God had done in Christ to annul sin and reconcile men to Himself, it at least recognised that to do something was necessary; it busied itself with the real problem, and men always hovered round it anew.[1] The old questions were asked with new depth and subtlety, and the work of Christ in reconciling man to God was never more eagerly studied than when sentence of futility seemed to have been passed on all previous efforts to understand it.

It is not possible to follow in detail the course of Christian thinking on reconciliation during the last century and a quarter; indeed it is not possible to say that it has had any definite course at all. But it does no injustice to other theologians, if we say that the original contributions which have been made to the subject are represented in Schleiermacher's *Der christliche Glaube* (1821), Macleod Campbell's *The Nature of the Atonement* (1856), and Ritschl's *Die christliche Lehre von der Rechtfertigung und Versöhnung* (1870-74).[2]

One characteristic of all these books is that, to a far greater degree than those which preceded them, they rest on the basis of history and experience. They are all conscious of

---

[1] *Aus meinem Leben: Dichtung u. Wahrheit,* Buch xv. *ad init.* See Bielschowsky's *Goethe,* ii. 95 f.

[2] An English translation has appeared of the first (the historical) volume of Ritschl's work, and of the last (the systematic); the second (the exegetical) has not been translated.

THE CHRISTIAN DOCTRINE OF RECONCILIATION

Jesus as well as of the Christ, and conscious that, whatever the work of the Christ may be, it must arise naturally out of the life of Jesus. He is not conceived as here to carry out any plan of salvation, but He is the Saviour by being what He is, doing what He does, and suffering what He suffers, as the relations in which He finds Himself require. There is nothing artificial in the work of the Saviour; it is ethical in its inspiration and its achievement from beginning to end.

It is ethical also in the mode of its appropriation. The two German writers, to avoid risks in different directions, lay stress here on the idea of the Church. Perhaps what Schleiermacher is most afraid of is magic, the kind of appropriation of Christ and His grace which is taught in the sacramental doctrines of the Church of Rome. We are conscious, he says, of all approximations to blessedness which occur in the Christian life, as being based on a new and divinely affected common life (*Gesammtleben*) which counteracts the common life of sin and the misery developed there.[1] It is this continuity with a collective and therefore objective Christianity which secures its historical, ethical, non-fanatical, non-magical character in the individual. Otherwise Schleiermacher emphasises what he calls its mystical character. But by mystical he only means that the truth of Christianity cannot be realised except through Christian experience; it cannot be antecedently demonstrated, on purely rational grounds, with a view to experience. Sacramentalism is not mystical but magical. Mysticism, on the other hand, in the sense of a direct and immediate contact between Christ and the believing soul, is Ritschl's bugbear, and the Church, in the ethical life of which the Christianity of the

[1] *Der christliche Glaube*, § 87.

individual is kept within sound moral limits, is part of his defence against it.[1]

Macleod Campbell distinguishes more emphatically than either Schleiermacher or Ritschl Christ's dealing with men on the part of God and His dealing with God on the part of men. It is in connection with the last that he introduces the peculiar phraseology which has proved at once so attractive and so repellent in the exposition of his ideas. "That oneness of mind with the Father, which towards man took the form of condemnation of sin, would, in the Son's dealing with the Father in relation to our sins, take the form of a perfect confession of our sins. This confession, as to its own nature, must have been *a perfect Amen in humanity to the judgment of God on the sin of man.* . . . Let us consider this Amen from the depths of the humanity of Christ to the divine condemnation of sin. What is it in relation to God's wrath against sin? What place has it in Christ's dealing with that wrath? I answer: He who so responds to the divine wrath against sin, saying, "Thou art righteous, O Lord, who judgest us," is necessarily receiving the full apprehension and realisation of that wrath, as well as of that sin against which it comes forth, into His soul and spirit, into the bosom of the divine humanity, and, so receiving it, He responds to it with a perfect response,—a response from the depths of that divine humanity,—and *in that perfect response He absorbs it.* For that response has all the elements of a perfect repentance in humanity for all the sin of man,—a perfect sorrow—a perfect contrition—all the elements of such a repentance, and that in absolute perfection, all—excepting the personal consciousness of sin;—and by that perfect response in Amen to the mind of God in relation to sin is the

---

[1] *Rechtfertigung und Versöhnung* (3rd ed.), iii. 107 f. Also 168 f.

wrath of God rightly met, and that is accorded to divine justice which is its due, and could alone satisfy it."[1] The main thing here is that Christ enters sympathetically, as His relation to man required Him to do, into the whole state and responsibilities of His sinful brethren, making their burden His own, as far as it was possible for love to do so; and this is undoubtedly a great thing whatever we may think of the description of it as vicarious repentance or vicarious confession. Something akin to it had been expressed long before by Jonathan Edwards the elder, a writer to whom Macleod Campbell owes much, as indeed we often owe much to those to whom we are most opposed. "A very strong and lively love and pity towards the miserable tends to make their case ours; as in other respects, so in this in particular, as it doth in our idea place us in their stead, under their misery, with a most lively, feeling sense of that misery, as it were feeling it for them, *actually suffering it in their stead by strong sympathy*."[2] In earlier theologians the idea that Christ was man's substitute or representative in the work of making atonement had too much lost its connection with love: it had become part of the plan of salvation, and its ethical character was impaired. But now, as Bushnell is fond of expressing it, vicariousness is seen to be only another name for love; under the influence of love men make the case of others their own; and even if we speak of Christ as our substitute, it is because love has impelled Him to make our situation His.

Side by side with the altered emphasis at this point comes a new sense that what Christ does for us must be more definitely related to what He produces in us. His identification

---

[1] *The Nature of the Atonement*, 5th ed., p. 116 ff.
[2] *The Atonement: Discourses and Treatises*, with an introduction by Prof E. A. Park, p. xxxix.

IN THE CHRISTIAN THOUGHT OF THE PAST

of Himself with us must have as its aim and issue an identification on our part of ourselves with Him. The vocabulary of imputation, if not displaced by that of identification, is interpreted through it. There may be a tendency to ignore limits and distinctions, but there is a genuine desire to secure a true and real union between Christ and those who are His. His work is to save men from their sins, not to save them from the experience of being saved, which only comes in proportion as they become one with Him. If He is not really changing us into His own likeness, and enabling us to enter into the experiences in which sin involved Him, He is not reconciling us to God, and our sins are not forgiven. This is maintained even while it is maintained at the same time that Christ does something for us which we could never have done for ourselves, and enables us to do in union with Himself what we could never do alone; and if our union with Him is His work, His position as Saviour is unimpaired.

It will not be denied that in such thoughts as these personality gets the place, or something like the place, which is its due. It had this place for a moment in the new experience of the gospel at the Reformation, but it proved unable then to assert it theologically. But now the personality of Jesus— the personal, which is also the ethical, character of all He does or suffers in relation to sin—the personal quality of the response made to Him and His work, the response of an indivisible faith in which we identify ourselves with Him, as He has identified Himself with us—all come out in a new relief. One advantage of this is that categories of quantity, which have no meaning where personality is concerned, are quite inapplicable to the work of Christ. The questions once so fiercely debated about the extent of the atonement have no meaning. The humiliating sophistries with which Scripture was tortured to make it mean the very opposite of what is written broad upon its face, need vex us no more. Of all books that have ever been written on the atonement, as God's way of reconciling man to Himself, Macleod Campbell's is probably that which is most completely inspired by the spirit of the truth with which it deals. There is a reconciling power of Christ in it to which no tormented conscience can be insensible. The originality of it is spiritual as well as intellectual, and no one who has ever felt its power will cease to put it in a class by itself. In speculative power he cannot be compared to Schleiermacher, nor in historical learning to Ritschl, and sometimes he writes as badly as either; but he walks in the light all the time, and everything he touches lives.

CHAPTER III

THE NEW TESTAMENT DOCTRINE OF RECONCILIATION

CHRISTIAN thinking on the subject of reconciliation, the course of which has just been outlined, was carried on as a rule in more or less close contact with the New Testament. It did not, indeed, attach itself immediately to the text of Scripture, and though the authority of Scripture would have been frankly admitted by all the theologians whose names have been mentioned, many of their forms of thought—for instance, the dominant one of "satisfaction"—come from elsewhere. The experiences, however, which really inspired all the intellectual activity we have surveyed, owed their origin to the gospel, and the great witness to the gospel was the New Testament. Moreover, as the experience of reconciliation was obviously the main characteristic of New Testament life, and as it brought with it, just as obviously, not only a spiritual but an intellectual regeneration, in which the new experience was interpreted by the first Christians to themselves, it is natural to ascribe to this primitive interpretation of the new life a great if not a decisive authority. We cannot, of course, simply borrow it to save ourselves the trouble of thinking; it is inconsistent with the nature of intelligence simply to borrow anything. But we may admit that it is entitled to the most serious consideration; and if our own interpretation of what we call the experience of reconciliation is inconsistent with it, we must feel that the question then raised is whether our interpretation is entitled to be called, in any properly historical sense, Christian.

It would hardly be profitable to discuss abstractly and *a priori* the kind of questions here involved. All we can do is to approach the New Testament with candour and to absorb what of it we can. There may be things in it which we cannot absorb, but which we can let alone without misgiving; but it would surely cause the most profound misgiving if the thing which is central and vital in the New Testament proved to be a thing which in the last resort we could only decline. This may not be a very adequate statement of the authority of the New Testament for Christian doctrine, but it is the actual basis on which most ministers of the New Testament at present stand, and it may serve for practical purposes—the only purposes which the gospel itself serves.[1]

A natural question to many in this connection is, Why limit to the New Testament the reference to Scripture? The New Testament writers do not make for themselves— or so at least it is often said—any claim to authority; rather do they appeal to the authority of what we call the Old Testament. What they preach, even about Jesus, is "according to" these ancient Scriptures. His death for our sins and His resurrection on the third day are set with the help of the Old Testament in the convincing and divine light which makes them authoritative for the conscience, a message of reconciliation and of eternal hope (1 Cor. xv. 3 f.). The

---

[1] On this see the instructive paragraph in Stade's *Bibl. Theologie der alten Testaments*, §§ 2. 5. But it is not merely "der vulgär-protestantische Fehler," as Stade calls it, which connects with the idea of religion, in the first instance, that of a doctrine (Lehre); the mistake is as common and as tenaciously held among Romanists as among Protestants.

NEW TESTAMENT DOCTRINE OF RECONCILIATION

apostles, it may be said, read the Old Testament as a Christian book, and we do not get into their minds till we can do the same. Would it not be proper, then, to take up here rather the Biblical than the New Testament doctrine of reconciliation, and to begin with an examination of the Old Testament by itself? This is not the view which on reflection has commended itself to the writer, and there are weighty considerations to be alleged against it.

It is true, no doubt, that there is a continuity between the Old Testament and the New, of which New Testament writers are well aware. It is one purpose of God which is being fulfilled throughout both, one people of God the story of which is being told from Abel to the apostolic age. There is one society of which God is the head, and in which God and man live in more or less perfect harmony with each other, sharing a common life, and achieving common ends. The Christian Church is conscious of being the true people of God, and as such the heir of all God's promises. The difference is that in earlier times the heir was a child, but now in the fulness of the time he has attained his majority and its liberty. But even where the continuity is insisted upon, the great thing is to understand the difference which has been made by the coming and the work of Christ; and though the apostles may use Old Testament ideas—sacrifice, redemption, propitiation, and such like—to interpret Christ to themselves, these ideas are all involuntarily modified by their application to Him. Instead of going to the Old Testament to find what He is in these characters, we have to fasten our eyes on Him to see what the essential truth of those Old Testament ideas amounts to. It is quite fair to say that we do not see Jesus truly unless we see Him in the perspective of the Old Testament, but it is quite fair also to say that we do not see the Old Testament truly unless we see it in the perspective of Jesus. To study reconciliation in the Old Testament, with our eyes closed to Him, would be to study it in vain. Our experience of it is only through Him, and the study of what it was, and of how it was conditioned, appropriated and realised, at a stage of religious history at which He had not yet appeared, and which even in imagination we can only doubtfully revive, can hardly be of decisive importance for our present pursuit. At all events, the use which New Testament writers make of the Old Testament can quite conveniently be referred to when the connections in which they use it come before us.

The propriety of this course is more evident if we observe that the New Testament is intensely conscious not only of its continuity with the Old, but of the fact that it transcends the Old. Paul, in particular, often defines the relation between them as one of contrast and even antagonism. In their spiritual effects, they are precisely opposed to each other; the New Testament does what the Old failed to do; it brings us to victory where the Old only led us to defeat. The one is embodied in the letter and the other in the spirit, and while the letter kills, the spirit makes alive. The ministry of the one ends in condemnation, that of the other in justification. The one has a transient, the other an abiding glory. The last word which the one wrings from human lips is the despairing cry, "O wretched man that I am! who shall deliver me?" The first word which the other inspires is, "So then there is no condemnation to them that are in Christ Jesus." This does indeed bring us to the point at which Paul is paradoxical to the verge of injustice, and perhaps beyond it, in his treatment of the Old Testament—expounding its religion, as he does for the moment, with the legalist life of the Pharisee under the law—but it shows at the same time that in approaching what is most characteristic of the gospel only through its continuity with the Old Testament, we are not necessarily entering on the most promising path. It is just as well to plunge at once *in medias res*. The New Testament gospel is related to human nature as well as to Jewish history, and much of it can probably be understood without a special historical training. Where this latter is indispensable as the key to peculiarities in the original construction and presentation of the gospel, we can consider as occasion requires.

To say this does not question the importance of the Old Testament nor its peculiar connection with the New. The idea of Schleiermacher, that the Christian religion was equally related to Gentile as to Jewish antecedents, and that there was an equivalent preparation for it in the pagan as in the Old Testament history, is quite unhistorical. Neither does it imply any assent beforehand to the arguments of those students of comparative religion who would persuade us that most of what is most characteristic of the New Testament, especially in its doctrine of reconciliation—the whole conception, for example, of a divine Redeemer, in whose death and resurrection men partake by mystical and sacramental means—is due to the infiltration into primitive Christianity of ideas which originated not in the Old Testament, but in the Hellenistic mystery religions. These arguments can be considered when they come directly before us: their validity does not need to be determined before we take the New Testament into our hands. On general grounds we can only hold that when the key to New Testament doctrines is sought anywhere rather than in the Old Testament, the presumption is that the search is misdirected. The sounder view historically is that nothing has a right to a place in the New

THE CHRISTIAN DOCTRINE OF RECONCILIATION

Testament which has not antecedents and affinities in the Old.

But in taking the New Testament into our hands, without prejudice of any kind, one vital problem arrests us. Is the New Testament itself a unity? Does it, to apply the question to our special subject, contain one doctrine of reconciliation, and no other? Does every part of it contain such a doctrine? There was a time, not so very remote, when these questions would not have been asked. The Christian Church of all ages and of all confessions believed that the Son of God, by His sacrificial death on the cross, had borne the sin of the world and reconciled men to God. It believed that by His resurrection from the dead men were born again to a living hope of eternal life. This was, in short, the gospel message; there was no gospel except in the Son of God, who was delivered for our offences and raised again for our justification. But in the last two generations another view has been widely held. The place of Christ in Christianity has been questioned and denied. It would not be of so much consequence if this were done by way of repudiating Christianity; what makes it important is that it purports to be done in the way of purifying and reforming Christianity, and that it professes to appeal to the authority of Christ Himself. It had its most startling expression in Harnack's well-known saying, that in the gospel as preached by Jesus the Son had no place, only the Father. Assuming that this was true, there would evidently be a schism in the New Testament itself. For in the gospel as preached by the apostles after the departure of Jesus, the Son is so far from having no place that He fills all things. To put it bluntly, in this view there are in the New Testament two gospels. There is the gospel preached by Jesus and the gospel preached by Paul, and so far as the

NEW TESTAMENT DOCTRINE OF RECONCILIATION

place of Jesus is concerned, the two are in direct antithesis to each other. In the one, Jesus is the ideal subject of religion, the pattern believer, who shows men through all the vicissitudes, temptations, wrongs, and agonies of life, and even in death itself, how to trust the Father and to love His children; in the other, Jesus is, in the first instance, not the pattern but the object of faith; we believe in Him as Lord and Saviour, as the propitiation for our sins, and not for ours only, but for the sin of the whole world. He does not merely announce, by His life and death He achieves, the reconciliation of men to God. Probably in practice no one born and brought up in the Christian Church is able simply to accept this antithesis. There is truth in the conception of Jesus as the pattern believer; the New Testament presents it, and the soul acknowledges its power. But there is truth also in the conception of Jesus as the object of faith, a redeemer, or reconciler, a sacrifice for sin; the New Testament presents this also, and the conscience of the sinner cannot shut it out. The impossibility of treating the antitheses as mutually exclusive is apparent even in Harnack himself. In the very context of the passage in which he declares that the Son has no place in the gospel, but only the Father, he is compelled to make a qualification so immense that it virtually annuls the declaration. The Son, he repeats, does not belong to the gospel as an element of it, but He has been "the personal realisation and the power of the gospel, and is still perpetually experienced as such. Fire is kindled only at fire, and personal life only at personal powers."[1] The same impossibility of ignoring entirely the value of the testimony borne in the New Testament to Christ as redeemer and reconciler is conspicuous in a lecture entitled *The Two-*

[1] Harnack, *Das Wesen des Christentums*, 91 f.

THE CHRISTIAN DOCTRINE OF RECONCILIATION

fold Gospel in the New Testament, delivered by Harnack at the Fifth International Congress of Free Christianity and Religious Progress, held at Berlin in 1910. Here he goes so far as to say that "this double gospel, as it is set forth in the New Testament, is just as necessary at the present day as it has been necessary in all periods of the past." [1]

But we can go much further than this. In his work *Jesus and the Gospel*, first published in 1908, the writer gave what he considers a sufficient proof of the unity of the New Testament. The argument is that there are not two gospels in the New Testament, but one; and that that one gospel is supported not only by the apostolic writers, but by the witness of Jesus Himself. It demonstrates, as he believes, that the attitude to Christ which has always been maintained in the Church—that in which He is regarded as the object of faith, the redeemer of men from sin and their reconciler to God through His death on the cross—is the one which is characteristic of the New Testament from beginning to end, and that this attitude is the only one which is consistent with the self-revelation of Jesus during His life on earth. If Jesus did not claim, He won and accepted this relation of men to Himself. It is impossible to resume this argument here, but its conclusions will be taken for granted. That there are relative contrasts within the New Testament is not denied, but there are no absolute ones—that is, there are none such as would justify us in speaking of two gosepls. It is more natural, for example, that our Lord should magnify the freeness of God's love to the sinful, and more natural that the sinners to whom it came should magnify its cost, as coming through Him and through His passion; and this, in fact, is what

[1] *The Two-fold Gospel in the New Testament,* a lecture by Adolf Harnack, D.D. (Williams and Norgate).

NEW TESTAMENT DOCTRINE OF RECONCILIATION

we find. But though there is a contrast between freeness and cost, there is no antagonism, and neither is there any antagonism between the gospel of Jesus and that of Paul, or Peter, or John. We get a better chance of being impressed with the truth in its native proportions if we approach the evangelists and apostles without such questionable preconceptions.

There is, however, at this point another difficulty on which the historical study of the New Testament has laid great weight, the difficulty of realising how historical events, like the life and death of Jesus, should have the significance which the New Testament and all Christian faith assign them. That something occurring in time and now lying in time far behind us should reveal eternal truth and have eternal value—that what was unquestionably human should be indubitably divine—that history, which is essentially relative, should here only be transcended, should for this once have absolute significance, never to be transcended—that the death of Christ should be at the same time the consummation of human sin and the final revelation of the love of God, a cruel unscrupulous murder and a voluntary atoning sacrifice; that it should be possible to explain the same thing in such inconceivably remote ways—on the one hand, through its historical causes in the ignorance, the pride, the hatred, the self-righteousness of men; on the other, through its final cause in the eternal sin-bearing, redeeming love of God;—there is the one difficulty of the Christian religion in which all others are summed up. How can the historical and human be eternal and divine? The New Testament, curiously enough, is aware of the contrasts here stated, but does not seem perplexed by them. The story of the Passion is told quite objectively—the timidity of the twelve, the malice of the

THE CHRISTIAN DOCTRINE OF RECONCILIATION

priests, the treachery of Judas, the vacillation and unscrupulousness of Pilate, all the historical causes of the death of Jesus, are presented quite disinterestedly; and side by side with this it is asserted that God gave Him up for us all, and forgiveness of sins is preached in His name. There was probably a latent sense of the disproportion between the historical facts and the divine meaning of them, but faith rather gloried in the paradox than wrestled with it. That a judicial murder, attended by many circumstances of squalor and horror, should also be the final sacrifice for the sin of the world, was strange indeed; but it was the Lord's doing, and wonderful in believers' eyes. No doubt the apostles were aware that in all its inner reality, in everything in it in which Christ was revealed, the passion was divine. When He said to the women on the Via Dolorosa, "Weep not for me, but weep for yourselves and for your children"; when He prayed at the cross, "Father, forgive them, for they know not what they do"; when He said to the penitent thief, "To-day shalt thou be with me in paradise"; when He bowed His head and cried, "Father, into thy hands I commend my spirit," they felt that nothing of this was without God. It was through eternal spirit—a spirit which in moral power could never be outgrown, and in which the final reality of God was made manifest—that He offered Himself without spot to the Father. But they do not reason upon this, they seem rather to have had an instinctive sense of its truth. The assertion that the murdered Jesus is the Lamb of God who takes away the sin of the world is too great not to be true, and the verification of it has been too wonderful to let us suppose it false. In the New Testament presentation of the gospel the final cause of Christ's death—what God does in it—completely overshadows the antecedent or his-

NEW TESTAMENT DOCTRINE OF RECONCILIATION

torical causes by which it was produced, and here it is the New Testament point of view which must determine our course.[1] At the same time, while we recognise that the historical in the New Testament is eternal and divine, we must not allow ourselves to suppose that when we have apprehended the eternal and divine we can become indifferent to the historical and let it go. The whole power of Christianity is in its historical character, and to replace its sublime and tragic facts by a system of ideas, however true and imposing, is to destroy it altogether.

In the first chapter reference has been made to the general character of the work of Jesus. In the widest sense it will not be questioned that it was a work of reconciliation. He received sinners. He declared, bestowed, and embodied forgiveness. He came to seek and to save that which was lost. Whatever else He did, He came to men who were alienated from God by their sins, full of apprehensions and distrust, and He brought them back to God and to the assurance of His fatherly love. This was the general character and result of His life work in relation to individuals. It was what His personality and His teaching inspired in the paralytic

[1] Cf. Grotius, *Defensio Fidei Catholicae*, etc., ed. secunda, p. 19: "Apostoli cum passionem Christi ad usus nostros referunt, non in ea respiciunt hominum facta, sed factum ipsius Dei." For another illustration of the disproportion between faith and fact in the New Testament, compare the following from Dr. Moffatt's note (*Expositor's Greek Testament*, vol. v.) on Rev. i. 18: "When one remembers the actual position of affairs, the confident faith of such passages is seen to have been little short of magnificent. To this Christian prophet, spokesman of a mere ripple upon a single wave of dissent in the broad ocean of paganism, history and experience find unity and meaning nowhere but in the person of a blameless Galilean peasant, who had perished as a criminal in Jerusalem. So would such early Christian expectations appear to an outsider." To understand the New Testament, and especially the wonderfulness of it, nothing is more important than to be alive to the stupendous contrast in it between appearance and reality, sense and faith, the visible and the divine.

man (of Mark ii.) and in the sin-burdened woman (of Luke vii.). The power which inspired the penitence and faith which these narratives reveal was exerted through His personality, during His ministry; and ever since, it has been signally exerted through His Passion. We may say that the reconciling virtue of His being was concentrated in His death, or that the reconciling virtue of His death pervaded His being; in any case, that the whole influence exerted upon sinners by Jesus is an influence by which, through penitence and faith, they are won from sin to God—in other words, is a reconciling influence—cannot be denied. How He exercised such an influence, and what it cost Him to do so, are ulterior questions.

When Jesus taught about forgiveness, what He emphasised was its freeness. This is the lesson of the prodigal son. The son did not buy his forgiveness, nor did anybody buy it for him. Nothing he could do could ever repay it. His father forgave him because he was his father and loved him with an indefeasible love, more strong and wonderful than all his sins. If there is any argument implied, it is the *a fortiori* argument from man to God which is habitual with Jesus. "If you, who are evil, can show such pardoning love to your children, much more will your heavenly Father freely forgive those who turn from their sins to Him." We have the same moral in the parable of the two debtors (Luke vii. 41 f.). "When they had nothing to pay, the creditor frankly forgave them both"; ἐχαρίσατο, he made them a present of the debt. But to emphasise the freeness of forgiveness is not to deny that it has other characteristics. It is not unconditional. God does not forgive the impenitent, who do not wish nor ask to be forgiven. He cannot do so, for forgiveness, like all spiritual things, cannot be given unless it is taken, and it can only be taken by a penitent and surrendered soul. Neither, as has been observed above, is the freeness of forgiveness inconsistent with its cost. Those to whom the assurance of forgiveness came through Jesus were not unconscious that it cost Him something. It came in a way which made them feel that they were His debtors, that He had put them under an infinite obligation, that they owed Him what they could never repay. It was not for Him to say this—that would have been morally unbecoming—but it was for them to feel it, and when the New Testament Church came to clear consciousness of itself and of its debt, it expressed its feeling in the doxologies to Christ, which from the beginning have been its truest creed. "Unto Him that loveth us, and loosed us from our sins in His blood, be the glory and the dominion for ever and ever."

The analogy, to which our Lord so often refers, between God's forgiveness of us and our forgiveness of one another, is very instructive in this connection. "Forgive us our debts," He taught His disciples to pray, "as we forgive our debtors." It is assumed here that we do forgive our debtors. Such a thing as forgiveness is actually known among men, and it throws real light upon the forgiveness of God. Here the mere fact is important, for we know how deep-seated is the impression that forgiveness is impossible. "Things are what they are, and the consequences of them will be what they will be; why then should we wish to be deceived?" To do wrong is to do what cannot be made right; it is to impair relations of trust and love which can never be the same again; its only end is despair. This is what we are apt to think and to feel, but the fact that we forgive each other is a practical refutation of this desponding logic. The father who forgives an erring son, and takes him into his confidence again—the wife who forgives the husband who has been disloyal to her, and makes possible again a common life in which there are no secrets—the friend who has been injured, and yet sees in him who has done the injury something quite inconsistent with it, and for the sake of that something cannot renounce the offender—all these show that there is something in the world higher than the formal obligations we owe to each other—higher, it may be said, than law or wrong—something which comes into the field to deal with emergencies to which law is unequal, and which deals with them effectively. And that something is the love which forgives and which reconstitutes the personal relations wrong had impaired. Here we may confidently argue on our Lord's favourite line: If we who are evil know how to deal with wrong so as to rob it of enduring power and to restore in love the bonds it has broken—if we who are so weak, and who live in the world of nature and its iron necessities, can give and receive the blessed experience of reconciliation with its incalculable power to neutralise and transcend the past—much more must the Father, the Lord of heaven and earth, be able to forgive sins and restore souls. When we see the children forgiving one another their trespasses, we can look up securely and say, "There is forgiveness with Thee."

There is another part of our Lord's teaching in connection with human forgiveness which is of great consequence, and which also throws light on the forgiveness of God. It is the duty of the offended person, of him who is in the right, to pave the way for reconciliation. He is not, because he is in the right, to wait passively and nurse his grievance till the offender comes and confesses that he is in the wrong. "If thy brother trespass against thee, go and tell him his fault; if he hear thee, thou hast gained thy brother" (Matt. xviii. 15 f.). Do not be discouraged by one rebuff. Bring every moral power at your disposal to bear upon him before you leave him to himself. Spare no pains to evoke in him the penitence on which forgiveness can be bestowed. This is a vital point in the teaching of Jesus about forgiveness between man and man: the initiative in the work of reconciliation must be taken by him who has been wronged, and he must not grudge any self-humbling that is necessary to win the offending brother. As has been already indicated, there would have been a want of moral decorum had Jesus obtruded the fact that this was what God was doing, and doing *through Him*. In point of fact, He did not obtrude it. The father, in the parable of the prodigal son, takes no initiative; he does nothing to inspire the prodigal with repentance; there is no elder brother in the family to go into the far country and make the prodigal's case his own, while he appeals to him in the name of the father and his love. But though all this is not put into the parable, it must all in some way be present in the facts, unless the reconciling love of God is a poorer thing than the reconciling love which Jesus requires of men. But He never requires anything that He does not exhibit, and that seeking love, which takes the initiative and is willing to spend and to be spent to the uttermost in the work of reconciliation, is the breath of His being. Of course it was not for Him to say this, but it was for sinners to see and to feel it. It is the plain truth that every one who knows, even in human relations, what it is to forgive or to be forgiven, knows also that it is the most costly and tragic of all experiences. Hence we are not afraid to argue again on our Lord's lines, especially when supported by His command to take the first steps to reconciliation, and to stop at no cost: "If we being evil pay the price we do pay to renew the relations wrong has broken, how much more will our heavenly Father be at cost to reconcile His offending children to Himself! How dearly bought must be that great forgiveness which is the highest achievement of the love which bears the sin of the world!" The divine forgiveness cannot be easier or cheaper than that which we know among ourselves, and it is not alien to it. It is of the same nature, but in cost as in worth it is above it as the heavens are higher than the earth. If we keep this in mind, we shall feel the ineptitude of disputing the ascription to Jesus of the words in which He speaks of giving His life a ransom for many, or of the cup at the supper as a new covenant in His blood. It became Him, who came to seek and to save that which was lost, and to take the initiative in the work of reconciliation, even at the cost of His own life, not indeed to parade His sacrifice, but in moving and mysterious words like these, on solemn occasions, to reveal or betray its presence in His soul. The fact and its repression and its manifestation are all in moral harmony with each other.

There is yet another aspect of human forgiveness to which our Lord directs attention, and here also we may point out the analogy between it and the forgiveness of God. It is fully and impressively exhibited in the parable of the unforgiving servant in Matt. xviii. 23 ff. Jesus teaches here that the experience of being forgiven, even when it is only one human being who forgives another, is or ought to be the most powerful of all motives in the life of the forgiven. It ought to bring into his very soul, to lodge at the heart of his being, the spirit of him from whom the forgiveness comes. This is what we normally find in our relations to one another. Nothing as a matter of fact strikes so deep into the human

NEW TESTAMENT DOCTRINE OF RECONCILIATION

heart, nothing evokes penitence so tender, so humble, and so unreserved, nothing carries with it such joy and such sorrow, in a word such inspiring and regenerating power. There is no such thing known to human experience as a dead, inert, fruitless forgiveness. If there is such a thing it is a moral monstrosity; it is not a real case of forgiveness, and does not deserve the name. And once more we may use the familiar analogy: "If we who are evil forgive with a forgiveness which regenerates—if the reconciliation with which we reconcile our offending brother makes him a new creature, with a new sense of loyalty to the relations in which we stand to each other—much more will the forgiveness of God bring with it the promise and potency of a new life." The only forgiveness Jesus recognises is that which makes the forgiven heart the home of the love which forgives; in other words, that by which a man is born again the child of God. Hence, forgiveness or reconciliation is in a strict sense everything in the Christian religion. It does not need to be eked out with anything else. God trusts to it to keep the sinner right with Him, just as we ourselves trust when we forgive. The child whom his father or mother pardons through pain cannot but be good while the sense of this forgiveness rests upon his heart, and it is this simple principle on which the whole New Testament rests. True forgiveness regenerates. Justification is the power which sanctifies. This truth, which we can verify in our forgiveness of one another daily, is the ultimate and fundamental truth of the gospel. The ignoring of it has led not only to unhappy practical consequences, to which the New Testament itself bears witness, but to many artificialities and confusions in theology. It has led to such sayings as that "all forgiveness is of the nature of fiction," [1] or even that forgiveness is

[1] Sanday and Headlam, *Romans*, p. 94.

a sort of formality. This may be in part a question of words; forgiveness by those who so speak is being taken in an abstractness foreign to its nature. But in a term so important, the more closely we can keep to the concrete reality and all its inevitable implications the better.

If we turn from the teaching of Jesus on forgiveness as between man and man and on the divine forgiveness as illustrated by it, to His conception of His own work as a whole, we get further light upon our subject. The vocation of Jesus is represented in the gospels in two ways. On the one hand, He came to reveal the Father, and by doing so to enable men to become children of God. In this relation He is spoken of *simpliciter* as the Son, to whom alone all others must owe it that they have the knowledge of the Father and a place among the children (Matt. xi. 27 ff.). On the other hand, He came to bring in the Kingdom of God and to secure for men their citizenship in this divine commonwealth. In this relation He is spoken of as the Son of Man. No expressions in the New Testament have been more discussed than Son of Man and Kingdom of God, but it is not necessary here to enter into any of the controversies connected with them. It will hardly be denied that the coming of the Son of Man in His glory, and the coming or consummation of the Kingdom, are coincident if not identical. Nor is it possible to contest the connection between the Son of Man in many gospel passages and the description of one like unto a Son of Man in Daniel vii., who comes before the Ancient of days, and has dominion, glory, and a kingdom given to Him. But there is one great and vital difference. The human form in the book of Daniel is nothing but glorious; in the gospels, the Son of Man is the subject of predictions in which Jesus declares not only His final glory but the path of rejection and treachery, of suffering and of death, which precedes and leads up to it. Whenever He speaks of these sufferings, as He does again and again, they are the sufferings of the Son of Man. To speak of them thus is to bring them into His vocation, and to represent them as essential to the coming of the Kingdom of God. Not apart from them, not in spite of them, but in virtue of them, does He establish that kingdom in which God rules over a community of forgiven and reconciled men.[1] The Son of Man (in short), in the teaching of Jesus, fuses in one person the glorious figure of Daniel, and perhaps of the later book of Enoch, with the suffering servant of the Lord depicted in Isaiah xlii., xlix., liii. This fusion pervades the story of the gospels more than is sometimes noticed. It comes out at the very beginning of the ministry of Jesus in the account of His baptism. The heavenly voice speaks to Him in the words not only of Ps. ii. 7, but of Isaiah xlii. 1; showing that from the very hour when He entered on His work as Saviour He was identified in His own mind with the suffering servant, and realised that in His calling to bring in the Kingdom of God a career like that of the servant was inevitable. The connection is made indisputable, when in the last hours of His life He applies to Himself the words of Isaiah liii. 12: I tell you, this that stands written must be fulfilled in me. He was reckoned with transgressors." And in the most wonderful of all the words in which He declares His consciousness of what He is here to do, the references to Isaiah liii. are numerous and undoubted: "The Son of Man came not to be ministered unto but to minister, and to give His life a ransom for many."[2]

[1] See the author's *Death of Christ*, 19 ff.
[2] *The Death of Christ*, p. 33, *note*.

It is the carrying on of kindred thoughts which we find in the Last Supper, though there they are attached to other passages in the Old Testament. Jesus speaks with His death in immediate prospect, and He calls His blood covenant blood. In the words as we have them in the different New Testament writers, there may be here or there a point at which the meaning is brought out more articulately than it was in the very terms employed by Jesus. But though it is possible that this is so, it is by no means certain. He may very well have said a great deal more—indeed it is difficult to believe that He did not say more—on the subject pointed to in the monumental words of institution. If He called His blood covenant blood at all, and no one questions this, it must have been the blood of a new covenant, and there is no reason why in conversation He should not have used the word *new* Himself. And if the word were used, or the idea of a new covenant suggested at all, it is inconceivable that any mind, nourished as was His on the Old Testament scriptures, should have failed to recall that sublimest of ancient prophecies in which Jeremiah describes the new covenant as it dawned on his horizon, with its primary and fundamental blessing of the forgiveness of sins (Jer. xxxi. 31-34). Possibly Jesus did not expressly say, as He is represented doing in Matt. xxvi. 28, that His blood was shed for many *unto remission of sins*, but possibly also He did use those very words. Even if He did not, there is no reason to believe that Matthew misinterpreted Him in using them. Expressions like "covenant blood," which was of course sacrificial blood, had their meaning in a system of ideas which was present to the minds of those to whom Jesus spoke, and immediate inferences from them were possible for such hearers which would not at once suggest themselves to us. It is at most such an immediate inference which is drawn by the first evangelist when he makes the death of Jesus refer to the forgiveness of sins, and it is gratuitous to question its correctness. He had Jeremiah at least to prompt him, and the whole of the New Testament supports him. If it were a case of calculating chances, the chances would be a thousand to one that Matthew was right in his rendering of the mind of Jesus, and that those who dissent from him at a distance of two thousand years are wrong. Hence when we take into account our Lord's conception of His work as a whole, and especially His conception of a Son of Man who comes to His kingdom through a Passion interpreted in such wonderful words as Mark x. 45 and Matt. xxvi. 28, we are able to say, with His authority behind us, that this Passion entered into the work of redeeming men, of forgiving them, and of reconciling them to God. Certainly we have no formal theology here, nothing abstract or speculative; but we have the consciousness, on the part of Jesus— the recognition, it may be said, in His words—of all the realities which present evangelical theology with its task. The problem of a doctrine of reconciliation has been set.

When we pass beyond the words of Jesus, the great preacher of reconciliation is Paul. The term owes its currency in the Church to him. It is he who describes what it is to be a Christian in the words, "we have received the reconciliation" (Rom. v. 10). It is he who says, "All things are of God, who reconciled us to himself through Christ." The apostolic ministry is for him "the ministry of reconciliation"; the apostolic gospel is "the word of reconciliation"; its appeal is condensed in the cry, "Be reconciled to God" (2 Cor. v. 18-20). The reconciliation is essentially related to the Passion. "He has made peace by the blood of his cross." "You who were once alienated and enemies in mind in your evil works, he has now reconciled in the body of his flesh through death" (Col. i. 20-22). Though he only uses the term in c. v. 10 f. (xi. 15), it is in the epistle to the Romans that Paul offers us the most systematic presentation of his gospel, and it is on it mainly that this statement of what he understands by reconciliation will be based.

Paul connects in the closest possible way the announcement of his gospel and the announcement of the necessity which it has to meet. "I am not ashamed of the gospel, for in it the righteousness of God is revealed . . . for the wrath of God is revealed from heaven against all ungodliness and unrighteousness of men, who suppress the truth in unrighteousness" (Rom. i. 16-18). The revelation of God's righteousness—which is the method of reconciliation—is necessitated by the revelation of His wrath; we require the gospel because apart from it this is what awaits us. It ought to be noticed that both the righteousness of God which constitutes the gospel, and the wrath of God to which men are exposed apart from the gospel, are spoken of as revelations. God is behind both and present in both. Both have a divine reality and objectivity. It is because the wrath of God is divinely real that those who are exposed to it need to have a real divine righteousness; while the divine righteousness must have such a character as to meet the situation created by the divine wrath. The bare statement of these facts at once raises the problem of Pauline and indeed of all New Testament theology. When God for man's salvation reveals a divine righteousness which somehow confronts and neutralises a divine wrath, we can only conceive it as *God taking part with us against Himself.* It is a divine wrath which makes the δικαιοσύνη Θεοῦ necessary; it is a prior manifestation of God's own nature by relation to which the δικαιοσύνη Θεοῦ has to be defined. When we try to put this into an abstract doctrinal statement it is not easy to escape at least the appearance of contradiction; perhaps it is not possible. But we must be true to the facts, and in interpreting Paul we must be true to the connection of ideas in his primary statement of his gospel. It is often said that the way to avoid these perplexing contradictions is to recognise that the work of reconciliation, the atonement, the δικαιοσύνη Θεοῦ, or however we phrase it, does not need to be defined by relation to God or to anything divine whatever: it is exhausted in man, and in the effect it produces in him. In other words, an objective doctrine of what Christ does—a doctrine implying that it is determined by anything divine—is a mistake: all we need is a doctrine of the way in which it tells upon sinners. That it must tell upon sinners is of course admitted by everybody, but to limit it so is certainly not in agreement with Paul. For him, it is not merely something in us that necessitates the revelation of divine righteousness, and determines it to take place in one way and not in another; it is something in God; it is the divine wrath revealed against every kind of sin. It is tempting when we preach the gospel to try to classify and simplify it so that every appearance even of contradiction shall disappear. But there is a real danger that in doing so we lose contact with the facts from which Paul started, and which have at least the semblance of contradiction; and when we lose contact with the facts we lose the power to evangelise. In spite of crudities and contradictions, men feel the power of the gospel through the most inadequate statement which implies that somehow or other it has to do with the wrath of God, as they do not feel it through the most lucid statement which defines it only by relation to the effect it is intended to produce in us. It is worth while therefore, for practical as well as scientific reasons, to direct attention to this point.

Nothing is commoner than the denial that the revelation of divine wrath is real. The wrath of God, it is constantly asserted, is an idea which is ultimately inconsistent with the Christian conception of God as a loving father. It is an illusion, a misunderstanding, the natural mistake of a bad conscience; and, like other mistakes, it is removed by explanation. Sin, against which it is supposed to be the divine reaction, has no such reality for God as this terrible word implies. It does not create a problem for Him the solution of which is costly and awful. The wrath of God, in short, is not a revelation but a bugbear. Well, this is a question of fact. Paul nowhere gives a definition of sin, or of the way in which it is related to the wrath of God, but he says this wrath is revealed from heaven against all ungodliness and unrighteousness of men; that is, it comes into human experience as a divine reality about which he, at least, has no uncertainty. It is revealed, as he explains in the first chapter of Romans, in the appalling spectacles of moral degradation which the world presents, and in which we see human sin, under the retributive judgment of God, exerting the most tremendous sentences upon itself. Three times over, in vv. 24, 26, 28, he says παρέδωκεν αὐτοὺς ὁ θεός—God gave them up, judicially abandoned them. He gave them up to uncleanness, to shameful passions, to a reprobate mind, meaning by the last a state of intelligence and conscience in which man's moral nature could only be rejected by *Him* because it no longer did the work it was meant for, but had been perverted against itself and its Author. Under God's judgment, the very light that was in men had become darkness. Was there no divine wrath in this? Paul believed in God as a living, acting, personal God, and while he probably would not have quarrelled with the expression that the degradation he describes was the natural and inevitable consequence of unfaithfulness to God, he would not have felt that it was any easier or truer to say this than to say, "Therefore God gave them up." We may take too easily to the conception of natural law in the spiritual world, or, in a case like this, to that of inevitable moral consequences. Sinful nature inclines unconsciously to everything which keeps God at arm's length. Many people, Erskine of Linlathen said, use their religion as a shield against God; many more in modern times use a conception like that of the moral order of the world as such a shield. There is a system of things, a method in which they operate, spontaneously and inevitably, to moral issues, but we do it wrong (it is said) when we introduce into it the personal voluntary action of God, especially with such associations as are inseparable from a term like wrath. But if there is a God at all, a living, personal God, the wrong, upon reflection, may well seem to be the other way. There is nothing good in the world but a good will, and nothing bad but a bad will; there is nothing moral at all except by the exercise of will. Moral consequences are consequences determined by a moral will, whatever the means employed to work them out, and we cannot hide from the will of God behind the very means which He is employing to express His will. It is not an impersonal characterless result when what we call the inevitable moral consequences of any line of conduct are brought home to a man; it is not a result at all, in the proper sense of the term, but the carrying out of a sentence; the proper way to describe it is by a proposition in which the living God is subject. This is what

THE CHRISTIAN DOCTRINE OF RECONCILIATION

Paul does here. He does not look at the moral world as something which he can always keep with its *quasi*-physical necessities between himself and God; the moral world is the very sphere and scene of God's working. The appalling fact with which we have to deal is that God has delivered men up to the awful degradation which we see, and in doing so has made a revelation of His wrath.

Further, this wrath is revealed in the solemn witness of conscience that they who do such things are worthy of death (Rom. i. 32): they have no right to be, and the final sentence will in due time be executed on them. This is what Paul means when he says that the wages of sin is death. This is not mythology, nor pseudo-science; it is the testimony of conscience that all sin, and all who identify themselves with sin, must confront the annihilating judgment of God. And finally, the wrath of God is revealed particularly in that commonplace of religion which to every one trained like Paul is self-evidently true—namely, that at the consummation of history God will judge the world and inflict the wrath which sin has merited (Rom. iii. 5). As the argument of iii. 5 shows, a person who does not admit this is a person with whom the apostle cannot argue for lack of fundamental common premises. It is mainly, if not always, in this eschatological sense that the wrath of God is spoken of in Paul.[1] It is the wrath to come. Jesus is our deliverer from the coming wrath (1 Thess. i. 10). We shall be saved from the wrath through Him (Rom. v. 10). And we must not say that this eschatological wrath is unreal, a picture painted on the clouds by an overheated imagination. If it is seen on the clouds, it is projected on them from the conscience, and the lurid colours are derived not from blank fear but from conscience itself, and from the

[1] See Haupt's note (in Meyer's *Kommentar*) on Col. iii. 6.

NEW TESTAMENT DOCTRINE OF RECONCILIATION

terrible experiences already referred to. When we take all these things together, it is idle to speak of the wrath of God as unreal. It is as real as any revelation of what God is, or of how He is affected in relation to man. Nothing that treats it as unreal can have any relevance as gospel to the situation of sinners.

This, though he gives no formal definition of sin, is the premiss of Paul's gospel of reconciliation. The two things in which he is mainly interested, so far as sin is concerned, are its universality, and the hopelessness of the problem it presents to man. Before he proceeds to explain how reconciliation is achieved by Christ, he exhibits to us the whole world guilty before God (ὑπόδικος τῷ Θεῷ, Rom. iii. 19: subject to His judgment and His wrath, lying under a terrible responsibility to Him). But his notion of sin is far more deeply tinctured by experience than the bare idea of universality suggests. Its universality is not more present to him than its virulence. This last is what is specially conveyed by his peculiar use of the term "flesh." He speaks of the flesh as flesh of sin (Rom. viii. 3): the two are or have become so related that the flesh is conceived as characterised by or belonging to sin. He says in c. vii. 16, "in me, that is, in my flesh, dwelleth no good thing." He says in c. vii. 8, "they that are in the flesh cannot please God." In Gal. v. 17, he tells us that "the flesh lusteth against the spirit," and in v. 24 that "they that are Christ's have crucified the flesh." Our first thought of this singular mode of expression is that it is only too effective for its purpose. If man is flesh, and if flesh is the seat and source of evil, then evil is native to man; it belongs to the physical and not to the moral world, and our conception of it as sin is illegitimate. It is certain, however, that this is not in line with Paul's use of the term, but the very reverse. What the flesh stands for with him is not in the first instance the universality of sin, though that is included; it is its virulence, its ingrained, deep-seated, constitutional character. If it were compared to a disease, it would not be a disease which had been accidentally caught and could be easily shaken off by a naturally healthy constitution; it would be a deep-seated congenital malady, against which the constitution had no resources within itself, and which could only have a fatal end. Not very much has been made by attempts to explain Paul's way of speaking about the flesh, either by reference to the Old Testament or to the dualism, metaphysical or ethical, in Greek philosophy. If there is any truth in his thought at all, it has no doubt antecedents and affinities in both—for men everywhere acquire self-knowledge—but these are not the key to his language. At this point nothing in Paul is speculative or second-hand. All he says is based on experience. All the passion of which his nature is capable comes out when he speaks of the flesh—a passionate loathing and repulsion, a passionate sense of bondage, a passion of ignominy and despair. He did not learn these things nor how to speak of them from any one, either in the Old Testament or in the philosophic world: he learned them within. "O wretched man that *I* am! who shall deliver *me?*" "I know that in *me*, that is in *my* flesh, dwelleth no good thing." The flesh, in the sense suggested by these expressions, is a synonym for human nature as it exists in this world. It does not describe only what we should call carnal sins; indeed, in the appalling picture of sensual degradation in Romans i. the term flesh is never used. But it does describe human nature as it is, and the man who has not in himself the key to Paul's doctrine is a man who does not know himself. "The flesh" may have a physical basis or relation, but it exists for Paul only in his moral consciousness. It does not ocur to him that when sin is thus closely connected with nature it loses the proper character of sinfulness; its sinfulness is assumed all along, and the sense of its close connection with nature does not make it less sinful but more dreadful and hopeless. It would not have seemed real to Paul to say that a man is not responsible for his nature: what else has he to be responsible for? We are all responsible for ourselves, and when Paul uses the word flesh in this connection, it is not to deny or to minimise our responsibility, but to make us feel how deep, all-pervading and desperate it is. The reality of sin and the reality of our responsibility for it, as that which evokes the condemnation and wrath of God and leaves us exposed to them, "condemned and unsheltered men," is the presupposition of Paul's gospel of reconciliation. The gospel does not deny these terrible realities; it confronts them and deals with them as what they are.

In the Epistle to the Romans Paul condenses his gospel, in this relation, in the brief phrase δικαιοσύνη Θεοῦ, the, or a, righteousness of God. This is what is wanted to match and overmatch the situation in which man stands subject to God's condemnation and to the ὀργὴ Θεοῦ, the wrath of God, in which that condemnation ultimately takes effect. Where Paul first uses the expression, condensed as it is in itself to the point of being enigmatic, he gives no explanation of it (Rom. i. 17), only introducing its relation to faith; but at a later stage (chap. iii. 21-26), he defines his thought with some precision. On one point there is no question. However the divine righteousness be conceived, it is on the basis of it, and through its appropriation to them on the ground of faith, that sinners are reconciled to God. It is in fact an outward or objective reconciliation, and in the believing acceptance of it (c. v. 10) men respond to the gospel call, "Be ye reconciled to God" (2 Cor. v. 20), and enter upon a reconciled or justified life.

At the present moment, the most current way of interpreting the divine righteousness is that which regards it as the righteousness of God Himself, His essential nature or character. Men are bankrupt of righteousness, they have none of their own, but the universe is not bankrupt. There is righteousness with God, inexhaustible and overflowing, and this is the sinner's hope. This has not been understood by the world, but it is the truth, and the truth revealed and proclaimed in the gospel. The divine righteousness is like a sun which shines on and on, pouring its radiance into lives darkened by sin, and making them bright. It is like a perennial spring of pure water flowing ceaselessly into a muddy basin and gradually washing it out and making it clean. Men are reconciled to God when they are made holy as He is holy, righteous as He is righteous, and when it is divested of technicalities and reduced to its simplest terms, this is the process.

No one can have any interest in disputing the truth there is in such a statement. There is none good but one, that is, God; and for all goodness all men are always indebted to Him. But it does not follow that this is what Paul meant by the divine righteousness which he preached as gospel to sinners. Paul was dealing with a moral problem, with the position of sinners against whom there had been and was a revelation of wrath, and the problem cannot be stated, to say nothing of being solved, as long as we confine ourselves to the use of physical categories such as those implied in the illustrations of the sun and the spring. Neither do we come closer to his thought when we speak of the δικαιοσύνη Θεῖν as the righteousness of God, "not as inherent in the Divine Essence, but as going forth and embracing the personalities of men. It is righteousness active and energising; the righteousness of the Divine Will as it were projected and enclosing and gathering into itself human wills." That this is the character of God's righteousness need not be disputed: we can say quite freely that "the whole scheme of things by which He gathers to Himself a righteous people is the direct and spontaneous expression of His own inherent righteousness: a necessity of His own nature impels Him to make them like Himself."[1] But to reduce the gospel to this is to ignore the distinction between man *simpliciter* and sinful man; it is to assume that sin makes no difference to God, or to the mode in which He makes men partakers in His righteousness. It is remarkable that such explanations of the righteousness of God can be given quite fully without introducing the name of Jesus. Room may be made for Him, no doubt, in the system of ideas which they exhibit; but at the utmost He is a shining illustration of the nature of the divine righteousness—it is in no way dependent on Him. But this is not the point of view of Paul. In Paul the divine righteousness which constitutes gospel for sinners exposed to the divine wrath is revealed in Christ, and nowhere else. It is not a vast idea which he possesses independently, and under which Christ can be conveniently subsumed; apart from Christ, and Christ crucified, he has no idea of a divine righteousness at all which he can preach to sinners as the way of reconciliation to God.

If it is possible to overlook this when we read the words in Rom. i. 16, it should not be possible when we come to deal

[1] Sanday and Headlam, *Romans*, p. 25.

with the apostle's own exposition of them in Rom. iii. 21-26. There the divine righteousness is defined as a righteousness through faith in Jesus Christ. Those who believe are justified (δικαιούμενοι) freely by God's grace through the redemption that is in Christ Jesus. And Christ Jesus in this particular connection is the Son of God whom God has set forth, as a propitiation, through faith, in His blood. The decisive word in this passage is propitiation—ἱλαστήριον— and without entering at this point further into the detail of interpretation, it will be admitted that it is only because Jesus Christ has the character or power of being a propitiation that there is revealed in Him a divine righteousness the revelation of which is gospel for sinners. Hence to comprehend ἱλαστήριον or propitiation as he comprehended it, is to have the only key to his gospel.

But there is a curious reluctance among many students of Paul to enter seriously into his mind at this critical point. Lightfoot, who has every disposition to agree with the apostle, formally declines the attempt. After noting that God's righteousness was manifested in the propitiation "inasmuch as sin required so great a sacrifice," he proceeds, "It is better not to go beyond the language of Scripture. All the moral difficulties connected with the atonement arise from pressing the imagery of the apostolic writers too far. Thus nothing is said here about appeasing divine wrath, nor is it stated to whom the sacrifice of Christ is paid. The central idea of that sacrifice is the great work done for us, whereby boasting is excluded."[1] It is in a similar tone of reverent renunciation that the authors of the *International Critical Commentary* on Romans refuse to construe the apostle's thoughts beyond his words. "Following the example of St. Paul and St.

[1] *Notes on Epistles of St. Paul*, p. 272 f.

NEW TESTAMENT DOCTRINE OF RECONCILIATION

John and the Epistle to the Hebrews, we speak of something in this great sacrifice which we call 'Propitiation.' We believe that the Holy Spirit spoke through these writers, and that it was His will that we should use this word. But it is a word which we must leave it to Him to interpret. We drop our plummet into the depths, but the line attached to it is too short, and it does not touch the bottom. The awful processes of the Divine Mind we cannot fathom. Sufficient for us to know that through the virtue of the One Sacrifice our sacrifices are accepted, that the barrier which sin places between God and us is removed, and that there is a 'sprinkling' which makes us free to approach the throne of grace."[1] In spite of its sincere humility one may doubt whether Paul would have appreciated this attitude to his exposition of the divine rigtheousness: it strikes one as rather English than either apostolic or philosophic. Scholars of a different type fight shy of the apostle in a different way. Deissmann, for example, who has devoted himself to showing that the New Testament is written in the ordinary language of the time, and that we ought to understand it as it would have been understood by the man in the street in Antioch or Ephesus, Rome or Alexandria, has an interesting note on ἱλαστήριον.[2] "Early in the imperial period," he writes, "it was a not uncommon custom to dedicate propitiatory gifts to the gods which were called ἱλαστήρια.' The author considers it quite impossible that Paul should not know the word in this sense; if he had not already been familiar with it by living in Cilicia, he had certainly read it here and there in his wanderings through the empire when he stood before the monuments of paganism and pensively contemplated what the piety of a

---
[1] Sanday and Headlam, *Romans*, p. 94.
[2] *Bible Studies*, p. 131 (English translation).

THE CHRISTIAN DOCTRINE OF RECONCILIATION

dying civilisation had to offer to its known or unknown gods. That the verb προέθετο admirably suits the ἱλαστήριον taken as *propitiatory gift*, in the sense given to it in the Greek usage of the imperial period, requires no proof. God has *publicly set forth* the crucified Christ in His blood, in view of the cosmos—to the Jews a stumblingblock, to the Greeks foolishness, to faith a ἱλαστήριον. The crucified Christ is the votive gift of the divine love for the salvation of men. Elsewhere it is human hands which dedicate to the deity a dead image of stone in order to gain his favour; here the God of grace Himself erects the consoling image, for the skill and power of men are not sufficient . . . God's favour must be obtained —He Himself fulfils the preliminary conditions; men can do nothing at all, they cannot so much as believe—God does all in Christ; that is the religion of Paul, and our passage in Romans is but another expression of the same mystery of salvation." All this is admirable: the crucified Christ *is* the votive gift of the divine love for the salvation of men. Possibly, as they read the word ἱλαστήριον, the statues or other propitiatory gifts to which Deissmann refers, and not the mercy-seat, which is designated by it in the Old Testament, did rise before the minds of the recipients of Paul's letter; but to say this is to stop short at the very surface of the Apostle's mind. According to Deissmann, the ἱλαστήριον neutralises the anger of a deity or secures his good will; every one knew that, and apparently thought no more about it. But the peculiarity of the passage in Romans is that Paul is applying the whole force of his intelligence, consciously and purposely, to this very point. He is explaining to himself and to others what a ἱλαστήριον is—what must be the nature of a votive gift which shall neutralise sin and enable God to receive as righteous those

NEW TESTAMENT DOCTRINE OF RECONCILIATION

who "believe" in it. It is not fair to him not to pursue his thought as far as he puts it in our power to do so, and it is surely more than unfair to say that he wishes us—much more that the Holy Spirit wishes us—to use particular words even though they do not convey to us any particular meaning. His meaning, however, in a highly argumentative passage like this, must be made out, not simply by reference to Old Testament words, like כַּפֹּרֶת or עֲוֹנָה, which the LXX renders by ἱλαστήριον, nor to words found in popular authorities approximately contemporary: it can only be made out from the connection of his thoughts.[1]

If we concentrate our attention upon this, some things become plain. Paul is supremely interested in the universal scope of his gospel. Before introducing the exposition of it in Rom. iii. 21 ff. he has taken pains to show that "all the world" is guilty before God, and in the course of his exposition he insists that there is no distinction between men, that all have sinned, that God is not the God of Jews only but of Gentiles also, and justifies both alike in precisely the same way. It seems a fair inference from this that the conditions for understanding the vital idea of propitiation are to be sought, not in any peculiarities of Jewish or of pagan

---

[1] In his later work, *Paulus*, Deissmann gives another illustration of what the writer can only regard as a refusal to take Paul's thoughts seriously. He makes the πίστις Ἰησοῦ Χριστοῦ—faith in Jesus Christ—"*Christusglauben*": not faith of which Christ is the object, but such faith as one can have in God only in virtue of being "in Christ"; and he even introduces into the grammar, where one had thought himself safe from such phantasmata, what he calls a *genitivus mysticus* to cover this interpretation. It is easy for him then—and in a manner it is quite legitimate—to regard justification, adoption, reconciliation, forgiveness, and redemption, as no more than various ways of presenting the same thing. The Christusglauben is the Kraftzentrum, von dem die vielen Einzelbekenntnisse über das Heil in Christus ausstrahlen. All these Christian blessings, however, depend on the ἱλαστήριον, and not to think out what it means on the apostle's lines is the gravest omission of all.

history, but in the human conscience which is common to both. If we have not the key to it in ourselves, no learning will put it into our hearts.

According to Paul, it is God who sets forth Christ as a propitiation, and as the propitiation in any case deals with sin for its removal, the setting forth of it is on God's part an act of grace. It is a manifestation of God in the character of a sin-forgiving God. Many modern interpreters of Paul find the meaning of the passage exhausted here. What the apostle insists upon is indeed that God makes in the propitiation a demonstration of His *righteousness*, but His righteousness, it is argued, is virtually identical with His grace. The meaning is that God would not be righteous—in other words, He would not do justice to Himself, He would not act in accordance with His real character—if He simply let sin take its course, and allowed sinners helplessly to perish under it. To be true to Himself, or, what is the same thing, to display His righteousness, He had to interpose in grace for man's salvation. It was by doing so, by enabling man to become a partaker in the divine nature, that He demonstrated Himself to be a righteous God; this, and nothing else, is the burden of the whole passage. No one, of course, can have any interest in disputing that God in setting forth Christ as a propitiation acts in harmony with His own nature: the gospel rests upon the character of God, and that character is revealed in it as it is nowhere else. God would not have done justice to Himself if He had not made Himself known as a Saviour. But though no Christian would dispute this, it is not a point on which stress is laid in the New Testament. Perhaps this is because it slips over too easily into the idea that salvation is something we are entitled to count upon, and that God would lose more than we if a way of salvation were not revealed. A temper to which such thoughts were habitual would hardly have seemed to the apostles a temper becoming Christian piety; the wonder of salvation was never so dulled for them that they could even seem to take it for granted. Salvation meant Christ; it meant Christ crucified, Christ the propitiation; and though they knew and declared that this Christ was the gift of God's love, it would never have occurred to them that God would have done Himself injustice—still less, that He would have done them injustice —unless He had so sent Christ. This is a theorem which they nowhere state, which they do not argue, and which it is permissible to think would have repelled rather than attracted them. Certainly it is not the theorem which Paul argues here. We do not need to be afraid that the apostle will lose the consciousness of God's grace because he does not in this way identify with it the divine righteousness. It stands on its own basis. We are justified freely by it. It is commended to us signally in Christ the propitiation, who when we were yet sinners died for us. But what is argued for, in connection with the propitiation, especially in Rom. iii. 25 f., is something different. To put it in a word, it is that in Christ as ἱλαστήριον justice is done not only to the grace of God but to His wrath —to that solemn reaction of God against all ungodliness and unrighteousness of men from which the apostle sets out in the exposition of his gospel (Rom. i. 18).

Paul is not preaching to men, but to sinners, to men who know what a bad conscience is, and who have a witness within them from which there is no appeal that the wages of sin is death. They have never analysed death, and have no interest in the ingenious distinctions which present it as temporal, spiritual, or eternal; to conscience it is one and indivisible, and whatever else it may be, it is God's annihilating sentence on sin. It is part of the total reality which sin is for the conscience; and as nothing can be of any use to the sinner in which the reality of sin, or any part of it, is ignored, so, it may be said, to a ἱλαστήριον death is vital. This is why God set forth Christ as a propitiation *in His blood*. This is why in every part of the New Testament such stress is laid upon His death. He *died* for the ungodly. He loosed us from our sins *by His blood*. In him we have our redemption *through His blood*, even the forgiveness of our trespasses. He put away sin *by the sacrifice of Himself*. There is a tragic reality in redemption, not inferior to, but rather identical with, the tragic reality of sin; and apart from this Christ would not have the character of a ἱλαστήριον. He would not do justice to God's attitude to sin, as one who not only forgives but inexorably repels and condemns it; He would not enable God to be in this sense just in the very act in which He justifies the man who can be adequately described as a believer in Jesus. This is the case which Paul argues in the passage with which we are now dealing. It is as though God's attitude to sin had up till now been equivocal, and had laid His righteousness open to impeachment. He had not dealt with men after their sins. He had been forbearing. He had passed by, if He had not pardoned, offences in times past.[1] But the ground on which He had so acted

---

[1] For the distinction of πάρεσις and ἄφεσις, on which the passage hinges, see Lightfoot's note *ad loc*. To take διὰ τὴν πάρεσιν as if it were equivalent to διὰ τῆς ἀφέσεως, in order to make forgiveness itself the manifestation of God's righteousness (*i.e.* His grace), is not to interpret the apostle, but to rewrite him. It is effectively refuted, to go no further, by the distinction between the past (τῶν προγεγονότων ἁμαρτημάτων), when sins were passed by in God's forbearance, in a way which puzzled, or might have puzzled, the onlooker, and brought God's righteousness into question, and the present (ἐν τῷ νῦν καιρῷ), when on the basis of the ἱλαστήριον His righteousness is evinced.

was not apparent. It might seem as though He had been arbitrary or capricious, and had disregarded moral reality as it presses painfully on sinful men. But now, it was no longer possible to say so. Forgiveness, or justification, in the new era (ἐν τῷ νῦν καιρῷ), has come to men in Christ, whom God has set forth in His blood as a propitiation; it has come in One who has realised to the uttermost in His own person all that sin meant, One who has drunk the cup our sins had mingled, One who has felt all the waves and billows break over Him in which God's reaction against sin comes home to us sinners. This is of the very essence of the ἱλαστήριον as Paul understands it. It bears witness, of course, to the goodness of God, for it is God who provides it, out of pure love, and it is the way of salvation; but it bears witness also to His severity, to His inexorable repulsion of evil, to a righteousness on which no shadow of moral unreality must ever fall. This is as important to Paul as that God should be a forgiving or justifying God. He must also be a true God, to whom sin is what it is, nothing else and nothing less; and in the propitiation which deals with sin as it is with a view to its removal He is revealed in both characters at once.

There has been much discussion in this connection of questions not really relevant to the apostle's thought. Thus it has sometimes seemed necessary to define righteousness—in the sense in which it is ascribed to God, when He is said to be "righteous himself" (Rom. iii. 26)—as retributive or distributive; and it has been argued that in virtue of it every sin must be punished, and that in the atonement the sum of all these punishments is laid on Christ, so that sinners may escape them. But all this is unreal. Quantitative categories are meaningless in the moral world. To say that the sin of the world in all its tragic reality was borne by Christ on

THE CHRISTIAN DOCTRINE OF RECONCILIATION

His cross, so that He is a propitiation for that sin, is one thing; to say that the penalties due to all men's offences were summed up and inflicted on him, is another and an entirely different thing. He came into our lot as sinners, and was baptized with our baptism; but this truth, essential as it is to the gospel, is spiritual, and not a truth to be expressed in terms of book-keeping.

Again, in this same connection, there has been much investigation of sacrifice, and of the ideas associated with it in Paul's mind. No doubt for him the propitiation was sacrificial; when he thought of Christ as set forth by God in His blood, he thought of Him as a sacrifice in which atonement was made for sins. But this is precisely one of the points at which it is easy to go astray. To investigate the history of sacrifice does not help us. There may quite well have been a time at which sacrifice had no relation to sin, or no peculiar relation to it which the worshipper could have defined. There certainly was a time when some sacrifices had a peculiar significance assigned to them as propitiatory or piacular: the later parts of the Jewish law illustrate this. But in the New Testament age sacrifice among the Jews was really a survival. It was prescribed in the law, and obedience to the law was a matter of conscience; but while in some vague sense all sacrifices, and not merely the sin or trespass offerings of the Old Testament, were probably regarded as having propitiatory power, there was no doctrine of the nature of sacrifice, or of the way in which it took effect.[1] We may say, indeed, as has been already remarked,[2] that the value of any sacrifice is its value for God, or that it makes an objective atonement; and so we may say of the propitiation in Romans

[1] *Vide* Holtzmann, *Lehrbuch des neut. Theologie*, i. 80 ff.
[2] *Vide supra*, p. 30.

iii. No doubt this propitiation has value also for men, and is intended to appeal to them, but what it does in the first instance is to meet divine necessities, the realities of the moral world as they exist in the order of God. If it did not meet these necessities, then forgiveness as the gospel knows and proclaims it could never come to men. God forgives our sins through Him who died for them.

This is the real basis in the New Testament for such a formula as that Christ by the sacrifice of Himself for sin satisfied divine justice. We must not seek for it as mere material or quantitative expression, but neither must we let it go. If we are to stand on New Testament ground, propitiation is a word which we cannot discard—there we must agree with Dr. Sanday—and propitiation can never be defined except by reference to God. It is a hasty inference to say that this means that Christ, with a love to sinners greater than that of the Father, bought from the Father the forgiveness He was unable or unwilling to bestow freely; and it is equally a hasty inference to say that because God provided the propitiation its sole reference must have been to men, not to Himself. Its reference is to sin, and what it signifies is that in the very process through which God's forgiveness comes to sinners justice is done, and must be done, to the divine order in which sin has been committed, and in which sin and death are one. In other words, it is divinely necessary—necessary not only with a view to impressing men, but necessary in order that God may be true to Himself and to the moral order He has established in the world—that sin, in the very process in which it is forgiven, should also, in all its reality, be borne. This is what is done by Christ in His blood. He enters into our lot as sinful men. In the unfathomable words of the apostle elsewhere, He is made sin for us. No element of the tremendous reality of sin, as that reality is determined in the divine order, is ignored or evaded by Him. On the contrary, sin is exhausted in His experience on the cross; the cup is not tasted but drained. The forgiveness which comes through Him will carry deep into the heart of man the same sense of sin's reality in the divine order, and in doing so it will be the basis of man's reconciliation to God. But in itself, the propitiation is the recognition of what sin is to God, in all its solemn reality; it is the acceptance of the facts of the case, as they are in the truth of God. It is the manifestation of the ultimate truth about forgiveness: namely, that sin is only forgiven as it is borne. He bore our sins in His own body on the tree: that is the propitiation. It is the satisfaction of divine necessities, and it has value not only for us, but for God. In that sense, though Christ is God's gift to us, the propitiation is objective; it is the voice of God, no less than that of the sinner, which says, "Thou, O Christ, art all I want; more than all in Thee I find." And this is our hope towards God. It is not that the love of God has inspired us to repent, but that Christ in the love of God has borne our sins.

Throughout the passage in which Paul explains the propitiation he makes constant reference to faith. The righteousness of God is through faith in Jesus Christ. It is for all who believe. God set forth Christ in His blood, as a propitiation, through faith. The man for whom the propitiation avails, the man who is justified by God, is he who can be characterised by his faith in Jesus. But what is faith? There is nowhere any definition of it in Paul, and it is idle to look for its meaning in the lexicon. It is obviously, in this passage, correlative to the propitiation; it is that which Christ in His character of propitiation appeals for and is designed to evoke in the hearts of sinful men. When the sinner stands before Christ on His cross, Christ a propitiation, bearing the sin of the world, what is he to do? What he sees there is the astounding truth that the last reality in the world is not, as he might have feared, sin, condemnation, estrangement, death, but a love which bears sin, taking it in all its dreadful reality upon itself, and, out of the very passion in which it does so, appealing to him. How is he to respond to this appeal? Paul has no difficulty in answering: he must respond by faith. He must trust himself to such love instantly, unreservedly, for ever. He cannot negotiate with God about it. He cannot suggest that perhaps upon reconsideration something else might be found which would suit all parties better than sin-bearing love on the one side and the unconditional acceptance of it and surrender to it on the other. He cannot suggest that less than the propitiation might meet the demands of his case, and that he might be saved in a way which did not make him so deeply Christ's debtor. He cannot qualify his indebtedness by the idea that a life of good works in future will enable him, at least to some extent, to clear scores with Christ, and to stand upon his own feet. There is a disproportion which makes them absurd and impious between all such ideas and Christ the propitiation, Christ in the love of God bearing the sin of the world. Once we see what that is, we see there is only one right thing to do with it: to trust it instantly, and to the uttermost. Of course we can turn away from it, and live—and die—in our sins. We can ignore it and harden our hearts against it, as we can against any appeal of any love. But that is wrong. The only right thing to do is trust it, to let go, to abandon ourselves to it, keeping nothing back. This is what Paul means by faith. And it is the whole of religion on the inner side, just as Christ the propitiation, or the sin-bearing love of God, is the whole of religion on the outer side—the whole, at all events, of the gospel, that is, of Christianity as the religion of redemption from sin. When a man believes in this sense, he does the only thing which it is right to do in the presence of Christ, and it puts him right with God. It really puts him right. There is nothing imaginary or fictitious about it. Sinner as he is, his whole being comes into a new relation to God through his faith, a relation in which there is no more condemnation. God justifies the ungodly man on the basis of his faith in Jesus, and there is nothing unreal about the justification. He proclaims and treats him as one who is right with Himself. And he is right with Himself. As long as he maintains the attitude of faith he remains right, nor is there any other attitude in which he can ever be right. Christ makes for ever the same appeal, which demands for ever the same response, and in that appeal and response Christianity, including the gospel message and the Christian life, is exhausted.

If this is, as the writer is convinced, the true interpretation of Paul, many of the questions which have been raised in connection with his gospel are unreal. The Catholic idea of a *fides informis*, as distinguished from a *fides caritate formata*, is unreal. The faith which is a response to love is in its very essence a *fides caritate formata:* there is no other kind of faith possible in the circumstances. In the soul's unreserved abandonment of itself to the sin-bearing Christ trust and love are indissolubly intertwined, and there would be no faith if either could be eliminated. Similarly the distinction of imputed and infused righteousness is unreal. The man who believes in Christ the propitiation—who stakes his whole being on sin-bearing love as the last reality in the universe—is not fictitiously regarded as right with God; he actually is right with God, and God treats him as such. He is in the right attitude to God the Redeemer, the attitude which has the promise and potency of all rightness or righteousness in it, and it only introduces intellectual and moral confusion to make artificial distinctions at this point. It is unreal also—and this is the modern form of these earlier unrealities—to argue that there are two gospels in Paul: one, the gospel of salvation through Christ the propitiation, a gospel open to be described as forensic, judicial, Pharisaical, non-moral, or by whatever opprobrious term we please; and the other, a gospel of mystical union with Christ, sublime, ideal, ethical, spiritual, and quite unrelated to the first. Broadly speaking, the first is said to be expounded in Romans cc. iii.-v., and the second in Romans cc. vi.-viii. There is no ground for this refusal to take a stereoscopic view of Paul's gospel. The word in which all its aspects are united and solidified is "faith"; and the faith which in Gal. ii., Phil. iii., or Rom. vi.-viii. is vindicated by appeal to its spiritual power and fertility is the very same which is exhibited in Rom. iii.-v. as the response of the sinful soul to Christ the propitiation. There was no other faith known to Paul than that of which he speaks in Rom. iii. 21-26; and it was that faith in virtue of which his whole being was absorbed, so to speak, in Christ who died for him.[1] To contrast a faith which unites sinners

---

[1] I have quoted elsewhere, but it is impossible to quote too often, the lines of St. Bernard in which the alleged two gospels in St. Paul are put in their true light, the gospel of the propitiation containing the power which evokes in the believing soul all the virtues which those who distinguish them ascribe to the other:

> "Propter mortem quam tulisti
> Quando pro me defecisti,
> Cordis mei cor dilectum
> In te meum fer affectum."

THE CHRISTIAN DOCTRINE OF RECONCILIATION

to Christ in His death and resurrection, and so enables them to die to sin and live to God, with faith in Christ as a propitiation for sin, is to draw a distinction which Paul would not have received, and could not have been made to understand. It was in His character of propitiation, the embodiment of sin-bearing love, that Christ appealed to Paul; and it was in that character, and no other, that His attraction was so irresistible, that Paul in the response of faith lost himself in His Lord. This is the only expression he can give to the one experience in which his whole Christian life was contained. "I have been crucified with Christ, and it is no more I who live; the life in me is Christ's. And the life I now live in the flesh I live by faith, faith in the Son of God who loved me and gave up himself for me." Nothing could show more clearly that faith is the whole of Christianity subjectively or experimentally, just as Christ is the whole of it objectively or historically, and that it is as impossible to supplement the one as the other. We must not eke out faith by works or love, any more than we must make good the deficiencies of the objective Christ by stray thoughts on the Spirit or the sacraments. Faith is the appropriation of Christ, and apart from Christ and faith, not only works and love, but sacraments and Spirit, are words without meaning. In experience, the Spirit is indistinguishable from the assurance that God is sin-bearing love; and to have that assurance in overpowering strength—as the apostle had it through faith in Christ—is to be full of the Holy Spirit. This again, it may be said, is everything in Christianity.

There are various peculiarities in Paul's presentation of his gospel which are often dwelt on, but they are not vital to his doctrine of reconciliation. The chief of these is his doctrine of the law. There are interpreters by whom this is put in the forefront of his gospel, and by whom, therefore, the whole doctrine of Christ as ἱλαστήριον is represented as incidental to the controversy between Judaism and Christianity. The controversy is dead, at least in the form it had in the apostolic age, and consequently the idea of the ἱλαστήριον or propitiation is dead along with it. So the argument runs. But it is quite unsound. As has been pointed out above, Paul preaches Christ as propitiation to all men alike, Gentiles as well as Jews, and he trusts, as every evangelist does, to something in the common conscience, not to any Jewish theologoumenon about the Mosaic law, to bear witness to its truth. When he argues in Gal. iii. 13, that Christ became a curse for us—that is, in the first instance for the Jews—through His crucifixion, because the law of Moses says, "Cursed is every one that hangeth upon a tree," it is quite evident that his argument is unequal to his thought. The cross no more exhausts what is meant by the curse, than the two criminals who happened to be executed along with Jesus exhaust what is meant by His being numbered with transgressors, or the ass on which He rode into Jerusalem is the full proof of His sovereignty. It is not Jewish law, in the legal or statutory sense, to which justice is done in the propitiation, though Paul would no doubt have admitted that the propitiation has its due application there; it is law in the large sense of the ethical necessities which determine all the relations of God and man. For law in this large sense Paul had the profoundest reverence. He knew that it could never be treated as though it were not, not even by God, and not even in the act of forgiveness. It is not to be sneered at, nor is reference to it to be decried, as though it were degrading the relation of God to man with that of a ruler to his subjects, or even that of a judge to the criminals at his bar. Law in this universal sense is the very element of the spiritual life which is common to God and man, and its sanctity is guarded in the Pauline gospel from the beginning of the Christian life to the end. Homage is paid to it in Christ the propitiation, as we enter on the way, and homage is paid to it at the close in that last judgment in which God renders to every man according to his works. The divine righteousness by which God justifies the ungodly is indeed revealed χωρὶς νόμου—no obedience to any statute contributes to putting us right with God; but it is not revealed outside of, but within, and always in harmony with, the constitution of a moral world in which God and man live a common life.

It would be an imperfect view of the Pauline doctrine of reconciliation which did not emphasise its absoluteness or finality. "There is therefore now no condemnation to them that are in Christ Jesus." The man who believes absolutely in Christ is absolutely right with God. He has in Christ an assurance of God's love which triumphs over everything. Neither sin nor death, neither the flesh nor the law, can depress or discomfort him more. This, at all events, is the ideal, and there are high hours, like that in which he wrote the eighth chapter of Romans, in which for Paul it seems to be realised. Yet for beings who live in time there must always be such a thing as suspense, and it will have its place even in the spiritual life. Religion is described by Hegel as a form of the absolute consciousness, or, as Halyburton says, Eternity is wrapt up and implied in all its truths; and so it is with that which here concerns us. Reconciliation to God, or justification, is an eternal blessing which is fully enjoyed in the present; having been justified by faith, we have peace with God through our Lord Jesus Christ. But when we think of the future, the justification which we have already received through faith comes again into a sort of suspense. Paul even conceives of it, in a very characteristic passage, eschatologically: "We by the Spirit in virtue of faith await the hope of justification" (ἡμεῖς γὰρ πνεύματι ἐκ πίστεως ἐλπίδα δικαιοσύνης ἀπεκδεχόμεθα, Gal. v. 5). Every word in this is significant. The emphatic *we* means that this is the Christian attitude as contrasted with the Jewish one which counted on statutory obedience, or works of law. Faith and the Spirit are correlative terms. The Spirit describes the Christian life as divinely determined, or as the gift of God; faith describes the very same life as humanly conditioned, a life which from first to last is one of trust in Christ. It is idle to try to separate these two from each other. There is no Christian experience whatever of which it cannot be said in the same instant that it is the Spirit of God and the faith of man. But this life at once divine and human is not yet consummated, nay, it is not lifted above all risks and uncertainties. We are saved in hope. The final sentence of δίκαιοι has not yet been pronounced, and we look out with eagerness for it. With eagerness, but not with misgiving; for faith and the Spirit bring the future into the present—give us an earnest of what is to come—and, by grasping the eternal love of God in Christ the propitiation for sin, raise us effectively above all that is disconcerting or disquieting in time. In this respect Paul's doctrine of the reconciled or justified life is like every other which recognises that both time and eternity are modes in which life has to be lived. The doctrine of justification by faith—in other words, of reconciliation to God, or acceptance with Him once for all, on the ground of abandoning self to His sin-bearing love in Christ—answers to the eternal aspect, and it is necessary if there is to be such a thing in life as that joyful assurance which is so characteristic of the New Testament. The doctrine of judgment according to works, on the other hand, answers to the temporal aspect, and it is necessary to be a check on presumption, and to maintain that tenderness of conscience and moral austerity which are equally characteristic of apostolic Christianity. It is a mistake to think of these doctrines—justification by faith and judgment according to works—as peculiarities of Paul, antinomies to which he was driven because he had principles at work in his mind which, though he did not know it, were ultimately incompatible. They were no more incompatible than man's power to live in time with all its suspense and uncertainty, and to realise in time the possession of divine and eternal good. And they are not peculiar to Paul. The doctrine of justification by faith is the doctrine of the parable of the prodigal son. The prodigal is made right with his father, absolutely and finally right, not by anything he has achieved, nor by anything he is going to achieve, but purely by trusting his father's love. His sins are freely forgiven, and no longer count against him in the least, and he knows it, and it is everything in his new relation to his father. Nobody questions the truth of the doctrine in an illustration like this. But it is not the only truth taught by Jesus. Jesus not only spoke of the parable of the prodigal son; he spoke also the most tremendous of all the parables—the builders on the rock and the sand. This is as true as the other, and it illustrates as perfectly the doctrine of judgment according to works. We need not quarrel with either, for whatever difficulty we may have in adjusting them logically, they are inevitable to our nature, and they are alike indispensable to our Christian life. They are forms of another—or other

NEW TESTAMENT DOCTRINE OF RECONCILIATION

forms of the same—Pauline doctrine: namely, that for the Christian law is abolished, and yet that in the Christian, and in him only, the just demand of the law is fulfilled.

The Pauline doctrine of reconciliation—if we should call a doctrine Pauline which the apostle himself tells us (1 Cor. xv. 1-3), was part of the primitive Christian gospel in which he and the Twelve were at one—can easily be distinguished in all parts of the New Testament. That Christ died for our sins, and by doing so reconciled us to God, can quite fairly be said to be the burden of the apostolic gospel. But there are other elements in Christ and His work to which a certain prominence is given in this connection, and which accordingly ought not to be ignored.

The Epistle of Peter, for example, uses what we might think characteristically Pauline language quite freely. We were redeemed with precious blood, the blood of Christ, as of a lamb without blemish and without spot (i. 19). He bore our sins in His own body on the tree (ii. 24). He died for sins once, the righteous for the unrighteous, that He might bring us to God (iii. 18). But Peter emphasises, as Paul does not, the example of Christ in His sufferings, and especially the power with which the innocence and meekness of the great Sufferer ought to appeal to wronged and suffering men. "He did no sin, neither was guile found in His mouth. When He was reviled He reviled not again; when He suffered He did not threaten, but committed Himself to Him who judges righteously" (ii. 22 f.). "It is better if the will of God so will, that you should suffer in well-doing than in evil-doing": it was so Christ suffered (iii. 17 f.). The idea here is that in the sufferings of the innocent Saviour there is something which has power to reconcile believers to the hardships and injustices of their lot; their patient and unresenting endurance of such wrongs is a fellowship in His sufferings and has in it the promise of participation in His glory (iv. 13).

In some respects the epistle to the Hebrews is remote from Paul: it gives a constant prominence, which is foreign to his mind, to Christ as the pattern rather than the object of faith. But it has its starting point and its centre where he also has his, in what Christ does as a propitiation. When the life work of the Son of God has to be condensed into a word, it is that "He made purgation of sins" (i. 3). When He is introduced as a merciful and faithful high priest, an idea of which Paul makes no use except in relation to the intercession of the risen Saviour for believers, it is "that He may make propitiation for the sins of the people" (ii. 17). He made sacrifice for the sins of the people once for all when He offered up Himself (vii. 27). By His own blood He entered once for all into the most holy place, and so obtained eternal redemption (ix. 12). Through eternal spirit He offered Himself without spot to God, and therefore His blood can do what that of animal sacrifices never could: it can cleanse the conscience from dead works to serve the living God (ix. 14). He has been once offered to bear the sins of many (ix. 28). Now once for all at the end of the world has He been manifested to annul sin by His sacrifice (ix. 26). When the author quotes the words of the 40th Psalm in which the doing of God's will is preferred to any kind of sacrifice, and applies them to Christ, he proceeds: "in the which will we have been consecrated"—constituted a people of God—"through the offering of the body of Jesus Christ once for all" (x. 5-10). The gospel is the final form of religion, for the God who is worshipped in it is the God of peace, who brought again from the dead the great Shepherd of the sheep, in the blood of an eternal covenant (xiii. 20). This is the heart of the epistle, and in all this the author and Paul are thoroughly at one. But it can hardly be questioned that he would have asserted, for other aspects of Christ's life which interested him, what may also be called a reconciling power. It is a great concern with him to bring out the extent to which Christ identified Himself with men. He does not save us, so to speak, from afar off; He does not stretch a hand to help us from a distant heaven. He comes as close to us as He can possibly come. He becomes a partaker of flesh and blood, because flesh and blood mean so much to us (ii. 14). He not only enters into our nature, He enters into our experience. He suffers what we suffer, and because we suffer. He is tempted in all things like as we are, yet without sin. His suffering is a discipline by which He is perfectly fitted for His calling to be a merciful and faithful high priest, a true captain of salvation. Even His death is presented in this sequence of thought. What would be the use to mortal men, who through fear of death are all their lifetime subject to bondage, of a Saviour who did not know what death was but by hearsay? He entered with us into the darkest place of all. He tasted death for every man. He took part in our flesh and blood in order to do so—"that through death He might destroy him that had the power of death." He learned obedience—that is, He learned what obedience is, and what the life is which the children of God have to live—through the things which He suffered. And all these things which add to His experience, and bring Him nearer to us, and perfect him in sympathy whether to deal for us with God or for God with us, add to His attractiveness and charm. The more we realise how He has identified Himself with us, the more we feel drawn to identify ourselves with Him. In this sense we may say that there is a reconciling power in Christ whenever we touch Him. *He* is our peace, and there is virtue in the hem of His garment as well as in His broken heart, or in the blood of His cross. But that does not shunt the cross either in the gospel or in the presentation of it in this epistle. The sympathy of Jesus is not something which displaces His death as a propitiation for sin; it is something which qualifies Him to bear sin in a way which is well pleasing to God and appeals with peculiar power to man. Christ does not cease to be a sacrifice for sin, because He is a perfectly sympathetic high priest. He offers Himself without spot to God. The way He opens for us into the holiest of all is through His flesh. The new and final covenant, with its fundamental blessing of forgiveness, is a covenant in His blood.

When we turn to the Johannine writings, we are confronted with an analogous situation. It used to be common to contrast Paul and John, and to argue that while Paul was concerned with the death of Jesus, John's interest was in His life; John was absorbed in the incarnation and Paul in the atonement. It was as characteristic of the one to say, "The Word was made flesh and dwelt among us full of grace and truth," as it was of the other to say, "One died for all." Especially, play was made with the categories of redemption and revelation for the purpose of distinguishing the two great New Testament writers. Both, of course, have both these ideas, but in Paul redemption is in the forefront, and it is through His redeeming work that Christ reveals the Father, while in John the obtrusive idea is revelation, and it is through the manifestation of what God is that Christ exercises His power to redeem. Further reflection does not add to the value or importance of such thoughts. Most students are agreed that the Pauline interpretation of Christianity underlies the Johannine one, and that the main differences between them are due to the fact that in Paul the essential Christian truth is exhibited directly in letters, while in John it is veiled or unveiled in the story of a life. But in the great epistle of John we find the same emphasis as in Paul upon Christ's work in relation to sin. Jesus Christ the righteous—the person who does justice in His life and death to the whole relations of God and man as affected by sin—is Himself the propitiation for our sins ($ἱλασμός$: compare $ἱλαστήριον$ in Paul), and not for ours only but also for the whole world (ii. 2). There is not, apart from this, a revelation of what God is which carries with it redeeming power; on the contrary, it is in the propitiation, and there only, that we have the revelation of redeeming love. In this is love, not that we loved God, but that He loved us, and sent His son a propitiation for our sins (iv. 10). Not only the truth here, but the form of thought in which it is conceived, is as close as possible to Paul's mind, as seen in Rom. v. 8: God makes good His love to us in that while we were yet sinners Christ died for us. Neither apostle thinks of arguing,—God does not forgive without a propitiation, and therefore He is not an absolutely loving God. They rather concur in arguing,—God, in order to forgive in consistency with Himself, provides a propitiation, and in doing so gives the supreme proof of love. The writer finds it impossible to take any interest in the attempts that have been made to assign the gospel and the epistle of John to different authors who are supposed to be discriminated, among other things, by the different views they hold on this subject. The one primary and comprehensive word of the gospel regarding it is given as the testimony of John the Baptist to Jesus: "Behold the Lamb of God which taketh away the sin of the world." A lamb which takes away sin is a sacrificial lamb, and it is not serious when one affects to find anything else here than what is suggested by the ἱλασμός of the epistle or the ἱλαστήριον of Paul. Even if we concede to the idea of revelation the prominence in John which is sometimes claimed for it, we are compelled to say that what is revealed is the same for both apostles, and that for both it is revealed in the same way. Both see in Christ the propitiation—and nowhere else—the truth that God is love. The meaning of that truth is discovered in the propitiation—and nowhere else. Alike to Paul and to John it signified the conviction that the utlimate reality in this world of sinful men was not after all sin, law, judgment, death, or hell, but a goodness in God which bears sin in all the dreadful reality it has for men, and in so doing wins them to trust it, delivers them from sin, reconciles them to itself, and makes them partakers in a divine and eternal life. In this all New Testament writers are at one. Perhaps it is an effect of the Johannine interest in revelation that when the Christian life is presented "mystically" it is as a life in God—Christ carries us, so to speak, beyond Himself to the Father; whereas in Paul it is as a life in Christ—the soul rests in the Saviour who died for us and rose again. But all such contrasts are relative. The mysticism of John xv., for example, is quite Pauline, concerned from first to last with abiding in Christ, while Paul addresses the Thessalonians as a church "in God the Father" as well as in the Lord Jesus Christ.

Though the primary form of reconciliation is the sinner's reconciliation to God, this carries with it other modes of reconciliation to which Paul in particular directs attention. Thus it involves the reconciliation of Jew and Gentile, or rather of all races of men to each other. It is when men are not right with God that they are most apt to fall out with each other, and in coming into right relations to God they discover that they are at one, in all that is deepest in their nature and their interests, with multitudes of whom they had been ignorant or from whom they had been estranged by prejudice and suspicion. The apostle regards this as an important truth. Through Christ we all have our access by one Spirit unto the Father: our reconciliation to God includes our gathering together as one body in Christ. The reconciliation of individuals creates the Church (Eph. ii. 14 ff.). It is not so much the carrying of this process one step further, in the way of experience, as a characteristic assertion of the absoluteness of Christianity, when we find Paul declaring to the Colossians, that it has pleased the Father through Christ "to reconcile all things to Himself . . . whether they be things on earth or things in heaven." The reconciliation achieved in Christ is so transcendent and wonderful, that there is no limit to its scope. Wherever we have to think of reconciliation, in the seen world or the unseen, in Him lie the love and power by which it must be achieved. Though we cannot tell precisely what Paul had in his mind when he spoke of things in heaven as needing reconciliation, we can understand his feeling; there is no problem of reconciliation too hard for the love which has borne our sins at the cross.[1]

The term reconciliation is not applied by the apostle to the process by which men (as we might say) are reconciled to the conditions of existence, but the truth which can be thus designated bulks largely in his mind. He expresses it in such daring words as, "All things are yours . . . the world, or life, or death"; or again, "All things work together for good to them that love God"; or most sublimely in the end of the

[1] *The Death of Christ*, 140 ff.

eighth chapter of Romans: "I am persuaded that neither death, nor life, nor angels, nor principalities, nor powers, nor things present, nor things to come, nor height, nor depth, nor any other creature, shall be able to separate us from the love of God which is in Christ Jesus our Lord." Reconciliation to God is not realised unless it includes reconciliation to the order of God's providence, and to the circumstances of our life as fixed for us by Him. We are not really reconciled to Him if we are at war with the conditions of human existence, and lead a resentful, querulous, or despondent life. True reconciliation confronts the world in another mood. It can say, "I have learned in whatever state I am therein to be content." It can say, "We glory in tribulations also." It can look the most painful things in the face—tribulation, distress, persecution, famine, nakedness, peril, sword—and cry, "In all these things we are more than conquerors through Him that loved us." It is of the utmost importance to keep this in mind when we think of the life of the justified or reconciled. There is a way of conceiving justification or reconciliation which reduces it as nearly as possible to moral nullity; it is something with the nature of fiction about it, something which speaks in terms of imputation as distinct from inspiration. This is not the Pauline view. If we fall into a mental attitude in which imputation seems to us a necessary stepping stone from the unreconciled to the reconciled state, let us be quite clear that the "imputation," if we call it so, is immediately creative, inspiring, and energising in the highest degree. Not only is God a new God, the world is a new world to the reconciled sinner; he is not at war with the conditions of life—at least he is not at a spiritless, angry, discontented war with them. He knows that if God is for him, no one can be against him, and that his

NEW TESTAMENT DOCTRINE OF RECONCILIATION

very badge as a Christian is that he can overcome the world, combining, as Paul so characteristically combined, much affliction with joy in the Holy Ghost. His faith in providence is an inference from his experience of reconciliation. "He who spared not His own Son, but delivered Him up for us all, how shall He not with Him also freely give us all things?"

In this survey of New Testament teaching on reconciliation, the writer is well aware that much will be contested by one type of student, and much missed by another. Especially, perhaps, this holds of the paragraphs on Paul. There are those for whom Paul is pre-eminently *"ein antik denkender Mensch,"* a being whose forms of thought and intellectual processes are remote and alien, and who, the more precisely he is reproduced, in that very proportion is incomprehensible and impossible. There are books on Paul which present him in this light. They are copious on the survivals of Pharisaical dogma in the apostle, and they are becoming copious on the infiltration into his mind of ideas derived from the Hellenistic mystery religions. But they do not set in any relief what it was that gave Paul his spiritual power while he lived, and has made him incomparably the greatest source of spiritual revivals in the Christian Church for nearly two thousand years. The writer frankly admits that his interest in Paul is not in the historical peculiarities which we cannot assimilate, but in that which gave him his place in the Church from the beginning, and has kept him in it ever since. It is this which he has aimed to reproduce in the foregoing pages. To say that Paul is unintelligible, or that he presents Christianity in a way which does it every kind of injustice and is finally unacceptable to us, is to fly in the face of history and experience. There have always been people who found Paul intelligible and accepted the gospel as he preached it. There are such people still, if not in theological class rooms, then in mission halls, at street corners, in lonely rooms. It is not historical scholarship that is wanted for the understanding of him, and neither is it the insight of genius: it is despair. Paul did not preach for scholars, nor even for philosophers; he preached for sinners. He had no gospel except for men whose mouths were stopped, and who were standing condemned at the bar of God. They understood him, and they find him eminently intelligible still. When a man has the simplicity to say, with Dr. Chalmers, "What could I do if God did not justify the ungodly?" he has the key to the Pauline gospel of reconciliation in his hand. What has been attempted in this chapter is to bring out what is vital in this gospel in its vital relations, ignoring everything else. It is not a chapter on the singularities of the ancient mind. It is a chapter on the gospel, as it has always been recognised in the Church, in the writings of the apostle. Anybody who likes may call it uncritical, although the criticism which pronounces a classic of religion, like Paul's epistles, antiquated and unintelligible is surely self-condemned. As has already been remarked, we do not lift our theology unreflectingly and indiscriminately from every word the apostles wrote. But a sinner who has been found by the apostolic gospel cannot think that anything at war with it is sound, nor can a Christian think that the Church which has been called into being by this gospel will disappear, or that its essential faith and motives can ever be anything but what they have been. Its Christ must always be He whom God set forth as a propitiation in His blood—the Lamb of God that taketh away the sin of the world.

NEW TESTAMENT DOCTRINE OF RECONCILIATION

It is natural at this point to refer to a subject which has been much discussed in this connection, though the New Testament hardly raises it in the form in which it is most familiar—the relation of the atonement, or of the work of reconciliation, to the incarnation. There are those who hold that the incarnation is too great a thing to be contingent upon anything else, and especially upon such an unhappy chance as the appearance of sin in the world. It would have taken place in any case: the Son of God would have become man even if man had never fallen; He would have come in flesh to consummate creation and give the human race its true head and a true unity. There is an ideal or metaphysical necessity for the incarnation which is independent of sin. In spite of the fascination which this view has had for some speculative or *quasi*-speculative minds, it may be doubted whether it has any Christian interest. There are hypothetical questions which it is idle to discuss, and they include those in which the hypothesis is that the world might have been something quite other than we know it to be. We know the world only as a sinful world, and we know the relation of Christ to it, experimentally, only as that of its Saviour from sin. Whether we can draw inferences, on the basis of this, to an original relation of the Son of God to nature and to the human race is, of course, an open question; and assuming that we could do so, it would be again an open question, but a very remote one, whether we could base on these inferences still further conclusions as to the probability or the inevitableness of the incarnation of the Son of God in a sinless world. The New Testament writers are not afraid to base the most far-reaching inferences on their experience of reconciliation. The Christ who has won eternal redemption, who has reconciled them to God with a perfect reconciliation, who has made all things theirs, is a Being by relation to whom all things have to be determined: they even say of Him, "In Him were all things created"; yes, in Him, and through Him, and for Him; He is the centre in which all have their unity (Col. i. 16). But they stick to the actual. They feel, as all serious thinkers feel, that the task of the mind is to understand and interpret what is, not to wander off into what might have been, as though it might find there truths sublime or more profound. The world we live in is the only world, and it is not thinking, but some other intellectual exercise, which concerns itself with a world we have never known and can never know. Probably this is why the New Testament ignores the question referred to, and when it speaks of Christ's coming connects it with His work of reconciliation, and contemplates it in no other light. He came to seek and to save that which was lost. He came to give His life a ransom. The meaning of all these expressions is that He came for us, and it is a Christian instinct which confines the New Testament to this point of view. It has been remarked above that though the work of reconciliation has its source in the character of God, so that it may be said that God would not have done Himself justice unless He had manifested Himself as He has done in Christ, this is not a mode of statement which has apostolic support; it approaches too closely to the feeling that the Christian revelation of God is a thing on which the sinner can of course presume. It is the same with the point which is now before us. An incarnation which would have taken place in any event is an incarnation which does not put the sinner under that obligation to Christ under which he is put by an incarnation which is necessitated and determined by the loving will to save sinners by bearing their sins. Schleiermacher, who takes both sides on every question, and is of all philosophers least exposed to the charge of being right in what he asserts and wrong in what he denies, tries to combine both points of view. The incarnation is natural, and it is also supernatural; it involves the redemption of man from sin, and at the same time the carrying out of the original idea of His creation; it consummates creation, as well as saves the human race. But he would be a bold man who ventured to maintain that the total impression made by Schleiermacher is in keeping with the total impression made by the New Testament. There is as much of Spinoza in his intellectual atmosphere as of Paul or John, and in his moral atmosphere there is more. But the real objection to the speculative theories of an incarnation independent of sin is that they assume us to know, in independence of the Saviour and of His sin-bearing work, what incarnation means. But this we do not know at all. What the writer understands, and alone can understand, by the incarnation, is the actual historical life and death of Christ. What many of those who use the term understand by it is the taking up of human nature into union with a divine person. In this sense, the incarnation is the presupposition of the life of Jesus, it is not identical with that life. There is a deep gulf between these two views, and when they express themselves, as they sometimes do, in similar language, it is apt to lead to misunderstanding. Nothing is commoner, for instance, than for those who conceive the incarnation as the taking up of human nature into union with the divine, to say that the incarnation is itself the atonement; in the person of the God-man humanity as such is reconciled to God. To the writer such expressions are as good as meaningless, and neither for the evangelist nor the theologian can he see that they have any value. But looking at the actual life and death of Jesus as the proper definition of the term incarnation—the sum of reality apart from which incarnation is an empty sound—he would have no difficulty in saying that the incarnation and the atonement, or the incarnation and the work of reconciling man to God, were all one. The traditional dogmatic conception of the incarnation, with which the idea of an incarnation independent of sin, and designed to consummate creation, is usually connected, does not lift us into a region of eternal or ideal truth; it does not enlighten our minds in the knowledge of Christ; it only lifts us out of the region of historical and moral reality. We have the practical interest of Christianity as well as the broad sense of the New Testament with us when we stand by the view that Christ Jesus came into the world to save sinners.

CHAPTER IV

THE NEED OF RECONCILIATION

THE sketch of reconciliation as a Christian experience, the survey of Christian thought upon it from the earliest times to the present, and the study of the manner in which it is exhibited and interpreted in the New Testament, contribute in various ways to the construction of a formal doctrine on the subject. It is this which we have now to attempt.

Every one who is familiar with systems of philosophy or theology must have been struck with the fact that there is no such thing in them as in other departments of thought would be called proof. The system as a whole is taken for granted, and the only proof offered for any part is that it is consistent with the whole, and becomes intelligible in the light of it. The central doctrine of Christianity is sometimes presented in this way. It must be deduced, it is said, from God and from His end in the ethical order, and be demonstrated to be merely the consistent carrying out of God's nature and purpose, not an exception to them. But against this it is fair to say that sin creates what for us can never be anything but an unanticipated situation, the dealing with which must always have something exceptional about it; and further, that we do not understand God's nature and purpose except by an inference backward from that very work of reconciliation which is supposed to be deduced from them. In other words, the supposed deduction is unreal. It is unreal to say, "God is love, and from the conception of love as such we shall deduce the idea and the necessity of reconciliation," when it is to the fact and experience of reconciliation, not deductions but *data*, that we owe the very idea that God is love. We must not in our treatment of a subject which has its reality in the world of history and experience be afraid of being empirical, or ambitious of being philosophical. In some respects Ritschl is the type of a positivist in theology, and any speculative strain in Christian doctrine is as abhorrent to him as mysticism. But in his exhaustive studies of what he calls the presuppositions of the Christian doctrine of justification and reconciliation he reaches some very giddy and some very obscure positions the vital relation of which to the doctrine to be deduced from them is not conspicuous. No doubt the reconciliation which we experience through Christ would be impossible if God were another kind of Being than we see Him in Christ to be; or if the providential order of the world, natural and moral, were something quite different from what it is; or if Christ were just a sinful man like ourselves, with no relation to God but our own; or if God had no moral purpose in creation at all. No doubt also, in their attempted definitions of the doctrine of reconciliation, theologians may have been discredited and baffled because they had not sufficiently Christianised their ideas on these subjects, and were operating *ab initio* with conceptions of them which were ultimately inconsistent with Christianity. It is not necessary, however vital and all determining for the Christian thinker as the experience of reconciliation through Christ must be, to make it the generative principle of a conception of God and the universe from which it can in turn be deduced by a kind of logical and natural necessity. It is a mere illusion that we

THE NEED OF RECONCILIATION

get new knowledge or new security in this way. The investigation of experience will lead to important inferences, but it is the experience which gives validity to the inferences, not *vice versa*, and the experience must be its own evidence. It is not arbitrary if we say that the essential questions connected with the doctrine of reconciliation will come before us if we consider in succession the need and the possibility of reconciliation; the work of reconciliation as achieved by Christ; and the purpose and fruits of reconciliation as exhibited in the life of the reconciled. The subject of this chapter is the first of these—the need and the possibility of reconciliation.

The need of reconciliation is given in the fact of alienation or estrangement. Man requires to be put right with God because, as a matter of fact, he is not right with Him. Such language implies, of course, the personality both of God and man. It implies that God is a Being who consciously deals with us as having responsibility to ourselves and to Him. It implies also that God is man's chief good, so that when we are in the right relation to Him we enjoy the life which is life indeed (ἡ ὄντως ζωή: 1 Tim. vi. 19), whereas if we are estranged from Him we have only an unhappy death in life.

Such language would have no meaning if there were anything arbitrary in the relations of God and man. Those relations are personal, but they must be determined on universal principles; in other words, they must be determined by law. It is absurd to object to this, that there can be no interposition of a statute book between the Father and His child. No one wishes to conceive the relations of God and man as determined by statute. We know that they are not determined in this way. But even if in the light of the Christian revelation we describe the divine and the human personality as Father and child, we do not eliminate from their relation that universal element which we call law. We know human families in which law in this great sense has disappeared—families in which the heart of the fathers is not toward the children, nor of the children toward the fathers; families in which there is no moral discipline, and in which no moral ends are being achieved; families in which natural affection, if it remains at all, remains as merely a physical instinct, and is never raised into a spiritual principle. This is not the nature of the family of God, in which law pervades all the relations of the Father and the children, though not in statutory or legal forms. The family exists in a world of universal moral necessities, and by these all the relations of its members are determined throughout. The 139th Psalm was written before the Christian era, but this conception of the personal relation of God and man, which is implied in the doctrine of reconciliation, and before it in the fact of estrangement, is expressed in it with transcendent power. "O Lord, Thou hast searched me, and known me. Thou knowest my downsitting and mine uprising. Thou understandest my thought afar off." This is not vague speculation, nor vague adoration, it is the most intimate and inevitable of experiences. The reader who has had the experience which makes it intelligible wants no other proof of the personality of God. When he says, "O Lord, Thou hast searched me and known me," he knows that he is not talking to himself: the "Thou" in his sentence has the same reality as the "me." If any one calls it conscience, then it is a conscience which is objective to his nature and his will—not one which belongs to him, but one to which he belongs. This is the point from which we

THE NEED OF RECONCILIATION

must start in defining the need of reconciliation. There is a relation between God and His human creatures, a relation of universal moral significance, on which the blessedness of man, and his attainment of his chief good, are dependent, and this relation is in point of fact impaired. Man is somehow wrong with God, and the task of reconciliation is to put him right again.

The consciousness of being wrong with God—in other words, the sense of sin—emerges in connection with some definite act, for which responsibility attaches to the actor. The act may happen to be one which is also a crime, a breach of some statute in the civil society to which the actor belongs; or without being legally a crime, it may be a wrong to another person, which that other is entitled to resent; but its character as sin comes into view only when we regard it as affecting his relation to God. It is not necessary in this connection to speculate either on the origin of evil or on a primitive state of man. Things are what they are, and we must take man as we find him, building on our present experience of sin as the one reality unquestionably within our reach. We have no right to assume that the origin of sin will ever be understood—in other words, that we shall discover the rationale of the irrational, or that we shall be able to resolve the ethical into unethical or infra-ethical elements, and so get rid of the specifically ethical problems it presents. But taking it as what it is, we can bring out its nature more clearly before our minds.

To do wrong gives us a bad conscience, and a bad conscience paralyses the moral nature. We know this even in our relations to one another. The child who has violated his father's will does not wish to meet his father, or to look him in the face. There is something in his heart he wishes to hide. But his whole moral health, strength, and happiness depend upon his having no secrets from his father; they depend, in fact, on his sharing with his father the common life of the family, without impediment or restraint. By his wrong act he has cut himself off from this, and till he overcomes it somehow he is morally crippled. He fears his father, for he knows he must disapprove of what he has done; he distrusts him, for he very possibly does not know that though his father's love has been wounded by the wrong he has done, it is great enough to bear his offence and to love him through it; and if he fears and distrusts and hides long enough, he is quite likely at last to hate—on the principle *odisse quem laeseris*. All this admits of easy and exact application to the sinner's relation to God. The bad conscience means definitely the sense of being wrong with God—of being estranged from Him by what we have done, yet unable to escape from Him, at once alienated and answerable. It is the fundamental truth with which we have to deal, that a bad conscience, or the sense of sin, induces moral paralysis. It disables the moral nature on every side. It dulls moral intelligence, so that unless we get deliverance from it the practical reason or moral sense becomes νοῦς ἀδόκιμος, a reprobate mind (Rom. i. 28), as Paul has it; or in the terrible word of our Lord, the light that is in us becomes darkness. It impairs even the power to repent, so that the more we need to sorrow for our sin with a sorrow which reaches the depths of our nature with healing pain, the less such sorrow is in our power. But above all, it relaxes and ultimately destroys the nerve of moral effort. One is good, that is God, and there is no such thing as doing good or being good, except in harmony with Him and in dependence on Him. How can any one be good who distrusts God the one spring of

THE NEED OF RECONCILIATION

goodness, who is afraid of God, who is hiding from God, who hates God? It is like asking, How can any one be good *in spite of God* the only source of goodness? It is this impossibility which makes reconciliation necessary if sinners are ever to achieve their chief end. A famous hymn cries,

> "Be of sin the double cure:
> Cleanse me from its guilt and power."

But its guilt and power are not co-ordinate. It is its guilt which gives it power. Its guilt alienates us from God, and it is in virtue of this alienation that sin reigns in us. Hence to be reconciled to God is the sinner's primary need. He overcomes the power of sin through having its guilt annulled, and his bad conscience stilled.

Thus far we have confined ourselves to the interpretation of the act in which the consciousness of sin emerges in the individual soul. But to limit our view thus—to speak as if God on the one hand, and the soul estranged from Him by a deliberate and isolated act on the other, were the only realities we had to consider—gives us a quite inadequate view of what is needed when we speak of the need of reconciliation. There is no such thing as the absolutely individual man with whose acts, as something between himself and God, we have been dealing. All men are members of a society in which they live and move and have their being morally, and in all they do, of right or wrong, they both affect and are affected by the body to which they belong. This has to be kept in mind, and it leads to two apparently contrary inferences.

On the one hand, the scope of the sinner's responsibility is immensely enlarged. He does not sin, any more than he lives, to himself. His act tells not only on himself and on

God, but on the society of which he is a member. It sets in motion a force which is beyond his control, and which acts according to its own laws, or the laws of society and human nature, in ever widening circles. There has always been some sense of this in the human mind, and it has been reinforced and deeply impressed on intelligence and imagination by much of the teaching of science. To see this has consequences for a doctrine of reconciliation. It means that reconciliation will be a greater work than might at first have been anticipated—more far-reaching and more difficult. It must embrace in its scope not only the individual sinner whose original bad action has estranged him from God, but the society to which he belongs, and in which that bad action has originated unmeasured evils which he never contemplated. It must deal somehow with the sin of his world, and trammel up the consequences which drive him to despair. We become conscious that the individual cannot be reconciled to God except by a reconciliation in which the interest of all his fellows is identical with his own.

On the other hand, the consideration of man's essentially social nature has sometimes seemed to extenuate his personal guilt, and by doing so to make reconciliation appear easier or less necessary. The development of a social or corporate conscience has been used or abused in this sense. Sinners of a certain type—sinners as classes rather than as individuals—have been disposed to say of their class: "Society is responsible for this, not we. We are more sinned against than sinning." The man who is looking for an excuse is not the best judge in questions of conscience, and the more general and imposing the excuse is, the less weight, probably, will it bear. Nevertheless there is something in the idea of corporate or social responsibility which needs to be

THE NEED OF RECONCILIATION

taken account of in considering the need of reconciliation. It does not imply that the individual can ever discharge himself entirely of responsibility for what he has done. His responsibility is that of a member of society, but it does not for that reason cease to be real. There is no such thing as a common or corporate conscience the existence of which excludes the individuals whose consciences live in it from the moral world and their responsibilities there. But while the responsibility of the individual remains real, and the need of reconciliation is therefore as unquestionable as ever, some light is perhaps thrown upon the possibility of it and the mode in which it may operate. If sin belonged to the individual alone, if his individual being were freely, fully, and finally expressed in it, reconciliation might well appear inconceivable. But the existence of a common or corporate conscience, of which his conscience for better or worse is a constituent, implies also the existence of a common moral life, with channels through which reconciling as well as disintegrating influences may flow. Wrong can be introduced into this common life by the act of an individual, wrong which works throughout the whole with alienating and debasing power, filling men with distrust and dislike of God. But if that is possible, much more—so must the Christian argue—is it possible that good should be introduced into it by the act of an individual, good which will work throughout the whole with reconciling power, restoring men to God in trust and love. That very constitution of society which, when we think of the diffusion of sin from one to another, or from the body to the members, seems to mitigate its guilt for those on whom it comes as distinct from those with whom it originates, provides at the same time the possibility that reconciling and restoring goodness may be poured through the veins of the guilty, and the evil of sin undone.

The distinction of an individual and of a corporate conscience, or of sin for which he who commits it must take the responsibility, and sin for which the responsibility falls on a society, does not exhaust the truth regarding sin, or show all that is meant by the need of reconciliation. The influence of sin in society may be regarded as due in part to the imitation of bad examples, the acceptance of bad teaching, the power of bad institutions, and so forth. In other words it is mediated, at least to some extent, through the freedom of the individual; he cannot simply disclaim responsibility for it, and say that he cannot help it. But a complete view of sin exhibits it in a light which at least brings the temptation to disclaim responsibility altogether. It is as though, when we saw what we mean by sin in its whole dimensions, the idea overbalanced itself, and ceased to be what it seemed at first. The individual man, whose sinful act is the starting point of our discussion, has not only all sorts of relations, voluntary and involuntary, to human society; he is related in a way intimate and profound to all that we mean when we speak of nature. It is through his birth that this relation is mediated to him, not through his choice, but it is none the less real for that. The idea of a pre-existent state, in which the individual existed as a spiritual monad—whether an atom or a God—and in which he freely determined to appear in flesh, or for some incomprehensible sin was doomed so to appear—is one which has indeed been appealed to as a way of escape from intellectual and moral perplexities at this point, but which will never convince any serious mind. Taking things as we find them, the simple fact is that we are born into the world, and into the constitution and course

THE NEED OF RECONCILIATION

of nature, and have to live out our life under its conditions. The saintliest man has the sap of nature in his veins. His roots strike down into its deepest and what will sometimes seem its darkest places, and he has in his own bosom the key to all that can ever appal him in the world. Human nature develops on the basis of nature in general, and our moral nature develops on the broad basis of human nature as it exists in human society; with the result that when the moral consciousness has come to any maturity, it is not only a consciousness that a given act is wrong, or that in virtue of some particular act I have incurred an abiding responsibility; it is a consciousness that what I call my nature is in some kind of antagonism to the laws of the moral world, and that sin in me is as deep as being.

The difficulty of construing such facts is obvious. On the one hand, we seem to be in contact with the most desperate and hopeless form of sin—sin which is identical with conscious human nature; on the other, sin is presented to us in a form in which the responsibility of the individual for it disappears—in other words, it ceases to be sin at all. If man is guilty, he is hopelessly guilty; reconciliation to a holy God is impossible, simply because human nature is what it is; and if we maintain that, in the sense in which we are now contemplating sin, the individual is not guilty, we must transfer the responsibility for his state from himself to his Maker, and, instead of urging him to seek reconciliation to God, advise him to be reconciled to himself—and to his sin. We must either say that man is born damned, or that he has no responsibility for being what he is.

The logical and ethical difficulties involved in these facts have given rise to some of the subtlest and most involved controversies in Christian history. Perhaps of all controversies they are those of which it may most truly be said that the disputants are right in what they assert and wrong in what they deny. Augustine and his followers in the fifth century emphasised the sinfulness of human nature as contrasted with isolated sinful actions, and they were right in emphasising it. Every sincere man is sorry not only for what he has done, but for what he is. The sin which weighs on us, which disables us, which defeats us, which makes us cry, "O wretched man that I am! who shall deliver me?" is more than isolated acts, it is deeper than the deliberate volition of this or that moment, it is as deep as our very being. It is *we* who need to be saved and reconciled, and we have never known ourselves but as subjects of this need. It is our very nature which needs to be redeemed and renewed: no intensity of conviction is too strong for this truth. On the other hand, the Pelagian opponents of Augustine were justified in maintaining that no doctrine of sin could be upheld which in the long run made God the author of it, or which involved the conclusion that redemption was impossible, or guilt unreal. It is not necessary to enter into the history of the controversy either in the fifth century, or in its renewal between the Jansenists and the Jesuits in the seventeenth. On the whole the Protestant Churches have been Augustinian in their sympathies; the Church of Rome, while professedly Augustinian both in the earlier and the later stages of the discussion, has in point of fact, under Jesuit influence, been much more Pelagian in its bias. In modern times the question has assumed other aspects and other dimensions. The obvious fact that the moral world has risen on the basis of nature has been set in the perspective of a general doctrine of evolution. The tendency then is to regard sin as inevitable; but when evolution, as is usually the case, is identified with "progress," or an optimistic view is taken of its general "upward" tendency—an "upward" tendency being a tendency to progressive moralisation—then, though inevitable, sin is not regarded as fatal. It emerges only that it may be transcended. A bad conscience is not an impracticable liability, a responsibility which we can neither meet nor evade; it is a kind of moral "growing pains" which in the course of nature will be outgrown.

If we could think of the world as a whole without thinking of any of the individuals in it, or of their definite and painful experiences, this vague conception of its physico-moral constitution would have a certain fascination for the mind. It is attractive enough to any one who is not vexed with a bad conscience, or who is not so vexed by it as to be driven to despair. But, as we have already seen, conscience not only brings a man face to face with himself, as a being whose very nature, rooted in the universal nature of things, is at variance with the moral law; it brings him face to face with the living God. Nothing is more real to conscience than its responsibility to God, and while the relation to nature may determine the particular cast or range of this responsibility, it cannot conjure away the thing itself. This is as true when we envisage nature through a doctrine of evolution as when we conceive it under any other category. Something in sin may be determined by the law of evolution, but not the very thing which makes it sin. It may have this or that form rather than another; it may be a mode of sensuality, or of pride, or of foolishness, because the evolutionary process has been what it has been, and not something different; but that which constitutes the sinfulness of sin, even when it is seen in the perspective of a natural evolution, is something which to conscience—and conscience is the only judge—is incommensurable with anything in nature. Rather than identify ourselves with it, we are bound to sacrifice anything in nature, including the natural life itself. Every one who knows anything about sin will admit that we should die rather than do wrong, and this is a conclusive proof that, however deeply our nature may be identified with sin, it is not finally one with it. We must be Augustinians without being Manichæans. We must be convinced that the need of redemption and reconciliation is desperate, and cannot be put too strongly, and at the same time that the possibility of redemption and reconciliation remains. Our whole nature is involved in sin, but not indistinguishably and irretrievably involved, and we disown the sin and protest against it even when we feel ourselves most hopelessly its slaves. On this the need and the possibility of redemption depend.

A serious injury is done to the Christian truth about redemption and reconciliation if either the one or the other element of the truth here indicated is ignored. This may be done in two opposite ways. On the one hand, for example, there is a widespread feeling that sin is natural and inevitable. But if it has a natural birth, so to speak, then in the course of nature it will, we may assume, die a natural death, and therefore there is no necessity for thinking about redemption or reconciliation as a way of getting rid of it. But experience disproves the assumption here made. Though sin may have a natural birth it does not die a natural death; in every case it has to be morally sentenced and put to death. The vague notion which prevails to the contrary would dispose of sin without having the sinner so much as come into God's presence, and there realise what it is. On the

THE NEED OF RECONCILIATION

other hand, there may be a doctrine of human depravity, not only seriously expressing serious facts, but so exaggerated and uncompromising as to exclude the very possibility of redemption. The Westminster Divines came at least perilously near to this when they spoke of Adam's posterity as "utterly indisposed, disabled, and made opposite to all good, and wholly inclined to all evil." The need of redemption is only too powerfully expressed here, but what becomes of its possibility? What is left in man for even redeeming love to appeal to? We must hold such a doctrine of sin as makes it evident that we cannot save ourselves, but not such a doctrine as implies that not even God can save us.[1]

It is not necessary to raise here any of the questions which have been so much discussed as to the primitive state of man. The basis of all theological doctrine is experience, and experience is always of the present. We may have all the experience that is necessary to convince us of the need of reconciliation, without having any opinions about the first man, or the state in which he was created, or the connection between his primitive and our present condition. Our life has its roots in nature, and we can form no conception of a being who originated in any other way; we cannot imagine what it would be to be created in some sense mature, instead of being born and growing into maturity, with all the

---

[1] This is recognised in the Declaratory Act passed by the General Assembly of the Free Church of Scotland in 1892, which states, *inter alia:* "that, in holding and teaching, according to the Confession of Faith, the corruption of man's whole nature as fallen, this Church also maintains that there remain tokens of his greatness as created in the image of God; that he possesses a knowledge of God and of duty; that he is responsible for compliance with the moral law and with the Gospel; and that, although unable without the aid of the Holy Spirit to return to God, he is yet capable of affections and actions which in themselves are virtuous and praiseworthy."

possible and inevitable mischances of this experience. But when we set our life in the perspective of an all-embracing natural evolution, it does not, in point of fact, lose for conscience its ethical character; it does not cease to need nor to remain capable of redemption. Within the lines of the evolutionary process, on the basis of it, we ourselves have fallen, not once but a thousand times. The disharmony between our nature and our vocation—between our nature as we know it in our moral consciousness, and our calling to live in union and communion with God—is the primary fact from which we have to start; and it is not made more real, more certain, or more intelligible, by any speculation about its origin. It does not take us an inch further on to say that our present condition is due to the disobedience of our first parents, to the corruption of their nature by the fall, and the transmission of that corrupted nature to their posterity. If this idea seems to be favoured by Paul in Romans v. 12 ff., the other or evolutionary view of all human nature may seem to be supported by the apostle in 1 Cor. xv. 44-9. "That is not first which is spiritual, but that which is natural, and afterward that which is spiritual." The spiritual life emerges from the basis of nature, in constant conflict with it, through experience of temptation, sin, despair, redemption, reconciliation; and there is no other way in which we can effectively think of it. We know immediately and at first hand the only things which are of any consequence: that sin is rooted in our nature so deeply, is so congenital and powerful, that we cannot save ourselves; and on the other hand, that God has made us for Himself, and has never left Himself without a witness in our consciences, so that the possibility and hope of reconciliation are not precluded. This is far surer and far more important than anything we can

THE NEED OF RECONCILIATION

find out about Adam, and it is quite independent of it. What Adam really represents is the unity or solidarity of the human race in sin; and the modern way of expressing this would rather be to say that the unity or solidarity of the human race in sin is involved in the vital organic connection of all men with each other, and in the disproportion which actually appears, in all men who have come to moral responsibility, between what they are, and what they know they should be.

We cannot say that man's nature is sinful, or that the common sinfulness of human nature is connected with the vital and organic unity of the race, without raising larger and if possible more difficult questions about the relation of the natural to the spiritual world. And these ulterior questions, as it happens, have played a large part in the discussion of the Christian doctrine of reconciliation. Probably the most widespread idea about the relation of the natural to the spiritual world is that which simply contrasts them. They are realities which stand apart, which do not interpenetrate, which are simply neutral to each other. At the utmost, nature is the stage on which the moral life is transacted. But it is quite indifferent to the quality of that life. The laws of nature are the same for the good man as for the bad; the flood drowns them both, and the lightning does not go out of the way of either. It is even argued that this moral neutrality of nature is necessary to protect the integrity of the moral life. If nature immediately sided with virtue and opposed vice, if she did poetic justice on her stage at every turn, disinterested goodness would be impossible; man would never be able to prove that they loved righteousness for its own sake. Without disputing the amount of truth there is in this view, it is apparent from what has been already said, that it is not equal to the depth and subtlety of the facts. Nature is not merely the stage of the moral life, but in some sense its soil. The moral life is not merely transacted in the face of nature, it is rooted in it, and grows up in profound and vital relations to it. The nature which is absolutely separated from the spiritual life—which does nothing but confront it in serene or scornful impartiality—is not the real nature in which we live and move and have our being; it is one of the abstractions which physical science constructs for its own convenience, but which are apt to mislead rather than enlighten in philosophy or theology. The only real nature is that to which we and our spiritual experiences are virtually related, and our problem is not to acquiesce in the idea of the ethical neutrality of nature—not to regard it as an ethical ἄπειρον or indeterminate quantity—but to see in it, in the last resort, the manifestation, the organ, the ally of God. It is not a hasty assumption but a more profound truth which views the world in this light. The universe is a system of things in which good can be planted and in which it will bear fruit; it is also a system of things in which there is a ceaseless and unrelenting reaction against evil. This view of nature is vital both to the doctrine of sin and to that of reconciliation. The natural and the spiritual worlds interpenetrate. The sense of their interpenetration comes out in the last words of which man is capable with regard either to good or evil. It is poignant and profound in the most solemn words of Scripture about sin—the wages of sin is death. It is equally poignant and profound in the sublime words of the Ode to Duty:—

"Thou dost preserve the stars from wrong,
And the most ancient heavens through Thee are fresh and strong."

THE NEED OF RECONCILIATION

Here we have Kant's two sublimes—the starry heaven above and the moral law within—fused into one, which, simply because it does justice to this interpenetration of the natural and the spiritual, transcends not only in sublimity but in truth all that could be felt or expressed of either nature cr spirit taken alone.

The importance of this for our subject is that it is only in this connection we can interpret the divine punishment of sin. In the divine government of the world under which we live, we have no experience of punishment analogous to those which human legislatures attach to crime. Such punishments are sometimes called "positive," because they are not determined by the nature of things, but in a way which is more or less arbitrary by the will of the lawgiver. He appoints certain losses or sufferings to follow upon certain prohibited actions, and the convicted offender becomes liable to them. In the government of God there is nothing parallel to this. The divine punishment is the divine reaction against sin expressing itself through the whole constitution or system of things under which the sinner lives. Some men are criminals and some are not, and therefore the punishments of human law come on some and not upon others. But we cannot say that some men are sinners and some are not. All men are sinners, and the whole race is sinful. There is a sin of the world in which all individuals are involved; and the divine reaction against sin—or, if we speak of it in such language, the divine punishment of sin—extends to every individual man, and to the race as a whole.

That there is such a reaction is hardly questioned, but there has been much disagreement as to its nature and extent. There are those who think that it is not only sensible in conscience, but that it begins and ends there. When a man does wrong, the bad conscience which attends upon his act is the divine reaction against it. It is his punishment, and all his punishment, and such an extension of this thought as would regard any reaction in the physical world as also penal, or as revealing or constituting part of the reality of sin for God, is a mistake. A bad conscience may, no doubt, cast a shadow on every good and distil poison into every pain, but nothing external as such is penal. Now no one would willingly make light of conscience, and its power to punish sin is a commonplace of moralists which it is superfluous to illustrate. But in spite of its plausibility, the idea that punishment, in the sense of the divine reaction against sin, is limited to conscience is both equivocal and untrue.

It is equivocal because conscience, if it may be so put, is not limited to itself. As has been pointed out already, a bad conscience is something which has effects on man's nature in the largest sense of the term. It dulls the moral intelligence, it paralyses the moral energies. These consequences of sin, which are involved in the divine reaction against it, are not doubt realised through conscience, but they are not identical with it. They would be there, whether they came into conscience (or consciousness) or not. But the untruth of the idea which limits the divine reaction against sin to the area of conscience is apparent when we consider that man's moral nature has developed on the basis of nature as a whole, and cannot be treated as if it had no vital or organic relations to it. It is a mere fancy that conscience can be insulated, or ever operates as if it were. On the contrary, the inmost conviction of conscience itself is the conviction that the natural and the moral world are one, and that the universe is in arms against the sinner. The fact that the

THE NEED OF RECONCILIATION

bad conscience in its panic gives expression to this conviction in arbitrary and capricious forms is no argument against its truth.

> "Suspicion always haunts the guilty mind;
> The thief doth fear each bush an officer."

The thief is mistaken, of course, when he takes the bush for a policeman; but he is not mistaken in his feeling that the world is no longer with him but against him. Conscience, if we will, is the weakest of all restraints, but it can summon to its reinforcement all the powers and terrors of nature.

> "Methought the billows spoke and told me of it;
> The winds did sing it to me; and the thunder,
> That deep and dreadful organ-pipe, pronounced
> The name of Prosper."

Wordsworth, who, in the lines quoted above, has given utterance to the very truth itself in words of deathless sublimity and beauty, narrates in the *Prelude* some escapades of his boyhood which illustrate its instinctive action in an imaginative and sensitive spirit. On one occasion he had appropriated the birds caught in another boy's snare;

> "And when the deed was done,
> I heard among the solitary hills
> Low breathings coming after me, and sounds
> Of undistinguishable motion, steps
> Almost as silent as the turf they trod."

On another, he took the loan of a boat without asking leave of the owner, and rowed out on the lake. There was an immediate reaction through conscience both within and without.

> "It was an act of stealth
> And troubled pleasure, nor without the voice
> Of mountain echoes did my boat move on."

THE CHRISTIAN DOCTRINE OF RECONCILIATION

The reaction became more intense and terrifying as he persisted in his troubled pleasure.

> "She was an elfin pinnace; lustily
> I dipped my oars into the silent lake,
> And, as I rose upon the stroke, my boat
> Went heaving through the water like a swan;
> When, from behind that craggy steep, till then
> The horizon's bound, a huge peak, black and huge,
> As if with voluntary power instinct
> Upreared its head. I struck and struck again,
> And growing still in stature the grim shape
> Towered up between me and the stars, and still,
> For so it seemed, with purpose of its own
> And measured motion like a living thing,
> Strode after me. With trembling oars I turned,
> And through the silent waters stole my way
> Back to the covert of the willow tree;
> There in her mooring-place I left my bark—
> And through the meadows homeward went, in grave
> And serious mood; but after I had seen
> That spectacle, for many days, my brain
> Worked with a dim and undetermined sense
> Of unknown modes of being; o'er my thoughts
> There hung a darkness, call it solitude
> Or blank desertion."

If we are determined to be rationalists, we may smile at the superstitious terrors of the child, but nature is even more determined than any resolve of ours, and may be depended upon to confound rationalism precisely at this point. It is not educating a child morally to deliver him from such superstitions; on the contrary, it is only through such superstitions, to call them so, that deep and ineffaceable moral impressions are made on the nature of man. What really terrified the boy Wordsworth was not Langdale Pike, regarded merely as a mass of stone, but the "dim and unde-

THE NEED OF RECONCILIATION

termined sense" that all nature was the expression of the same power which made itself felt in the inward trouble the moment he took the boat, and was therefore in arms against him as long as he was in the wrong; and though this took a form determined by circumstances and by an imaginative temperament, and not to be verified by science, it was essentially right and true. Indeed it is not too much to say that it was not merely *a* truth to Wordsworth, but *the* truth which made him the poet and philosopher he was. And it is not against its truth that it can only be illustrated by reference to poetry. "I myself," says Höffding, "occupy a standpoint from which the fact that the poetic form is the only possible one is a sign that we are in the presence of the highest."[1]

If the punishment of sin under the divine government is not "positive," but comes in the form of the reaction against sin of the whole order under which we live—a reaction instinctively appreciated by conscience—it is clear that many of the questions discussed in connection with the Christian doctrine of reconciliation, as to the nature and purpose of punishment, are irrelevant. Starting from the idea of criminal law and the punishment it inflicts, and looking especially to its history and the gradual process by which it has been humanised, an argument *a fortiori* is often applied to the government of God with the intention of excluding from it any such idea as that of retribution. If we who are evil are learning at last that retribution does no good, and that punishment should not be vindicative or vindictive, but educative, disciplinary, reformatory, much more may we assume that this will be the character of all punishments under the government of God. But we cannot com-

[1] Höffding, *Philosophy of Religion* (English translation), p. 207.

pare in this way the positive punishments instituted and inflicted by human society with the inevitable reactions of the divine order against evil. The latter are not positive; they are in the strict sense reactions. They are the sin itself coming back in another form and finding out the sinner. They are nothing if not retributive. That does not prevent them from being disciplinary or reformatory; on the contrary, their whole power to correct or to educate depends on the fact that they are retributive. A penalty which is only connected with sin through a good intention of the legislator to benefit the criminal is connected with it in a way of which the criminal may never become conscious, and which might do him no good if he did; the only punishment which has the promise of beneficial results in it—the only one which in the nature of things *can* have a remedial virtue—is that which is the natural, inevitable, divine reaction of the sin itself. In other words, the only hopeful penalty is that in which the sin finds out the sinner and makes him see all that it means; the only way of salvation here, as always, is through the truth. The one fact which penologists seem to be agreed upon does bring the human administration of criminal justice into a certain analogy with the divine. It is apparently accepted among them that what really prevents crime is not the severity of punishment, but the certainty of detection. Now just in proportion as detection is certain, a human government is assimilated to that of God. Under the divine rule, the reaction is inevitable: man can be sure his sin will find him out; retribution is as certain as wrong. But under ordinary human administration the reaction is not inevitable. The offender may never be found out, and if he is, he may be unable to see in his punishment anything that belongs to his sin; it may appear arbitrary, cruel, absurd; anything but retributive, or his sin in another form. Ordinary legal punishments—the sentences of the criminal courts—do little good to the criminals, not because they are purely retributive, but because they are hardly retributive at all. The conscience of the offender is not on their side; he does not feel instinctively, "This is what I was doing," and consequently he has no motive for doing otherwise. In his sentence, it is not his sin which has come back to him to show him all it is; it is just a cursed spite which has befallen him, from which others, worse than he, have had the luck to escape. The more, by securing infallible detection, we can assimilate human to divine methods of reacting against sin—in other words, the more we can make our legal penalties in the proper sense retributive, the recoil of the sinful act—the more it will be possible to look for disciplinary or educative results to follow from them. But benevolence which seeks to secure its ends by evading the idea of retribution seeks to attain apart from conscience that which cannot even be conceived except through conscience.

The fact that there is, in the whole constitution of things under which we live, an incessant reaction against evil is one which cannot be proved, so to speak, by adducing evidence from without. It is one our assurance of which is identical with our faith in God, or our possessing or being possessed by a conscience; apart from it, the very conception of the world as the scene of moral government or moral education would be impossible. The final form in which Scripture gives expression to this assurance is "the wages of sin is death." The reaction against evil is persistent, inexorable, absolute; when it goes on to the end, this is the end. Sin is something which is finally repelled by God.

THE CHRISTIAN DOCTRINE OF RECONCILIATION

Part of its reality, of what it essentially is, remains unknown till this is recognised. Sin is essentially a thing against which an annihilating sentence of God lies. Those who identify themselves with it come under the sentence. The end of such things—of the doings of the sinful life—is death.

This Biblical and experimental doctrine has been much misunderstood. It is not natural science, though it has sometimes been taken as if it were. There is a phenomenon known to biologists as death, and it is a legitimate subject of inquiry for them to ask what it is and what is its origin. But it would be no answer to any question they ask to say that death was due to sin—that a physical phenomenon had nothing but a moral antecedent. As far as we can see, death in the sense of the biologist is part of the mechanism of what we call life; it is an essential wheel in the course of nature, and we can conceive no natural system, no system of birth and growth, in which decay and death should not also have their place. But to assert this without qualification does not touch the certainty that nature is so constituted as to react ceaselessly, inexorably, and at last fatally, against evil. It was not sin that introduced death, in the sense of biology, into the world—though it is plausible to say that this was in Paul's mind when he wrote Romans v. 12 ff.; nevertheless, sin is fatal to man, and that is what is meant by saying that the wages of it is death.

Further, if this Bible doctrine is not natural science, neither is it mythology. At all events, it is not mythology if we mean by that term the answers which the human mind gives to scientific questions before it has any scientific method of finding the true answers. We can easily imagine that primitive man was awed by the mysterious fact of death, and questioned dimly how it came to be, and it is not hard to conceive that they answered it by a mythical story of some god or gods who had attached this penalty to some arbitrary transgression of their will. But no sympathetic and intelligent reader of the story in the third chapter of Genesis would say that this answers to the intention of the writer. The moral significance of the story is far too wonderful and profound. There is too great a sum of tragic moral experiences beneath it to comfort with such a comparatively childish rendering. It is not the origin of death the author is interested in, but the origin of evil; this involves death, indeed, but only because evil cannot dwell with God. It is repelled and inexorably repelled from Him with whom alone is the fountain of life.

Probably a certain amount of difficulty has attached to this subject from the modern habit of distinguishing various senses of death, and looking at these as if they were independent entities. Thus it is common to speak of "physical" death, or death in the sense of the biologist, and to argue that this has no relation to sin. This has just been admitted, but it must be pointed out that when we come to speak of man, who is a spiritual being, there is no such thing as merely physical death. Even in the case of creatures which have been intimately associated with man—domesticated and taken in a measure into the human family—the term ceases to be appropriate. The death of a pet canary is not a "merely physical" event, and when we know all that the doctor puts into the death certificate, we know very little about the death of a man. The Bible does not draw our distinctions. It does not speak about physical death at all. It knows that for man death is not an event only, but an experience, and that it depends on the man who dies what kind of experience it shall be. It is one of the signal mercies of God to sinful men that, though sin is fatal, He enables men to win victory over death even in dying. They can die as heroes, as saints, as martyrs. But there is no such victory over death which is not at the same time a victory over sin, and that is part of the proof of an intimate connection between the two. We do not vanquish death by reducing it in our minds to something merely "physical"—in other words, by reducing ourselves *pro tanto* to the level of animals and discharging the debt of nature as animals do, which have no conscience of sin. We vanquish it only as sin is transcended in reconciliation, and in the power of the spirit of Jesus. This does not refute but confirm the truth that death is the only expression we have for the culmination of the divine reaction against sin. All that is works ceaselessly for its destruction and for the destruction of all who are identified with it. This is part of what sin is in the mind and world of God.

Many of the difficulties connected with the ideas of sin and punishment in the divine order are due to the fact that men have essayed to interpret God's providential government, and to read character through circumstances, with a precision which no calculus at our command enables us to attain. To say that there is a divine reaction against evil tempts the naïve and inexperienced mind to say that wherever there is suffering there is sin. The appearance of physical evil is an index of the presence of moral evil; if the moral evil is as yet concealed it will nevertheless one day be brought to light. It was not enough to say, with the book of Wisdom (xvi. 24), "The creation, ministering to thee its Maker, straineth its force against the unrighteous for punishment, and slackeneth it in behalf of them that trust in thee for beneficence"; the truth was applied as if it meant

THE NEED OF RECONCILIATION

that all the pain, disease, or disaster by which the type of this or that individual was attended were the immediate reflex or counterpart of his individual guilt. The depth to which this mode of thought had penetrated is shown by the fact that the necessary protest against it evoked the sublimest work in all literature, the Book of Job. Job is in essence a protest, but while it is a magnificent vindication of the place of agnosticism in the true religion, it cannot be appealed to against the general truth which is here asserted. Job cannot find the moral interpretation of his own sufferings and sorrows, and he will not allow his friends to put an interpretation on them at which his integrity revolts: that is all. When the same problem was brought before our Lord, he expressed himself variously, according to circumstances. That there were cases in which the connection between sin and the divine reaction against it was traceable He evidently allowed, as when He said to the impotent man whom He cured, "Sin no more, lest a worse thing come unto thee" (John. v. 14). That there were cases in which it is presumptuous and uncharitable so to judge is proved by His answer to the disciples' question: "Who did sin, this man or his parents, that he should be born blind?" "Neither," He said, "did this man sin nor his parents, but [he is lying here blind] that the works of God may be manifested in him" (John ix. 2). In a sense, this is only a rebuke to the disciples. We are inhuman, if a man suffering from blindness is nothing to us but an occasion for speculating on the connection between physical and moral evil; what such a spectacle calls for, according to Jesus, is the manifestation of the works of God on the blind; we must open his eyes for him, or, if that is beyond our power, do him such services as he requires and we can render. But though this is the burden of Jesus' answer, the form in which it is expressed suggests another reflection. "Who did sin," the disciples asked, "this man or his parents?" The answer implies that the question is put too narrowly and too simply. The moral problems raised by the state of an individual cannot be answered if our vision is limited to him and to his parents. The human race is one, and there is no answer—no complete answer—to problems arising out of the individual life until we take into account the common sin of the race, the universal divine reaction against it, and also the redemptive will of God as illustrated here by Jesus when He restored the man's sight. We have no calculus for working out the problems involved in any particular case. What human suffering ought always to prompt in the first instance is help, not the investigation of character or a verdict upon it, and just as little general speculations on the relation of physical to moral evil. But we may recognise all this without modifying our conviction that there is in the nature of things a reaction against sin which when it has had its perfect work is fatal, that this reaction is the divine punishment of sin, and that its finally fatal character is what is meant by Scripture when it says that the wages of sin is death.

Modern theologians have generally been cautious, not to say timid, in their attitude to this question. Their tendency has been to say that strictly speaking nothing but the consciousness of guilt is a divine punishment. Other "evils" may be described as penal if we are compelled by our own conscience so to consider them, but we are never in a position to extend to others and their fortunes the kind of moral verdict which we may be compelled to pronounce against ourselves. The danger in this is that when we acknowledge our inability to pass judgment in the case of others as to the connection between physical and moral evil, and when we admit, as we are bound to do, the fallibility of our verdict on such connection even in our own case, we are apt to fall unconsciously towards the view that after all the connection is a matter of more or less doubtful interpretation, and that in any event it has only subjective, not objective, validity. But this is a thoroughly false view. Conscience is not subjective; it is the most objective and independent authority of which we have any knowledge, and its very being would be denied if we questioned the objectivity of a divine reaction against evil pervading the whole nature of things. In any given case, his own or another's, a man may misread the reaction; he may see the resentment of God where it is not, and fail to see it where it ought to be felt; but as long as his conscience is alive he cannot question the objectivity of the reaction itself. He certainly cannot be made to feel that he is being punished except through his conscience. It is through his conscience that he belongs to the moral world and can conceive such an idea as that of punishment; but though it is true to say that all punishment is through conscience, it is quite unreal to say that it is limited to conscience. The divine reaction against sin is instinctively understood by conscience, but in itself it is independent of it, and it may be most poweiful and inexorable when the conscience is seared and unconscious of it. It is part of what sin is for God whether any given sinner understands it as such or not.

To be born human is to be born into vital and organic relation to the human race, and to that whole system of nature on the basis of which humanity has been evolved. It is to be born into a state in which the need of redemption and reconciliation is a universal and urgent need. We do not require to ask or answer any questions about Adam and his fall; that moral evil is present in the race, that it is diffused through all its members, that there is a divine reaction against it, ceaseless and uncompromising, are facts independent of our knowledge or ignorance of the first man. Being what they are, they create for us the need of redemption and reconciliation. Of course we are not conscious of this need except as we come to years of moral maturity, and serve ourselves heirs, by voluntary acts, to the *damnosa haereditas* which is ours as members of the human race. All the difficulties of this doctrine, and all that can be advanced in mitigation of them, are concentrated if we say that the *damnosa haereditas* is ours as members of the human race, and yet is not ours, or not fully ours, till by free action we make it our own. We have no means of solving these difficulties, because we have no means of tracing a process by which merely animal rises into conscious life, or merely rational into moral intelligence. The perplexities and incredibilities of all Church doctrines about the salvation of infants are due to the refusal to recognise the limitation of our faculties here, and the determination to have articulate answers to all questions arising out of a system. The orthodox systems, Catholic and Protestant, emphasised the idea that the *damnosa haereditas* was ours by birth; we inherited it apart from any action of our own; simply by being born into the human race we were born lost souls. This was a hard saying when it had to be applied to those who were not only born but died before the moral nature could declare itself. The doctrine that the baptism of infants cleanses them from the sin into which they are born as members of the human race, and so secures their salvation, spares the feelings of those who can believe it, and who can close their minds

THE NEED OF RECONCILIATION

to the thought of the infinitely greater number who die unbaptized, and who according to the Romish doctrine are damned, though it is with a *damnatio mitissima*, a *poena damni*, not *sensus;* but who that has part in the intellectual life of the world to-day can believe it? Our mental and moral perplexities are not to be got rid of now by barefaced magic. Just as little are we helped by such an expression as that in the Westminster Confession (c. x. iii.): "Elect infants, dying in infancy, are regenerated and saved by Christ through the Spirit, who worketh when, and where, and how he pleaseth." On the logical principle that the exception proves the rule, the specification of "elect" infants here implies that infants are not as such elect; it is only when elect that they are regenerated and saved. But apart from this, to introduce election or predestination into the course of a moral argument is to dismiss argument altogether. The salvation of infants is just as much a blank mystery to the Westminster Assembly with its doctrine of election as to the Council of Trent with its regenerating sacrament; predestination in the one case and magic in the other are but different ways of marking the limit at which intelligence gives way. The wise course is to confess that there are questions here which we cannot answer. No doubt our mature moral life is continuous with the life of infancy, but it is not identical with it, and it is our mature moral life with which we have to do. All adult human beings have identified themselves by free acts of their own with the sin of the world; not only by birth but by choice they are incorporated in a system of things in which evil is omnipresent, and in which God is ceaselessly reacting against it. It is in this situation that the need of reconciliation becomes sensible, and that we cry "What must I do to be saved?

THE CHRISTIAN DOCTRINE OF RECONCILIATION

O wretched man that I am! who shall deliver me?" And it is not too much to say, even at this stage, that as we so cry we become conscious that the essence of salvation and deliverance is reconciliation. It is in the restoration of a right relation to God that all promise for our future lies. It is not meant that we can anticipate in our sin what the divine way of deliverance will be, but only that there is something in our necessities to which the way of deliverance must appeal and which is therefore prepared to understand and appreciate it. In the last resort, nothing reconciles but love, and what the soul, which has been alienated from God by sin and is suffering under the divine reaction against it, needs is the manifestation of a love which can assure it that neither the sin itself nor the soul's condemnation of it, nor even the divine reaction against it culminating in death, is the last reality in the universe; the last reality is rather love itself, making our sin its own in all its reality, submitting as one with us to all the divine reactions against it, and loving us to the end through it, and in spite of it. Reconciliation is achieved when such a love is manifested, and when, in spite of guilt, distrust, and fear, it wins the confidence of the sinful.

There are two questions which inevitably arise when we think of sin as constituting the need for reconciliation. One is the question whether there is any kind or degree of sin which precludes reconciliation because it lies beyond the limits of forgiveness. In all that has been already said of the consciousness of sin it has been assumed—it has at some points been expressly affirmed—that sin is not one and the same with human nature. In the heart of the sinner generally —in the heart of humanity as a whole, if one may use such an expression—there is not only the consciousness of sin,

THE NEED OF RECONCILIATION

but a resentment of it, a protest against it, a real even if it be an ineffectual longing for deliverance from it. Where there is such a longing, resentment, and protest, for grace to appeal to, the question does not arise. God has not left Himself without a witness in the sinful heart, and His witness is being heard. The way to reconciliation is not closed. It is putting the question in another form if we ask whether there are sinful states in which the inward witness for God in the soul has been finally stifled, so that there is nothing in the sinner to which God can appeal. No one would willingly answer this question in the affirmative *a priori*, and if we tried to answer it on the basis of experience we should have to admit that no experience of ours was adequate to provide the answer required. We may have known astounding instances of human sin, but perhaps also instances as astounding of God's winning just such sinners for Himself.

But we are bound to remember that there is no physical necessity of salvation, and that the longer evil is persisted in the greater is the difficulty with which it is overcome. The potter, to use Jeremiah's figure, if the vessel is marred in his hand, can put it on the wheel again and fashion it anew; but if the clay has been through the furnace, it is past remodelling; he can only shatter it irremediably (Jer. cc. xviii. and xix.). There are aggravations of guilt which tend to make forgiveness doubtful and even desperate. Sins of sensuality and profanity when associated with religion come under this head. "I have sworn unto the house of Eli that the iniquity of Eli's house shall not be purged with sacrifice nor offering for ever" (1 Sam. iii. 14). So does the sin of insensibility or indifference to the voice of God in a time of moral crisis. "In that day did the Lord, the Lord of hosts, call to weeping and to mourning and to baldness and to girding with sackcloth; and behold, joy and gladness, slaying oxen and killing sheep, eating flesh and drinking wine: let us eat and drink, for to-morrow we shall die. And the Lord of hosts revealed himself in mine ears, Surely this iniquity shall not be purged from you till ye die, saith the Lord, the Lord of hosts" (Is. xxii. 12-14). Passages like these are not infrequent in the prophets, yet it is hardly possible to make them the basis of doctrine; they rather exhibit the heinousness of sin under special circumstances, and the intensity, in these circumstances, of the divine repulsion of it, than tell us whether any sin, and if so what sort of sin, is absolutely unpardonable.

Neither can we base much immediately on the distinction drawn in the Old Testament law between sins of ignorance or inadvertence (sinning בִּשְׁגָגָה) for which atonement could be made and forgiveness obtained, and presumptuous sins (sinning with a high hand, בְּיָד רָמָה), the perpetrator of which was to be inexorably cut off from his people (Num. xv. 22-31). This distinction is not indeed without religious or theological import, but it is applicable in the first instance only within the sphere of Israel's national life. It means that violations of the law in certain cases were not fatal or irremediable, while in other cases they were; but it does not mean that in these last cases the breach of the law, defiant or presumptuous as it might be, was for God an absolutely unpardonable sin. Yet the distinction was present to the mind of some New Testament writers who evidently felt that something analogous to it might emerge under the Christian dispensation. We find "ignorance" made a plea for mercy. "Father, forgive them, for they know not what they do" (Luke xxiii. 34). "I wot that through ignorance ye did it, as did also your rulers" (Acts iii. 17). In both these cases the reference is to the crucifixion, in which sin, we might have been disposed to say, showed itself exceeding sinful, guilty with a guilt which nothing could excuse or attenuate. If what was done by Caiaphas and Herod and Pilate can in any way have the benefit of the plea of "ignorance," is there any sin which can be excluded from that benefit? All the people who had responsibility in connection with the death of Jesus knew something of what they were doing, or they would have had no guilt and no need of forgiveness. But they did not know everything, or their guilt would have been final, and forgiveness impossible. It is remarkable that unpardonable sin in the New Testament is always represented as sin against Christ, and against God's salvation as present in Him. This holds, for example, of that sin against the Holy Spirit, which, according to the word of Jesus, has forgiveness neither in this world nor in that which is to come (Mark iii. 28-30; Matt. xii. 31 f.). For the Holy Spirit in this passage is the power of God actually at work in Jesus delivering men from the tyranny of evil; if a man deliberately misinterprets and maligns this, he has rejected God's final appeal to our race, and has no hope left. The same reflection may be made on the passages in Hebrews which deal with a fatal form of sin. The sinners are in the first passage (c. vi. 4-6), those who after having proved the blessings of the Christian dispensation, "crucify to themselves the Son of God afresh and put him to an open shame." They are apostates from the gospel, and their sin is the deliberate and heartless rejection of the Saviour after a real experience of His power. It does not need to be proved that the deliberate rejection of Christ is unpardonable; it is in point of fact the deliberate rejection of pardon, for it is in Him that we have our redemption through His blood, even the forgiveness of our trespasses. The other passage in Hebrews (x. 28 f.) is in the same key. "If he who set at naught Moses' law died without mercy on the word of two or three witnesses, of how much sorer punishment shall he be thought worthy, who has trodden under foot the Son of God, and counted the covenant blood in which he was consecrated a profane thing, and done despite to the Spirit of grace?" The sin is deliberate and wanton, and it is a sin against Christ and His Passion; it is fatal and beyond forgiveness, simply because it is a contemptuous rejection of the very way of forgiveness. This is probably the key to the passage in the first epistle of John (c. v. 16 f.) in which the distinction is drawn between sin unto death and sin which is not unto death. The latter is the incidental sin into which any Christian may be surprised, and for which we have an advocate with the Father—an advocate in whose intercession for the sinner the brethren are here exhorted to join; the former—the sin unto death—must be some mode of that denial of the Son on which the apostle lays such stress throughout the epistle, and which carries with it, *ipso facto*, exclusion from the life eternal which is in Him.

The consideration of these passages taken collectively seems to favour the view of Ritschl, that in the sense of the New Testament all sins are sins of ignorance except the final and obdurate rejection of Christ. The sins of those who are saved never go beyond the degree of infirmity, and in the full and absolute sense sin can only be committed against the Christian salvation.[1] What we need to guard against in this statement is the impression it is apt to leave, that because sin is pardonable it is not serious—as if nothing were serious but final damnation. Ritschl's doctrine is not

[1] *Rechtfertigung und Versöhnung*, iii. § 43.

THE NEED OF RECONCILIATION

misrepresented if we say that according to him the sins which can be and actually are pardoned are not properly sins at all—they are ἄγνοιαι or inadvertences, for which forgiveness is a matter of course; while when we come to what really is sin, an offence against the Christian salvation, there is no such thing as forgiveness conceivable. To exclude such inferences we require a definition of sin which shall be applicable to sins of ignorance as well as to the unpardonable sin, and shall not extenuate sin's seriousness at every stage but the last. It is unreal to define sin by relation to an original righteousness which is inaccessible, and it is not adequate to define it simply by relation to Christ and His salvation, for then it is defined in a way by which salvation from it is precluded. We must think of it as something which emerges and asserts its character at all stages or levels of human life; something from which at every stage we need to be delivered, and from which we cannot at any stage deliver ourselves. In the words of the Shorter Catechism, we must conceive it as *any* want of conformity unto or transgression of the law of God; it is moral evil, or unfaithfulness to the moral ideal, regarded in its relation to God. The moral ideal, it will no doubt be said, varies; different people have different ideas of what is God's will. That is quite true, but it only means that there are differences of endowment and of privilege in men; it does not affect the truth that at every stage of our life we have the responsibility of subordinating that life to moral ends which for us have absolute authority. The law of God is not a statute; it is an ideal which defines itself through conscience in a form appropriate to each successive moment of our existence; and the obligation of it, as so defined, is never less than unconditional. We ought not to do any wrong for the world.

THE CHRISTIAN DOCTRINE OF RECONCILIATION

We ought to die rather than do any wrong whatever. It is as truly sin to neglect the duty of the moment as finally to turn one's back on Christ and His salvation. In this respect sin is death—any sin, and not only the unpardonable sin of which the New Testament speaks. It is deadly until it is repented of and forgiven; whereas the other is deadly in the sense that in its very nature it excludes repentance and forgiveness. It belongs to a true estimate of redemption and reconciliation to apprehend all sin in all its seriousness. The Ritschlian elaboration of the contrast between sins of ignorance and the unpardonable sin tends, in the writer's opinion, to reduce the former to a sort of insignificance; and when the sins which can be atoned for are generically not fatal, the shadow of insignificance readily falls on the atonement itself.

The second question to be raised in connection with sin and reconciliation is how far the consequences of sin are reversible when the sinner is reconciled to God. It would be easy to answer the question if we assumed that the consequences are to be traced in conscience alone. In this case these consequences would simply disappear. There is no condemnation to them that are in Christ Jesus. In the overpowering sense of God's love in Christ distrust and fear vanish away. But this is not the view which has been taken of the subject in these lectures: the reaction of God against sin, it has been argued, is a reaction through the whole system of things in which we live; nature as well as conscience is involved in it; there are relations of physical and moral evil which we may not be able to define in particular cases, but which on the whole it is impossible to deny. Now, that the natural consequences of sin are irreversible is a commonplace of moralists. It has a plausible support in

THE NEED OF RECONCILIATION

the words of Scripture: "Whatsoever a man soweth, that shall he also reap" (Gal. vi. 7), and there is nothing in Scripture which experience more promptly confirms. But there are other words of Scripture, and other experiences also. "He hath not dealt with us after our sins, nor rewarded us according to our iniquities" (Ps. ciii. 10). "I will restore to you the years that the locust hath eaten" (Joel ii. 25). Irreversibleness holds true of all consequences in that abstract nature with which the physical deals, but how far it is true of nature entering as a constituent into a moral system is a question which no one can answer beforehand. There are healing as well as fatal reactions in nature, and the change in the soul's relation to God through reconciliation is a change so profound that we should anticipate far-reaching reverberations of it even in the natural world. This anticipation is encouraged in the New Testament. The work of Christ is not in the limited sense of the term a spiritual work: the bodies of men are no less His care than their souls. When He says to the paralytic, "Courage, child, thy sins are forgiven thee," He says in the same breath, "Take up thy bed and walk." There is only one work of redemption, one reconciling and restoring power of God in Christ, but its virtue extends to palsy as well as to sin. The reaction of God against sin through nature may be terrible and crushing; but His reaction against it through the Redeemer is more profound and wonderful. It transcends nature, in the sense in which science uses the term, and raises hopes which leave it out of sight. It holds out the prospect of a mode of being in which not only sin will have disappeared, but in which there will be no more death, neither sorrow nor crying, neither shall there be any more pain. In the world of reconciliation all things are made new. The pitiless idea that for ever and ever even the saved will bear the scars and the disablements of their sin is not supported by anything in the New Testament, and is quite out of harmony with its sense of triumph in Christ. Immortality is of the essence of Christianity, and once we accept an idea which is so purely supernatural as that of immortal life, it is idle to revolt at the reversal of any consequences of sin on the ground that they are inconsistent with the laws of nature. With the laws of nature, in the sense of biology or physics, immortality itself is inconsistent; nature has no example of it. But Christians are pledged to faith in immortality, and though it doth not yet appear what we shall be, we believe that we shall wear the image of the Heavenly, and that the wounds of sin shall be healed till not even a scar remains.

This, of course, does not answer the questions which can be raised as to the effect, here and now, of reconciliation upon what may be regarded as the natural consequences of sin. When a man recognises that in such consequences his sin has found him out, he recognises them as penal. They are the just award of his deeds, his sin returning to him in a new form, and showing him what it fully and really is. As long as the man is alienated from God they retain this character; they are depressing, tormenting, ominous. He resents them, fears them, struggles against them, but his bad conscience, or the sense of estrangement from God underlying them, forbids his facing them in any mood but that of despair. They are tokens of a condemnation from which there is no appeal, and they lie with a disabling force upon his life. Now reconciliation makes a radical change here. Not that it suspends or arrests the divine reactions against evil which the sinner has found as distressing, but it enables him, in words which have been already quoted from the

THE NEED OF RECONCILIATION

Old Testament, to "accept" them as "the punishment of his iniquity"; and, as he does so, they acquire a new virtue in his life. They are not a divine judgment of his sin, terminating in itself; they are part of the discipline of his Father's house, which has his moral advantage in view. In the language ordinarily employed to express this contrast, they have ceased to be punishment, and become chastisement. And if, as has been argued, the natural and the moral worlds are organically related in the government of God, to take them in the new character makes a difference in them through and through. The unreconciled man kicks against the pricks, and his punishment is made by that very fact the more severe. The reconciled man, bowing to the divine will which reacts against his sin, finds the reaction, through God's mercy, to be on his side; in proportion as he consents to bear it, he is able to do so; it finds its place among the things which work together for his good; he can believe that when it ceases to be necessary it will pass, and that in the world beyond death, at all events, all the pain, shame, and disablement which the sinful life has brought in its train will certainly disappear.

The attitude taken throughout this chapter on the question of the divine reaction against sin will inevitably raise in some minds questions about the wrath of God. As has often been pointed out, the wrath of God in Scripture is mainly, if not exclusively, an eschatological idea. There is a day of wrath. The wrath itself is often spoken of as the wrath to come. Jesus is our deliverer from the wrath to come. Having been justified now in His blood, we shall be saved by Him from that wrath. What is the relation between the wrath of God so conceived and that ceaseless and omnipresent divine reaction against evil on which we have hitherto insisted? There is undoubtedly a connection between them. Apart from present experiences to which we can attach the idea of a divine wrath—a divine resentment and repulsion of evil—we could attach no meaning to a wrath of God which was merely eschatological. There is no such thing as a future which is not the future of the present. The key to everything in the future—even to the future and final wrath of God—must be found in the present. The divine reaction against evil, of which we are conscious now, is continuous with the coming wrath, but it is not identical with it. It prophesies that the wages of sin is death, and in the day of wrath the prophecy is fulfilled for those who have identified themselves with sin to the last. The wrath of God which awaits the finally impenitent makes its weight felt even now upon all who live in sin. The sum of the divine reactions against evil in the human race is the wrath of God so far as yet revealed; working, so to speak, from behind a screen; working, in the forbearance of God, with some kind of self-restraint, so as to give opportunity as well as motives for repentance (2 Pet. iii. 9); but not capable of being really misunderstood in the conscience. In so far as it lies immersed in sin, the whole world lies exposed to the wrath of God; to live in the world, to be a member of the human race, is to know to that extent at least what the wrath of God means. We cannot evade this conclusion by arguing that the world is the object of God's love, and therefore cannot be the object of His wrath; the very task of Christian thought is to do justice to both ideas. The world is undoubtedly the object of God's love—the whole world; but it is a love which inexorably judges and repels evil. Our own experience is at one with the New Testament in revealing to us both these truths, and it is therefore inept to play off the one against the other. It is not necessary to say they must be reconciled, for that assumes that there is an antagonism between them, but they must be recognised and combined in any true doctrine of sin and reconciliation.

The old difficulty about the relation of sin and death emerges here in another form. If the wrath of God is finally revealed only in the day of wrath—if it is then only that we see all that sin is to God—apparently we ought to say, not the wages of sin is death, but the wages of sin is the second death, the death involved in the wrath of God, the death which has no life on its horizon. This, it might then be argued, would deprive the first death—the death which all men die in this world, the death which Jesus died on the cross—of any significance in relation to sin. Instead of being in some mysterious way one, sin and this death would have nothing to do with each other. But this would be a hasty conclusion. To say that sin and death have nothing to do with each other is to repudiate the whole argument of this chapter, that what we distinguish as the physical and the moral worlds are elements organically related and interpenetrating each other in one divine system; and without repeating the argument the writer must stand by it. Not in the world of the physicist, and not perhaps in that of the moralist, but in the world of God, in which nature and spiri cast lights and shadows on each other and call for a common and continuous interpretation, death comes, and must come, into the divine reaction against evil. It is not only physical or moral, it is spiritual, prophetic, sacramental; to pass through it, even at peace with God, is to realise something which could not be realised otherwise of what sin means to Him. That is why death must enter into a forgiveness or reconciliation in which sin is not extenuated or condoned, but acknowledged by the sinner as all it is to God. No one can ever save us who does not know what sin is, and no one knows what it is who has not bowed to the divine reactions against it as far as they come upon a race which not only needs but remains capable of salvation.

Up till now, in speaking of the need of reconciliation, account has only been taken of that need as felt by man. Man needs to be reconciled to God if he is not to perish in his sin. There is a kind of equivocation if we speak of reconciliation as necessary to God, yet in some sense most theologians have had this idea or its equivalent represented in their systems of thought. If man is not reconciled to God, it is argued, then not only does man perish in his sins, but God's purpose in man's creation is frustrated; He has made His noblest creature in vain. But this, we must assume, is an intolerable thought. The divine purpose must be carried into effect if God is to remain God, and therefore reconciliation is as indispensable to Him as it is to sinners themselves. This can be put in more naïve forms, as by Anselm,[1] who thinks it was a matter of divine necessity that the number of the fallen angels should be replaced by an equal number of redeemed men—the angels being irremediably lost; or in a more philosophical form, as by Ritschl, who holds that the realisation of the Kingdom of God among men, which is unconditionally necessary, carries with it the same divine necessity for the reconciliation of sinners; but in no form does it make a very strong appeal to the Christian conscience. Salvation is of grace, and anything that impairs its absolutely gracious character raises an instinctive protest in the Christian spirit. The ideas just indicated cannot easily be expressed without seeming, at least, to compro-

[1] *Vide* Rivière, *Etude théologique*, pp. 348 ff.

THE NEED OF RECONCILIATION

mise the freeness of God's reconciling love. They lay a necessity on Him at the very point at which the Christian spirit requires to contemplate Him as free. If it be replied that the necessity is one of the kind which is identical with freedom—the work of reconciliation arising out of what God is, and being therefore at once free and inevitable—it must be answered that the necessity that God should act in accordance with His true character, and the necessity that His design in creating man should not be frustrated, are not identical; they do not make the same appeal either to the intellect or to the emotions of man. Further, the logic of the argument leads inevitably either to the conclusion that all men must be saved, if God's purpose in creating them is not to be defeated, or that God's purpose in creating man included only the salvation of some. But neither universalism nor a particular predestination carries its own evidence to the Christian conscience. Both indeed reason about the moral world as if it were not a moral world at all, as if it could have all its riddles read *a priori* by the use of abstract categories which leave its reality untouched. The Christian conscience does not dwell on the fact that, being what He is, God must reconcile man to Himself, and can therefore be said to need reconciliation as well as the sinner: its final utterance is that of adoring amazement: "Behold, what manner of love the Father hath bestowed upon us." A theology which is out of tune with this is beside the mark.

It is more legitimate to insist that once the freeness of God's reconciling love has been recognised, a necessity of some kind attaches to the mode of its manifestation. To be real, and to stand in a real relation to the necessities of sinners, his love must appear in a fashion determined by these necessities. To save a drowning man you want a rope, to save a starving man a loaf, to save a sick man a medicine; and to save a man involved with a bad conscience in the divine reaction against the world's sin, you need a manifestation of help which has a necessary adaptation to his case. It is here indeed, when we speak of the method of salvation, that the proper place appears for emphasising necessity in connection with God's work as Reconciler. It is misleading, to say the least, to preach that God must save men, because He cannot see His purposes frustrated; but it is in keeping both with Scripture and with Christian conscience to teach that, given the free unmerited reconciling love of God, the circumstances of man, or, if we prefer to put it so, the relations between God and man, necessitate its manifestation having one character and not another. It is in the interpretation of this secondary kind of necessity that we deal with the doctrine of reconciliation in the proper sense of the term. And even so, we cannot deal with it *a priori*.

CHAPTER V

RECONCILIATION AS ACHIEVED BY CHRIST

THE need of reconciliation, in the only sense in which the term "need" can properly be used in this connection, lies, as we have now seen, in man, and in his relation to God as affected by sin. The source of it, as Scripture and experience combine to teach, is to be found purely in the love of God.

This ultimate truth about reconciliation is not touched by the fact that the Christian experience of it comes to us through Christ. For Christ, in achieving the reconciliation of the world to God, is doing the work that the Father gave Him to do. The one term by which His work can always be described in relation to God is obedience. He is the righteous Servant of the Lord. He is in the world not to do His own will, but the will of Him that sent Him. He is not wringing favour or forgiveness for men from a God who is reluctant to bestow it; He is manifesting the love which God eternally is and eternally bears to His creatures. Neither does the achievement of reconciliation by Christ imply that there is any schism in the divine nature, as though it would be wrong to forgive freely, or unmerciful to treat sin as what it is. In the divine nature justice and mercy do not need to be composed, they have never fallen out.

These universally accepted truths, however, are sometimes made to support questionable inferences. Thus it is argued that on the basis of them we must admit that the reconciling work of Christ has reference to men only, and that its meaning and virtue are exhausted in the effect it is designed to produce upon sinners. We must give up all that is meant by an objective atonement—that is, a work of Christ as Reconciler which tells upon God as well as upon the sinful. We must abandon as misleading the use of such terms as ἱλασμός, ἱλαστήριον, propitiation, expiation: they are all tainted incurably with the idea that the Son represents mercy and the Father judgment, and that forgiveness has to be extorted, so to speak, from one to whom it is not natural to forgive. If we continue to speak of an "objective" atonement at all, it can only be in the modified—one should rather say the irrelevant or evasive—sense, that it is an atonement provided by God and not by the sinner from his own resources.

Notwithstanding the volume and the emphasis of such argument in recent times, and notwithstanding its relative justification in the disregard by some preachers and theologians of the truth that even in the work of reconciliation the Father and the Son are one, there is something in it which tends to obscure the truth about the work of Christ. The work of Christ is not designed to impress men *simpliciter*. It is designed to impress them to a certain intent, to a certain issue; it is designed to produce in them through penitence God's mind about sin. It cannot do this simply as an exhibition of unconditioned love. It can only do it as the exhibition or demonstration of a love which is itself ethical in character and looks to ethical issues. But the only love of this description is love which owns the reality of sin by submitting humbly and without rebellion to the divine reaction against it; it is love doing homage to the divine ethical necessities which pervade the nature of things and the whole order in which

RECONCILIATION AS ACHIEVED BY CHRIST

men live. These divine ethical necessities are in the strictest sense objective. They are independent of us, and they claim and receive homage from Christ in His work of reconciliation, whether that work does or does not produce upon men the impression which is its due. This is an objective atonement. It is a homage paid by Christ to the moral order of the world established and upheld by God; a homage essential to the work of reconciliation, for unless men are caught into it, and made participant of it somehow, they cannot be reconciled; but a homage, at the same time, which has value in God's sight, and therefore constitutes an objective atonement, whether any particular person is impressed by it or not. Even if no man should ever say, "Thou, O Christ, art all I want; more than all in Thee I find," God says it. Christ and His work have this absolute value for the Father, whatever this or that individual may think of them; and as it is only on the basis of Christ and His work that reconciliation becomes an accomplished fact, it is strict truth to say that reconciliation—in the sense of man's return to God and acceptance with Him—is based on an objective atonement. It is because divine necessities have had homage done to them by Christ, that the way is open for sinners to return to God through Him. When they are forgiven, it is *propter Christum* as well as *gratuito*: it is not by unconditioned love—an expression to which no meaning can be attached which does not obliterate the distinction between right and wrong—but by a love the very nature of which is that it does absolute homage to the whole being and self-revelation of God, and especially to the inexorable reactions of the divine nature against sin.

It is a serious objection to the contrary view that it removes God from the centre of religion and puts man in His

THE CHRISTIAN DOCTRINE OF RECONCILIATION

place. Instead of God being man's chief end, man is made God's chief end. God has no *raison d'être*, so to speak, but to look after us; the type of religion becomes hedonist rather than ethical: there is a loss of reverence, of awe, of solemn worship, of concentration on the moral life. There is a plausible appearance of the contrary when all the emphasis is laid, in the work of Christ, on the moral effect produced by it upon men. But this is one of many cases in religion in which the proverb holds, that the longest way round is the shortest way home. What pursues man in his sin and appeals to him is not love which is thinking of nothing but man, and is ready to ignore and to defy everything for his sake; it is a love which in Christ before everything does homage to that in God which sin has defied. No other love, and no love acting otherwise, can reconcile the sinner to a God whose inexorable repulsion of sin is witnessed to in conscience and in the whole reaction of the world's order against evil. We cannot dispense with the ideas of propitiation, ἱλασμός, ἱλαστήριον: we cannot dispense with a work of reconciliation which is as objective as Christ Himself, and has its independent objective value to God, let our estimate of it be what it will. The world with Christ and His Passion in it is a different place from the world without Christ and His Passion in it. It is a different place to God, and God's attitude to it is different. Is there any other way to express this than by saying that Christ and His Passion constitute an objective atonement, and that it is on the basis of this that men are reconciled to God?

It is true that in the New Testament God is never spoken of as the object of reconciliation. Man is reconciled to God, but we never read that God is reconciled to man. God is always the subject of the verb "to reconcile." "All things

RECONCILIATION AS ACHIEVED BY CHRIST

are of God who hath reconciled us to Himself through Christ." "God was, in Christ, reconciling the world to Himself." This is the uniform style of speech, if we can speak of uniformity when we have only one or two instances to argue from. What underlies it, of course, is the sense that God takes the initiative in the work of reconciliation, that Christ is the gift of God, and the gift of His love. It is on this free gift that everything in Christianity depends. All the New Testament writers would have said, with Augustine, "*Jam diligenti reconciliati sumus.*" But the inference sometimes drawn from this, that it is wrong to speak of God in the passive as reconciled, surely overlooks the fact that it is possible at the same time to love and to be justly estranged; yes, and at the same time also to work for the winning again of the offender against love. When we say that because God is love, immutably and eternally love, therefore He does not need to be and cannot be reconciled, we are imputing immutability to God in a sense which practically denies that He is the living God. If sin makes a difference to God —and that it does is the solemn fact which makes reconciliation of interest to us—then God is not immutable, and His love is not immutable, in the sense assumed. He has experiences in His love. To have His love wounded by sin is one, and to forgive sin is another. If to be forgiven is a real experience, so is to forgive: it makes a difference to God as well as to us. An earthly father's readiness to forgive—the fact that he is *jam diligens*—is not the same as his actual forgiveness. When he actually forgives, he not only loves his penitent child as he always loved him, but his attitude to him is changed; as a matter of fact it is other than it was when he was only waiting for the opportunity to forgive. The only natural way to express the difference is to say that now he is reconciled to the offender. No one thinks that this is inconsistent with his always having loved him, and if we do not think so in the case of an earthly father, there is no reason why we should make difficulty about it in the case of the Heavenly Father. Unchanging love is taken for granted in both cases; but in both cases also sin makes a difference, and so do penitence and pardon. In the experience of forgiveness, as a matter of fact, not only are we reconciled to God, but God is reconciled to us. He is not reconciled in the sense that something is won from Him for us against His will, but in the sense that His will to bless us is realised, as it was not before, on the basis of what Christ has done, and of our appropriation of it. Christian creeds of every type have freely expressed this without any sense that they were compromising the love of God. It is natural that St. Paul in the few places in which he speaks of reconciliation should make God its author and man its object; but it is not less natural nor less legitimate for the Christian who feels that he owes to Christ his experience of God's pardoning love to say that through Christ he possesses a reconciled God and Father. It is in virtue of his Christian relation to Christ —what this is will be considered in the next chapter—that God has for him the character of a reconciled, propitious, or gracious God; and without impugning the essential love of God which gave Christ to the world, he would be doing less than justice to the difference Christ makes, if he did not include in it the difference made not merely in our thought of God, but in God's real relation to us. There have, no doubt, been exaggerated and unconsidered expressions given to this, but the fact remains, and it is not easy to do justice to it if we repudiate *simpliciter* an objective atone-

RECONCILIATION AS ACHIEVED BY CHRIST

ment. Reduced to its simplest expression, what an objective atonement means is that but for Christ and His Passion God would not *be* to us what He is. This seems to the writer the unquestionable Christian truth. The alternative is to say that quite independent of any value which Christ and His Passion have for God, God would still be to us what He is. But this is really to put Christ out of Christianity altogether, and needs no refutation.[1]

What we have now to do is to exhibit as clearly as possible the content of the work of reconciliation as achieved by Christ. The question to be answered is not "What is Christ doing to reconcile men to God?" but "What did He do for this purpose in His life and Passion?" In other words, we are concerned here with what used to be spoken of as the finished work of Christ. The unfinished or progressive work—that which is still going on in the restoration of men to God—is, of course, not in dispute; only, it is assumed that it proceeds on the basis of the other. The other, the finished work of Christ—what has just been described as the objective atonement—is precisely what is meant by καταλλαγή in the New Testament.[2] It is on its completeness and finality that the finality and perfection of the Christian religion depend. It is this which justifies the evangelist when he says "Receive the reconciliation" (Rom. v. 11), or "Be reconciled to God" (2 Cor. v. 20).

To begin with, Jesus was born into the world and the race in which sin and the divine reactions against it were the universal experience. This is not just the same as to

[1] Cf. McLeod Campbell, *The Nature of the Atonement*, p. xxvi—"that divine love which, while as love it is unchanging, yet must, because of its very nature, ever change in the look with which it regards us according to our changing selves."

[2] *The Death of Christ*, p. 103.

say that He was born in our nature, or that in Him a divine person took humanity into hypostatic union with Himself. Much has been written in this sense by Catholic theologians both in ancient and in modern times, but except to those who bow without question to the authority of what is regarded as orthodox tradition it is entirely unimpressive, and it is not the key to the problem before us. To speak of this taking of the human nature into union with the divine as the incarnation, and then to argue that the incarnation in this sense virtually contains the atonement, is quite unreal. Reconciliation is not the nature of Christ, but His task. It is not something which is identical with this metaphysical union of the human and the divine, it is something which has to be morally achieved. It is as a member of our race, sharing our nature and our lot, that Christ accomplishes the moral task of reconciling the world to God; but His being is not identical with nor a substitute for the fulfilment of His task.

Strange illustrations could be given of the unreal conclusions to which theologians are led who in discussing the atonement emphasise the value of the incarnation, in this bare metaphysical sense of the personal union of the human nature with the divine. What is apparently their intention is to represent the hypostatic union—the incarnation, as they call it—as giving an infinite value to all the experiences of Jesus. But instead of giving them an infinite value, on their own showing it renders them superfluous. "What was necessary," asks M. Rivière, "that the Word incarnate might achieve this work of reparation?"—that is, the work of moral reparation in which, as he properly insists, a due satisfaction is made to God for sin. His answer is, "In principle, nothing but His presence in humanity; the least

RECONCILIATION AS ACHIEVED BY CHRIST

of His actions had a sufficient value." [1] Elsewhere he writes: "Although, strictly speaking, a single act of the incarnate Word would have sufficed for this end"—that is, to counterbalance the fault of our first father, or to neutralise the introduction of sin into the world, with all its consequences in the relations of God and man—"God nevertheless has willed, if one may so say, to make the measure of reparation superabundant, as if the humanity had been bound to provide it alone"—that is, apparently, apart from the Word.[2] One can only say that these are extraordinary statements. In the interest of a dogmatic theory—the theory of the hypostatic union in Jesus of the human and the divine—the whole life and death of Jesus, as the gospels exhibit them, the whole story of the evangelists through which Jesus has lived and has exerted His reconciling power in the world, is pronounced in principle superfluous. It may be hoped that not many Christians have courage equal to this logic. The obvious inference from a doctrine which makes all that we read in the evangelists, except perhaps the first two chapters of Matthew and Luke, in principle superfluous, is that that doctrine is wrong. No matter how well intentioned it is, no matter what pious usages have coalesced with it, it is wrong. Every one has encountered the kind of devotional utterance which this doctrine of the incarnation justifies and inspires. It is as common among Protestant pietists as among Catholics: that one drop of Christ's blood, one pang of His agony, one sigh of His sorrow, is a superabundant satisfaction for the sin of the whole world—in virtue of the hypostatic union. Such utterances stand in no relation to the realities with which we have to

---

[1] J. Rivière, *Le Dogme de la Rédemption: étude théologique*, p. 373.
[2] *Ibid.*, p. 292.

deal in interpreting the reconciling work of Christ. They thrust into the place of these realities, which include the life, sufferings, and death of the Saviour, a set of fictitious and feeble extravagances which pall when they do not nauseate. They ought to be dropped with the whole theory of the incarnation which implies that you can multiply the human by the divine, and so infinitely increase its value. There are no quantities in the case, and the multiplication therefore has no meaning. The reconciling power of what Jesus did and suffered—its value alike for God and man in the situation in which man is estranged from God by sin and the world is full of divine reactions against that sin—is not in point of fact dependent on any idea as to the constitution of Christ's person. To say, with M. Rivière,[1] that the principles of a moral biography of Jesus are to be taken from the classical treatises on the incarnation—treatises in which the incarnation means the hypostatic union—is to turn our backs upon history and reality. The only incarnation of which the New Testament knows anything is the appearance of Christ in the race and lot of sinful men, and His endurance in it to the end. Apart from sharing our experience, that sharing of our nature, which is sometimes supposed to be what is meant by incarnation, is an abstraction and a figment. But everything in that sharing of our experience is essential. We dare not say that anything is "in principle" superfluous, and stands in the life of Jesus and in the story of the evangelists only because "God willed, if one may so say," to make the measure of reparation "superabundant." This bare will of God, in which there is no principle and no rational or moral necessity, is really nothing at all, and we cannot use it to buttress an interpretation of

[1] *Le Dogme de la Rédemption: étude théologique*, p. 289.

the life and death of Jesus by which they also are robbed of reality. Everything in the story of Jesus belongs to the gospel as the word of reconciliation, and everything in it has in principle the same meaning, necessity, and value as everything else. But how are we to work this out further, keeping in view the fundamental truth that reconciliation is not the nature but the task of the reconciler?

From the very beginning Christians have believed that Christ lived in our nature, and under all the conditions in which we have failed, an absolutely sinless life. He was tempted in all things like as we are, but He knew no sin (2 Cor. v. 21); to His conscience and will it remained absolutely foreign. It assailed His will, but was never able to obtain the slightest advantage against it. This is not the place to develop an argument for the sinlessness of Jesus: it will be enough to remark that the strength of such an argument would lie not in such direct assertions by others, as have just been quoted from Paul, but in the complete absence, from the self-revelation of Jesus, of anything which betrays on His own part the consciousness of sin. The importance of it in the present connection is that the sinlessness which is here contemplated is contemplated as a moral achievement. Not as though Jesus had been born sinful, and overcame sin in Himself, attaining to purity through conflict and victory; but as a member of our race He had to live in a world and in a society in which sin was omnipresent, in which it had great bribes to offer, great powers of intimidation to exercise, great sufferings to inflict, and He won a continuous and complete victory over it by resisting unto blood. In spite of all the seductions and all the importunate pressures of sin He lived, as a member of our race, a life in which sin had no place and no power.

THE CHRISTIAN DOCTRINE OF RECONCILIATION

In doing so, it is sometimes argued, He reconciled humanity to God. His sinless life and death—or, to bring out more unambiguously the moral character of it as an achievement, His life and death of victory over sin—are the work of reconciliation. Ideas of this kind have probably never been strange to the Christian mind. No doctrine of Christ's Person can hide from a simple spectator the truth that He had a battle to fight, and that we men, in whose nature He fights it, are interested in His victory. Athanasius puts it with the one-sided emphasis on death as the enemy, rather than sin, which is characteristic of the Greek fathers. When all men were perishing because of the transgression of Adam, Christ came, and, by dying and rising again, won for humanity a victory over death. He won it in our nature, in our flesh; in Him, in union with the Word, our nature or flesh overcame the last enemy. Hence Athanasius can apply the idea of salvation to Christ Himself, and speak of His victory as something He achieved for Himself as well as for us. Πρώτη τῶν ἄλλων, he writes, ἐσώθη καὶ ἠλευθερώθη ἡ ἐκείνου σάρξ, ὡς αὐτοῦ τοῦ λόγου σῶμα γενομένη.[1] In other words, He saved human nature in His own person, in order that it might subsequently be saved in the persons of others. Christ Himself illustrates not only what it is to save, but what it is to be saved; indeed it is only the Christ in whom the human nature which He has assumed is saved who is able to be the Saviour.

This point of view, however, becomes much more significant, when it is transposed from the metaphysical key in which it deals only with death to the moral one in which it deals with sin. Sin is regarded here, not in the first instance—indeed not directly at all—as the sin under which

[1] Athanasius, c. *Arianos*, ii. 61.

others suffer, but as a power which assails and tries to subdue Christ. He is in conflict with it on His own account, and His task is to put it under His feet. The most strenuous representatives of this view in modern times have been Menken and Du Bose. Ordinarily the human nature of Christ is regarded by those who take this line as identical with human nature in other men. It has the same latent possibility of sin in it, the same susceptibility to the temptations which sin can offer, the same liability to be intimidated by the cruel power sin wields. But in Christ the latent possibility of sin is never allowed under any temptation to develop or emerge in a sinful act. He was never bribed or coerced into doing anything which left a stain on His conscience, or rose as a cloud between His soul and God. He not only maintained a perpetual conflict against sin, He achieved an unbroken victory over it. He saved human nature in His own person: saved it in spite of all it was as the nature of Adam, and of all that beset it in this present evil world; and in so saving human nature in His own person He reconciled humanity to God. It is a *Christus salvus factus*, a Christ who is saved, who becomes *Christus salvos faciens*, Christ the Saviour. He saves Himself by His divine energy, resisting unto blood, striving against sin; and He saves us as He inspires us by His example to walk in His steps.

It was a commonplace of Christian teaching a generation ago to contrast Christ as our atonement and reconciliation with Christ as a "mere" example; the latter was the Socinian, the former the evangelical view. But Christ, as the evangelical view sometimes led its adherents to forget, after all *is* an example; and it is at least possible that to be insensible to the inspiration of His example is to lie outside

THE CHRISTIAN DOCTRINE OF RECONCILIATION

of His reconciling power. The emphasis laid by the writers just referred to on the conflict by which Christ achieved and maintained that perfect life which we contemplate in the gospels has its own justification; it keeps us in the world of moral reality from which our want of moral nerve is always tempting us to slink. Whatever reconciliation may be, it is something which for Christians must have the character and virtue of Christ in it, and everything does us a service which brings into fresh prominence aspects of that character and virtue which have been somewhat overlooked.

But while this appreciation is due to writers like Menken and Du Bose, it is not possible to accept the view that Christ's personal victory over sin, regarded as a power tempting or assailing Him, is His complete work of reconciliation. Such a formula as that He saved human nature in His own person is of no value; it assumes a whole incredible philosophy about natures and persons, and all it means is that the man Christ Jesus won a perfect victory over sin. The Biblical support of this doctrine of reconciliation is meagre and dubious. Two passages are quoted in its favour from the epistle to the Romans, both, as Holtzmann remarked, among the *cruces* of Paulinism. The first is Rom. vi. 10: "The death that He [Christ] died, He died unto sin once for all." In ordinary circumstances when Paul speaks of dying to sin, he has in view people who once lived to sin. They are to change their attitude and relation to it, now that they are Christians; they are to reckon themselves dead to it, to become every day more insensible to its appeal. But it is more than doubtful whether Paul ever associated this ethical dying to sin with either the life or death of Jesus. He certainly could not do so if the assumption were that Jesus had once lived to sin; and it would not be natural for him to use the expression "dying to sin" to describe the victorious conflict with temptation, which is one aspect of the whole career of Jesus. Further, though he would not have denied that the death of Jesus crowned that victorious conflict which filled His life, the whole context of thought in which he says that the death which He died (on the cross) He died to sin once for all shows that something quite different from this was in his mind. When He died, He was done with sin; He had cleared all scores with it, and passed into a region where it could make no claim upon Him more; His life now was determined altogether not by sin and its responsibilities, but by God. This is quite remote from a daily crucifixion of the flesh such as is contemplated in Christ by the theory under review.

Similar considerations apply to the second passage which has been adduced to support the theory (Rom. viii. 3 f.), "What the law could not do, in that it was weak through the flesh, God, sending His own Son in the likeness of sinful flesh and as an offering for sin, condemned sin in the flesh; that the ordinance of the law might be fulfilled in us who walk not after the flesh but after the spirit." The general idea here is that what the law could not do—viz., bring men to righteousness and life—God took another and more effective way of doing: He sent His Son. The main proposition is that in which God is said, by the mission of His Son under the circumstances described, to have condemned sin in the flesh; and this is interpreted, by the advocates of the theory under discussion, as the result of Christ's life and work. He appeared in the world "in the likeness of sinful flesh and in connection with sin." He had the very same nature which we have, with the same latent possibilities of evil in it; He had the same flesh which we have, with all its natural antipathy to the spirit. But in Him these latent possibilities were never allowed to emerge in act; the flesh was crucified every instant before any one of its impulses could declare itself as actual sin. Everything that in us might have and would have ripened into sin was in Him extinguished before it could begin to grow, and it is in the light of this that we have to interpret the phrase "condemned sin in the flesh." What it means is that Christ proved by His sinless life in the flesh that sin was not inevitable in the flesh; sinful men need not feel themselves shut up to despair; there was a possibility for them of escape and victory. By living in the flesh—in the very human nature in which it is our lot to live—a life without sin, Christ had reconciled that nature to God in His own person, and He held out in the gospel a similar reconciliation, in a similarly triumphant life, to all who were doomed to call sinful flesh their own. They could crucify the flesh as He had done, and have the just demand of the law fulfilled in them as it was in Him.

The passage is difficult, but there are many objections to this rendering of it. For one thing, it lifts it off the hinges, and interprets it as if there were no system of Pauline thoughts in which it must find its place. For another, it disregards the expression περὶ ἁμαρτίας, the natural meaning of which is that it is Christ in the character of a sacrifice for sin, and not merely of one who allowed sin no place in His will, to whom salvation is due. Further, it is a very forced construction which contrives to draw hope for sinners from the doctrine that the sinless life of Jesus condemns sin in the flesh. The natural inference from such an expression is not that sin is not inevitable, and that therefore men may hope to live without it; but that sin is not inevitable, and that therefore those who live in sin, as all men do, are inexcus-

RECONCILIATION AS ACHIEVED BY CHRIST

able. This is the moral suggested by the analogous use of "condemn" in the familiar gospel passage: "The men of Nineveh shall rise up in the judgment with this generation and shall condemn it" (Matt. xii. 41). If we read Paul's words in the context of his own thoughts they yield quite a different sense. It is not Christ's sinless life in the form of our sinful flesh by which sin is condemned; it is condemned by God in sending Christ in our nature and as a sacrifice for sin. How this sacrifice is made, and how it tells, according to Paul, are matters for further explanation: the point with which we have to do here is that it is not done simply by Christ's personal victory as a man over sin. This might be inspiring, or it might, as just explained, be the quenching of the sinner's last hope. It is certainly not for Paul an exhaustive account of the moral task of Jesus in reconciling the world to God.

The truth which is the inspiration of this view is, however, a real and important truth which must have its place in any adequate doctrine of reconciliation. If it is not fairly deducible—as to the writer seems obvious—from any of the Biblical passages cited, it is fairly covered by the term ἀρχηγός, as the New Testament applies it to Jesus. This picturesque word is variously rendered in the English version. "Ye slew *the Prince* of life" (Acts iii. 15). "Him God exalted as *a Prince* and a Saviour" (Acts v. 31). "It pleased God to make *the Captain* of our salvation perfect through sufferings" (Heb. ii. 10). "Looking unto Jesus *the Author* and finisher of faith" (Heb. xii. 2). There is something peculiarly felicitous and suggestive in Dr. Moffatt's rendering, *the Pioneer*, though all the associations of the English term pioneer are not equally appropriate in all the contexts. But what it invariably implies is that Jesus has trodden the path which all who are to be saved must tread. He has made the path by treading it Himself, and apart from this He would not have the power He actually exercises to bring men to the Father. Moral power, as Bushnell is never tired of telling us, must be won by moral means; it is the victory of Jesus over sin which is the basis of His power with sinners. His power, too, must be exercised in constraining sinners to face the same foes, to fight the good fight till the last breath, to resist even until blood striving against sin; it is thus, and only thus, that He becomes for them a living way to the Father. Nevertheless to describe Him as ἀρχηγός or Pioneer does not exhaust His significance as Reconciler. It conceives of Him too exclusively as on a level with us, and as having the same battle to fight which we have. He and we are both face to face with sin in the world, and are conceived as having the same task with regard to it. But this does not answer to all the facts. The world not only contains sin in the sense of a power hostile to Christ and to us, a power which He has vanquished in bloody conflict, and which we must vanquish in His train; it contains *our sin*. Besides its relation to sin abstractly considered, the work of the Reconciler must have some specific relation to sin in this latter aspect; it must deal with sin not merely as a power at work in the world, but as something for which responsibility already lies upon us. The Reconciler must not simply overcome sin in His own person; He must do something bearing upon *our* sin, and the sin of the whole world.

Nothing is more conspicuous in the New Testament than that the life and death of Jesus are to be interpreted in this light, and that as we approach this apprehension of His work we are approaching the secret of reconciliation. The

RECONCILIATION AS ACHIEVED BY CHRIST

Jesus who was born into our race and our lot made Himself one with us in love to the uttermost. Nothing in the life of men was alien to Him; there was nothing but touched Him profoundly. He did not look on His own things only, but on the things of others also; He loved His neighbour as Himself. In all this there was nothing artificial, no carrying out of a programme: it arose inevitably and spontaneously out of His situation as a man among men, or rather as the beloved Son of the Father in a family of alienated children. He took all the burdens of the race upon Himself in passionate sympathy. Above all He took that heaviest burden under which the race was sinking with despair and death. He bore our sins. In every sense and to every extent to which love could do so, He made them His own. Can we develop what this means, and say whether here is the ultimate secret of Christ's reconciling power?

We are at least supported in making the attempt if we look at the life and death of Jesus as they are represented in the gospels and interpreted in the apostolic writings. But for the sin of the world, that life and death would not have been what they were; they were determined by sin to be what we see them to have been. The very act in which Jesus comes upon the stage of history—His baptism by John—is in this respect of profound significance. No doubt the baptism has many aspects which can be independently emphasised: it was the anointing of Jesus as the Messianic King, it was an hour in which He was signally conscious of His relation to the Father and of His Messianic calling, it was in some sense a great act of self-dedication or self-consecration to a work which only time and Providence would define: but no such conceptions of it enable us to answer the question which evidently exercised the mind of the Church from the beginning,—Why did the sinless one come to be baptized with what was explicitly declared to be a baptism of repentance looking to remission of sins? There is no answer to this question, equal to its importance, but that which allows us to see Jesus, at the very outset of His career, identifying Himself, as far as love enabled Him to do so, with sinful men. We might have expected that where the work of God was being done, as through the prophetic ministry of John, Jesus would be present; but we should have looked for Him at John's side, confronting the people, assisting the prophet to proclaim the word of God. Yet nothing is more true to the character of Jesus and to the spirit in which He carries through His mission than that He appears not at John's side, but among the people who came to be baptized; His entrance on His work, like the whole work from beginning to end, was an act of loving communion with us in our misery. He numbered Himself with the transgressors, and made the burden of our sins His own.

A similar relation to sin is implied in all Jesus' dealings with sinners for their forgiveness and restoration to God. Nothing is more certain than His power to win sinners from their sin and to bring them to the Father, and nothing is more certain than that such power depends absolutely on the bearing of sin in the sense at present in view—on entering lovingly, sympathetically, and profoundly into the sinner's experience, and realising through love and sympathy the crushing weight which sin is for him. This is the vital difference between Jesus and the Pharisees, between goodness which bears the sinner's burden and says, "Come unto Me, and I will give you rest," and goodness which has no sympathy with the sinner, which bears no burden for him, which says, "Stand by thyself; come not near me, for I am holier than thou." Pharisaic goodness has no redemptive power in it just because it has no love in it and bears no burden; the sinner is not moved by it except to curse it, and in doing so he shows at least some sense for what goodness is. For God also curses it as a wicked slander upon Himself. But the goodness of Jesus has the redeeming virtue which unquestionably belongs to it just because love is the soul of it, love which in its very nature makes the burdens of others its own, whatever these burdens be. If sin is the most fatal and crushing of all, then sin will weigh heaviest upon Him. When Jesus received sinners in the gospel they were conscious of this. He did not talk about sin-bearing love; He exhibited it. They knew in His presence what forgiveness cost. They saw it in His face, and heard it in the tones of His voice. They were aware that He had carried on His own spirit the weight which was lifted from theirs, and that their debt to Him was immeasurable. That was why they poured their precious ointment on His head, and wet His feet with tears. If there was not an articulate word in the New Testament on the subject of Christ bearing sin, we should argue quite confidently from the redemptive power of goodness as displayed in Him, that He did unquestionably bear it. He bore it in a love which entered victoriously into sinful hearts and reconciled them to God.

But there are articulate words in the gospels which exhibit the whole life and calling of Jesus as having relation to sin, and therefore give to this bearing of sin a central and decisive significance in His work. "I came," He says in one of those great utterances in which the purpose of His presence in the world is disclosed, "I came not to call the righteous, but sinners." Sinners are for Him the centre of interest on earth, and to bear their sin in a sympathetic sense of what a burden it is for them must lie at the very centre of His work. Again He says, "The Son of Man came to seek and to save that which is lost." The very words used to describe the state of the sinful—that which is lost—are a pathetic expression of Christ's sense of their situation. Nobody could have hit upon them whose heart had not been burdened by the contemplation of the life which men lead when sin has separated them from God. The sinners themselves do not always feel the burden. There are states of levity and stupidity in which men are insensible to what they are, and to the responsibilities which lie upon them; but the burden only weighs the heavier then upon Him who can feel it, and who knows through what soul travail the dull heart must be awakened to penitence and faith, and so be reconciled to God. And once more, there is the great word in which Jesus near the close of His life again defined the end and the method of His mission in the world. "The Son of Man came not to be ministered unto but to minister, and to give His life a ransom for many" (Mark x. 45). The liberation of sinners is the end which Jesus has in view; and though the giving of His life a ransom may include more, it includes at least that spending of His being in love and sympathy with the sinful which can be described as bearing their sins. It is true that in the Synoptic tradition of Jesus' words the precise expression, "to bear sins" does not occur. It is true also that where it does occur in later apostolic thought, it has to be interpreted in its own context, and may be found to carry other ideas than those which modern psychology finds it congenial to attach to the words. But, words apart, it cannot be questioned that there is something in the facts of the life of Jesus, something deep, per-

RECONCILIATION AS ACHIEVED BY CHRIST

vading, and decisive, which we can naturally express by saying He bore our sins; and that this something enters, essentially, into His reconciling power.

The more the life of Jesus as well as His death has been taken into consideration in studying His work, the more has this view been emphasised. Even when we wish to interpret the death of Jesus, we feel that we can do no more than regard it as the consummation of His life. We find it indispensable to set it in the light of the whole impression made on us by the life. That impression is not in the least ambiguous. The life of Jesus, from beginning to end, is in all its relations to others a life of love. It is love, then, we have to understand. Without love, there could be no reconciliation, and what we have to discover is how love functions—what it does, suffers, or promises, in relation to man as a being in need of reconciliation to God.

We have two books in our language by men of original spiritual insight and intellectual power which make a noble contribution to this study. One is Bushnell's *The Vicarious Sacrifice*, the other is McLeod Campbell's *The Nature of the Atonement*. The former dates from 1865, the latter from 1856, and it may be questioned whether anything has been written since to rival either as an interpretation of Christ's reconciling work purely through the idea of love. In Bushnell the idea is taken more broadly. He views the vicarious sacrifice as "grounded in principles of universal obligation," and He illustrates the love of Christ in relation to other burdens which He bore as well as to the burden of sin. Thus to him, as to the first evangelist, it is the key to Christ's healing ministry. "Himself," says Matthew, after narrating typical specimens of our Lord's work as a physician, "himself took our infirmities and bore our sicknesses" (Matt.

viii. 17). He was not sick or infirm Himself, but He felt in genuine sympathy what sickness and infirmity meant to others, and in love He made their burdens His own. He had no medical science, no professional skill; when He healed it was through His personality and at a personal expense; virtue went out of Him, and He felt the drain upon His strength. It is not exaggerating to say that He really made His own the pains He relieved; it was at His cost that the sufferings of others were lightened. This conception, obviously, can be extended by analogy to Christ's sympathy with the moral sickness and infirmity of men, His feeling with them under the burden, the disablement, and the alienation of sin. He did not become a sinner out of His sympathy with the state of the sinful, any more than He became a sick man out of His sympathy with the diseased; but He took on Himself, in the one case as in the other, as far as the nature of things admitted it, the weight under which men laboured. He bore our sins, as He bore our diseases, on His loving heart. He identified Himself with us, as far as love made it possible for Him to do so, in the whole circumstances of our stricken life. This identification of Himself with us is the very meaning of love, and its power to win men from sin to God is self-evident. It does not need any explanation: to ask for explanation is like asking for a candle by which to see the sun.

McLeod Campbell would have had no call to disown anything Bushnell says of the essentially vicarious nature of love, but he studies the love of Christ more exclusively in relation to sin, and he thinks more constantly of what sin means to God as well as of what it means to man. Perhaps there is a certain degree of artificiality in his treating separately, both with regard to the retrospective and the prospective

RECONCILIATION AS ACHIEVED BY CHRIST

aspects of the atonement, Christ's dealing with men on behalf of God, and His dealing with God on behalf of men. For there is just one body of fact to deal with—namely, the life of Christ, as a life inspired throughout by love—and we do not get new material under the two heads, but only a new point of view. If the life of Christ is inspired throughout by love, it is a revelation of God, for God is love; and in this sense it is an appeal to men in the name of the Father. But it is also a revelation of man, for love is the true law of the human being, love to God and love to His neighbour; and in this sense the life of Christ may be said to constitute an appeal to God in the name of men, or an appeal to the Father in the name of the children. But the appeal to God and the appeal to man are made by the one life of love, and though theologians may emphasise the one or the other as they reflect upon the method and the power of reconciliation, it can hardly be questioned that, consciously or unconsciously, both will influence their thoughts.

Broadly speaking, Bushnell emphasised the appeal to man in the name of the Father: what to him is conspicuous in Christ is the love which identifies itself with man and his interests; man, so to speak, is the sole object and concern of that love. With McLeod Campbell it is otherwise. He thinks not only of man but of God as interested in sin, and as necessarily related to it. Apart from this thought of God, there is a tendency to regard sin as a misfortune rather than a fault; sympathy with the sinner is apt to lapse into an extenuating or condoning of sin; it becomes emotional or sentimental, and ceases to be, what it always was in Jesus, ethical and austere. We may think what we will of the peculiar form in which McLeod Campbell expresses his mind on this subject, but there can be no question that he is dealing in it with something which is as essential to reconciliation, in the Christian sense, as Christ's sympathy with men in the calamity, the burden, the ruin of their sin. When He identifies Himself with God's interest in the situation as well as man's, Christ sees sin as something which God righteously condemns, and cannot but condemn, and He acknowledges in human nature the justice of that condemnation. He sees it as something from which, in the divine order, there is but one way of escape, that of an adequate repentance; and seeing further that for man left to himself there is no hope, because the very sin which calls for repentance has disabled him spiritually and made him incapable of a repentance really answering to his guilt, in a very agony of love He takes this responsibility of man to God upon Himself, and makes in the place of sinful men that deeply felt acknowledgment of human sin which is the repentance due from the race but beyond its power to render. It is best to give this in the author's own words: it is the original and creative element in his mind which has entered as a ferment into all Christian thinking for the last two generations. "That oneness of mind with the Father, which towards man took the form of condemnation of sin, would in the Son's dealing with the Father in relation to our sins, take the form of a perfect confession of our sins. This confession, as to its own nature, must have been *a perfect Amen in humanity to the judgment of God on the sin of man.* Such an Amen was due in the truth of things. He who was the truth could not be in humanity and not utter it. . . . He who so responds to the divine wrath against sin, saying, "Thou art righteous, O Lord, who judgest so," is necessarily receiving the full apprehension and realisation of that wrath, as well as of that sin against which it comes forth, into His

RECONCILIATION AS ACHIEVED BY CHRIST

soul and spirit, into the bosom of the divine humanity, and so receiving it, He responds to it with a perfect response— a response from the depths of that divine humanity—and *in that perfect response He absorbs it.* For that response has all the elements of a perfect repentance in humanity for all the sin of man,—a perfect sorrow—a perfect contrition— all the elements of such a repentance, and that in absolute perfection, all—excepting the personal consciousness of sin;—and by that perfect response in Amen to the mind of God in relation to sin is the wrath of God rightly met, and that is accorded to divine justice which is its due, and could alone satisfy it." [1] Discounting the questionable nomenclature here—the use of the term "repentance" to describe a spiritual state or act in which there is no personal consciousness of sin—it does not seem to the writer open to question that this description of what is involved in Christ's relation to sin, considered not as man's misfortune but as an offence against God, is sound. Christ saw what sin was to God as we because of our sin itself could not see it; He felt what it was to God as we for the same reason could not feel it; He owned the justice of God in condemning it and repelling it inexorably, even while He yearned over His sinful children, and longed for their reconciliation. It was unhappy, to say the least of it, to call this repentance, or vicarious repentance; but it is a description of facts in the experience of the Saviour, and of facts on which His power to reconcile us to God is essentially dependent. If He had not thus seen and felt what sin is to God, if He had not thus acknowledged God's justice in condemning it, we could never have been brought through Him to the same insight and sorrow, to the same confession and acknowledgment,

[1] *The Nature of the Atonement,* pp. 117-119.

apart from which the reconciliation of sinners to God is self-evidently an impossibility. For to be reconciled to God means at all events that God's mind about sin, which is revealed to us in Christ, through Christ becomes our own.

Although McLeod Campbell is often classed with writers who view the work of Christ only in its relation to man, this is clearly unjust. He certainly would have said that the orthodox writers on the atonement viewed it too exclusively in its relation to God. They dealt with it almost wholly in what he calls its retrospective aspect; it was an appeal to God which issued in the forgiveness of sins on His part. They were less alive to its prospective aspect, to the fact that it included an appeal to man which evoked eternal life. But though he laid a new emphasis on the truth that the atonement is meant to regenerate men, and to do so directly, and that a doctrine of atonement which is not essentially related to the new eternal life is fatally defective, he never held that the work of Christ had reference only to man. In His reconciling work Christ dealt with God on behalf of men as well as with men on behalf of God; His "repentance," to use the objectionable name for the indubitable and essential facts, was addressed to God and had infinite value to Him; it was on the basis of it, and on the assurance that it could be reproduced in sinners, that God was able to forgive sins; in the strict sense of the term it was an objective atonement. McLeod Campbell puts this quite unambiguously when, after summing up all that enters into the life of Jesus, alike as a dealing with us on behalf of the Father and a dealing with the Father on our behalf, he says that here "we have the elements of the atonement before us as presented by the Son and accepted by the Father, and see the grounds of the divine procedure in granting to

RECONCILIATION AS ACHIEVED BY CHRIST

us remission of our sins and the gift of eternal life." He has the same difficulty in combining this objective atonement with the free gift of Christ to the world by the Father that earlier theologians have in combining the merits of Christ with the grace of God. His disposition, perhaps due to the circumstances of the time, is to emphasise grace, "the ultimate foundation in God for that peace with God which we have in Christ";[1] but he never eviscerates the "in Christ" so that it ceases to signify something which weighs with God. He would have felt that to do so was to deal deceitfully both with the gospel facts and with the apostolic interpretation of them, and to cut the nerve of the reconciling power in Christ.[2]

No one can question, so far as it goes, the truth and power of this explanation of the process by which Christ achieves the work of reconciliation. Without such a process—without a love which entered thus profoundly and sympathetically into all that sin is both for God and man, and took upon its own spirit the crushing weight of it—that work could never have been accomplished. All that is positive in the doctrines of Bushnell and McLeod Campbell, not to speak of the numberless writers who have learned from them, is to be welcomed without reserve. We are to think of the work of atonement or reconciliation as a work arising out of the situation in which Christ found Himself as a member of the human race; as one with us He spontaneously, under the impulse of love, makes all our burdens His own. He

---

[1] *The Nature of the Atonement*, p. 287. "To stop at the atonement, and rest in the fact of the atonement, instead of ascending through it to that in God from which it has proceeded, and which demanded it for its due expression, is to misapprehend the atonement as to its nature, and place, and end."

[2] *Ibid.*, p. 151 f.

makes the burden of our sin His own as far as that can be done by one who Himself knows no sin, and to whom no part of the burden of sin ever comes home through a bad conscience of His own. Stress is laid on both parts of this conception, and all with the idea of preserving for the work of Christ in reconciliation a purely ethical character. Such a character, of course, belongs to it as the spontaneous manifestation of love, determined by the relations in which Christ stood to God on the one side and to man on the other; but this character, it is agreed, can only be maintained if it is made quite clear that the burden Christ bore under the inspiration of His love cannot be described as *penal*. Punishment is something which can only exist in and for a bad conscience, and the sufferings into which His love led Him, and in and through which His reconciling work is achieved, do not come to Him through a bad conscience, and therefore are in no sense penal. That the innocent, moved by love, should suffer with the guilty and for them, is in line with all we know of the moral order under which we live; it is the triumph of goodness in its highest form. But that the innocent should be punished for the guilty is not moral at all. It is in every sense of the term impossible. As an incident in the divine administration of the world it is simply inconceivable.

All this may be admitted without reserve, and we may reflect with pleasure that it excludes a great deal by which the Christian conscience has often been shocked in discussions of the atonement. It excludes the idea that the Son of God, with whom the Father was well pleased, should be regarded at the same time as the object of the Father's displeasure, the victim of His wrath, on whom the punishment of all the world's sin was inflicted. It excludes all those ideas of equivalence between what Christ suffered and what

RECONCILIATION AS ACHIEVED BY CHRIST

men as sinners were under an obligation to suffer, which revolt both intelligence and conscience in much of what is called orthodox theology. It excludes all those assimilations of the sufferings of our Lord in the garden and on the cross to the pains of the damned, which cast a hideous shadow on many interpretations of His Passion. It may not be out of place to quote one or two of the most signal instances of this perversion to show how essential it had become to emphasise the purely ethical character of the work of Christ. Luther, for example, carried away by the passion with which he exulted in Christ's identification of Himself with men, could write that "in His tender innocent heart He had to feel God's wrath and judgment against sin, to taste for us eternal death and damnation, and in a word to suffer everything which a condemned sinner has merited and must suffer eternally." "Look at Christ," he says again to the sinner dreading wrath and death, "who for thy sake has gone to hell and been abandoned by God as one damned for ever." This is his interpretation of "My God, my God, why hast Thou forsaken Me?"[1] Calvin, less passionate, is more cautious, and guards against the idea that God was ever *adversarius* or *iratus* in relation to Christ; yet He can allow himself to write of the *descensus ad inferos* that here Christ endured in His soul the dire torments of a condemned and lost man.[2] M. Rivière, who holds that the orthodox Romish doctrine is that the work of redemption is an act of moral reparation, and that nothing that is not moral can enter into it or have any relevance to it, ascribes the appearance in Catholic preaching of ideas like those just illustrated to the pernicious influence of Protestantism on the true Church.

[1] Thomasius, *Christi Person und Werk* (3rd ed.), ii. 177.
[2] *Institutio*, 11. xvi. 10.

THE CHRISTIAN DOCTRINE OF RECONCILIATION

The *abandon* with which they are expressed in the writers from whom he quotes seems to show that they found in Catholicism a soil at least as congenial as that which he regards as native to them. "Jesus," says one, "appears in the eyes of His Father as the universal sinner, *comme le péché vivant*, as a being accursed. . . . God no longer sees in Him His well-beloved Son, but the victim for sin, the sinner of all times and of all places, on whom He is about to bring down in all its weight the rigour of His justice." "Spare Him, Lord," cries another, "it is thy Son." "No, no," is the answer; "it is sin; it must be chastised." A third, commenting on the text *Oportet Christum pati*, is bolder still. He depicts Jesus between the sin of the world on one side, from which He shrinks in horror, and the inexorable justice of heaven on the other; He stands there face to face with the divine decree that lays all this sin on Him that He may satisfy this justice. It is hardly possible to translate to the end what follows. "Il faut qu'il s'ouvre à ce double déluge du péché et de la peine, qu'il mange ce pain amer de nos iniquités, qu'il boire jusqu' à la lie ce vin âpre de la colère céleste; il faut qu'il absorbe et cette fange humaine et cette vengeance divine; il faut que lui, qui est le sanctuaire du monde et le cœur de l'humanité, il en devienne l'égout." A still more revolting extravagance in the same direction may be added. "Become le péché universel, He has a sort of likeness to evil, to Satan, to all the reprobate; for the righteous, for the angels, for the immaculate Virgin, He is an object of repulsion; God Himself is about to launch His anathema against Him; He will be *l'excommunié universel, le maudit*."[1] It might be supposed that excesses like these would cure themselves, but it is good to have

[1] Rivière, *Le Dogme de la Rédemption: étude théologique*, pp. 232 ff.

RECONCILIATION AS ACHIEVED BY CHRIST

them barred out by such a conception of Christ's relation to sin, in its bearing alike on God and man, as we have just been considering. It keeps within the limits of the moral world, and of moral reality and sanity, and we can have no sure standing ground if this is withdrawn from us.

The question remains, however, whether it exhausts the truth about Christ's achievement of reconciliation. It emphasises the fact that the work of Christ is an ethical work, that love is its motive, that it is transacted from beginning to end in the moral universe, and that it makes a rational and moral appeal to us. On the other hand, in the minds of many of its advocates it has been associated with a tendency to overlook, or to depreciate, the Passion of Christ as a concrete historical fact, or to separate the physical aspects of the Passion—the mere physical death, as it is sometimes called—from the spirit of love and obedience in which Christ died, as though this spirit were the only thing which counted in the work of reconciliation. This is done consciously and on principle by many Roman Catholic theologians, who emphasise moral reparation as the proper work of Christ. Thus M. Rivière asks point blank, "If the Christ had not suffered, if He had not died upon the cross, would He nevertheless have redeemed us?" and he proceeds unhesitatingly, "To this question Catholic theologians unanimously reply in the affirmative. It follows with perfect clearness that neither the suffering, the death, nor the cross represents the essential, or, to use the language of the school, the formal element in redemption. They are so many contingent circumstances, the reason for which is to be sought *dans les convenances du mystère, non dans ses exigences absolues.*"[1] That is, they were in keeping with the wonderful work which

[1] *Op. cit.,* p. 260 f.

God was doing in Christ, but it was not really dependent on them. It would not have looked so well if the Redeemer had died in His bed, or if He had not died at all, but the work of redemption would have been accomplished all the same. "*Non mors,*" as St. Bernard says, "*sed voluntas placuit sponte morientis.*" Much Protestant teaching, without rising to the audacity which Mr. Rivière ascribes to all Catholic theologians, has a bias in the same direction. Perhaps it is due to a reaction against the tradition which treated the cross and the death of Christ as purely objective and penal inflictions, and not as consequences brought upon the Saviour by the love in which, in a sinful world, He identified Himself at once with God and with man. Such a reaction would be legitimate in itself, for that Christ's Passion enters into His ethical life is indubitable, and it is as part of His ethical life that it has power to win men to God; but it is not legitimate if it goes so far as to say that the ethical element —the spirit in which Jesus suffered—is everything, and that it would have made no difference, or none that was vital, if He had not suffered at all.

There is, in point of fact, something so artificial and unreal in this abstract separation of the death of Jesus from the spirit in which He died, that even those who lay the greatest stress upon it find it difficult to express themselves with any approach to consistency. The language of Scripture and the common sense of men assert themselves against the arbitrary element in such distinctions. McLeod Campbell himself is a signal illustration of what is here meant. In one place he tells us that a certain passage in Scripture "prepares us to find in the moral and spiritual elements in the sufferings of Christ, the atoning power that was in them; and to see how, though there is nothing of an atoning nature in death, the

RECONCILIATION AS ACHIEVED BY CHRIST

wages of sin—not in the death of all who have died since death entered the world, nor in all death that may yet be endured; yet was the death of Christ, who tasted death for every man, because of the condemnation of sin in His spirit, an atonement for the sin of the whole world." Here death is roundly pronounced irrelevant to atonement, and then in the same breath we are told that Christ tasted death for every man, and that this, in virtue of "the condemnation of sin in His spirit," was itself the atonement.[1] There is undoubtedly a want of unity in this statement which needs elucidation. The same remark applies to another passage in which he approaches the death of Christ, so to speak, from the opposite side. Dealing with the contemplation of our Lord's sufferings during the hour and power of darkness, he writes: "Feelings of a strong and solemn as well as tender character, have doubtless been thus cherished; and doubtless, the element of gratitude has been present: yet there was not, for there could not be, in images of physical suffering anything of the nature of spiritual light,—however such light may have been present along with them, being received otherwise."[2] The last words, "being received otherwise," strike curiously on the mind. They are as much as to say that the Passion of Jesus, in its concrete reality—for no human soul, contemplating it as it was, ever in the act and process of contemplation regarded it as a "physical" experience as distinct from a moral one—is unable to speak for itself. But this is simply not true. Whatever the cross of Jesus does, it speaks for itself. It is not by the help of light "received otherwise," but by its own light, that we see and feel what it means. But that is only to say in other words that the absolute distinction of physical and spiritual—the

[1] *The Nature of the Atonement*, p. 105. [2] *Ibid.*, p. 220.

abstract separation of the death of Jesus, as non-significant, from the spirit in which He died, as infinitely valuable to God and prevalent with man—needs to be revised. And as we proceed in McLeod Campbell's work, we find that he is driven almost unconsciously to this point of view. He not only speaks of Christ as tasting death for every man, he says the peace which became perfected on the cross is set forth to us as made there;[1] he speaks of death as Christ passed through it as the perfecting of the atonement,[2] and of "the death of Christ as filled with the divine judgment on sin."[3] What is more striking, he explicitly and formally goes beyond the abstract view which disregards the "physical" aspects of the Passion and which lays exclusive emphasis on the "spiritual" or "ethical" ones, when he writes: "It was not only the divine mind that had to be responded to, but also that expression of the divine mind which was contained in God's making death the wages of sin."[4] It is impossible for any one who attaches the slightest importance to the New Testament presentation of the facts to question that this last utterance is that which is most in harmony with the apostolic gospel. The one thing that the apostles have to tell about Christ—what they deliver first of all to all men—is that Christ died for our sins. He suffered for them once, the just for the unjust, that He might bring us to God. We are reconciled to God by the death of His Son. He is placarded before our eyes on earth as Χριστὸς ἐσταυρωμένος, Christ in the abiding reality and power of His cross. He is seen in heaven as the ἀρνίον ὡς ἐσφαγμένον; the aspect in which He is of eternal interest to us is that He was slain as a sacrifice, and that the virtue of His sacri-

---

[1] *The Nature of the Atonement*, p. 249. [2] *Ibid.*, p. 262.
[3] *Ibid.*, p. 268. [4] *Ibid.*, p. 261.

RECONCILIATION AS ACHIEVED BY CHRIST

ficial death abides in Him for ever. There is no dispute in Scripture about the spirit in which He died, about His obedience to the Father or His love to men; but in Scripture these things are not separated even in imagination from the cross; they radiate from the cross; they are the meaning and message of the cross, and are not revealed in all their dimensions except through the cross. To insulate them from the cross is to lose them. To a really philosophical mind as well as to a simply Christian one the question, "If Christ had not suffered, would He nevertheless have redeemed us?" is puerile and unreal. The work of redemption has actually been done by Christ who died, and the consent of all Catholic theologians, that He would have redeemed us all the same even if He had not died, adds nothing to our knowledge or understanding. Intelligence is given us, not to ask and answer fancy questions about a world which has never been and never will be, but to interpret the actual world and things as they are. The fact being that Christ has redeemed us to God by His blood, to argue that He would have redeemed us nevertheless, though there had been no cross or passion, is neither profound nor sublime, but irrelevant. To an unsophisticated Christian, to talk of a redemption to which the death of Christ is not essential is to talk about nothing at all. The simplest evangelist here will always confound the subtlest theologian; the foolishness of God is wiser than men.

Plainly what is wanted here is a more concrete, less analysing and abstract way of looking at the death of Christ, than has sometimes established itself in theology. The experiences of a human being are not physical merely, or spiritual merely, they are human; and in humanity the physical and the spiritual coalesce or interpenetrate; they are indissoluble elements in one reality. The same consideration has to be extended to all our thoughts of God's relations to man. God does not deal with us as merely physical or as merely spiritual beings, He deals with us as what we are, beings in whom the physical and the spiritual interpenetrate in the way just described. He deals with us as beings whose life is rooted in the vast world of nature, and vibrates to every throb in its constitution. There are not two abstractly independent worlds, a physical and a spiritual one; to believe in God means to believe that what we call the physical world is caught up and integrated into a system which is spiritual, and that it can and does in the last resort serve as the instrument for expressing the mind and will of God. When we say, for example, that God condemns sin, we do not say something the truth of which is exclusively spiritual; God's condemnation of sin finds expression, in innumerable ways in which not only conscience, or the spiritual element in man as we distinguish it from the physical, is His organ or the sphere of His operations, but the whole constitutional course of nature. When we say that Christ acknowledges the justice of God's condemnation of sin, we do not mean only that He thinks it right that the man who sins should have a bad conscience, and that he should shrink from meeting God and find that fellowship with Him is impossible; we mean further that He acknowledges as just the whole divine reaction against sin which expresses itself in the nature of things, as well as in the soul of man. And He not only acknowledges it as just in itself, He acknowledges it as just while Himself living under it and enduring all that it involved for sinful men, though Himself without sin. Short of this, we do not really get to the Biblical conception of atonement. We do not get to that in the experience of

RECONCILIATION AS ACHIEVED BY CHRIST

Jesus which, as the most unfathomable proof of love, has both supreme value to God and supreme influence with men.

The case may be stated thus. Christ's death was once presented in theology too abstractly, in no relation to His life, simply as the doom of sin, which He came to earth to undergo for us. Apart from His death He was really a sort of lay figure. His whole object in being here was to die, to have the punishment of our sins inflicted on Him at the cross, and so to deliver us from them. It is no wonder that a view so inadequate provoked reactions, and that one more intelligible, more human, more ethically interesting, took its place. The death of Christ was now treated as the culmination of His life, and the key to it was sought in His life. His career was interpreted through categories which are immediately applicable to other lives as well as His, and in this way it seemed to become at the same time more intelligible and more inspiring. It was a career determined throughout by love to God and man; to use ancient terminology, it was the achievement of an infinite merit. His death simply crowns it; it was an act of heroic fidelity in which He resisted unto blood striving against sin. That all this is true, and that there is something in it which appeals to men with reconciling power, is not to be denied. But it is another question whether it is the whole truth, and whether the former view, repellent and inadequate as were many expressions of it, was not occupied with a reality to which the latter fails to do justice. The death of Christ *was* an act of heroism and fidelity, the crown of a life by the whole course of which humanity was ennobled; and when we look at it in this aspect we are moved to think with joy and pride of the heights to which human nature can rise. But it will hardly be asserted that this is the aspect in which the Passion is exclusively or mainly presented to us in the New Testament. The lights there are more solemn, subdued, and awful. There is indeed in the fourth gospel the conception of a triumph pervading everything: "Now is the Son of Man glorified," "now is the Prince of this world cast out." But there is also even there, and still more in the other gospels, the sense of something dreadful and mysterious; a soul trouble of Jesus, a sorrow under which He is dismayed and ready to die, an agony of prayer, a bitter cup from which His whole being shrinks, an uncomprehended necessity for drinking it, a dark experience of being forsaken by God. There is no intention, in recalling these things, either to deny the truth of the view that Christ's death is the moral consummation of His life, and is to be interpreted as such, or to withdraw what has been said above about the *penal* character of His sufferings. They were not penal in the sense of coming to Him through a bad conscience, or in the sense that God was angry with Him personally, as if He had really been a guilty man. But they cannot be ignored; and it seems to the writer that if we contemplate Christ's life and death solely as a moral triumph throughout which He must have enjoyed the approbation of the Father, they must either be ignored, or regarded as due to misapprehensions on the part of Jesus as to the true relation subsisting between Himself and God. Some shadow of unreality would then fall upon His soul trouble, His deadly sorrow, His agony, His sense of dereliction. It is impossible to accept any such view. These solemn things, in which so much of the power of the gospel is hidden, must not only have their complete reality recognised, but their justification sought out. And when we come to the point along

RECONCILIATION AS ACHIEVED BY CHRIST

this line, can we say anything else than this: That while the agony and the Passion were not penal in the sense of coming upon Jesus through a bad conscience, or making Him the personal object of divine wrath, they were penal in the sense that in that dark hour He had to realise to the full the divine reaction against sin in the race in which He was incorporated, and that without doing so to the uttermost He could not have been the Redeemer of that race from sin, or the Reconciler of sinful men to God? When we look at our Lord's life and death from the side of His own initiative, so to speak—when we think of His career from beginning to end as one of truth, love, and fidelity to righteousness, which involved Him in all kinds of suffering and finally in a martyr's death—questions of this kind may never arise, or may be swept away on a flood of evasive eloquence. But when we look at these same things, as we are bound to do, from the side of the divine order—of the constitution of the world as a system in which there is an unceasing, dreadful, and finally fatal reaction against sin; when we see the events of Jesus' last hours, not only as a supreme moral triumph (justifiable as such a view is), but as an experience in which He knew what it was to be appalled, in an agony, stricken and desolate—such questions cannot be repressed. There is no getting past the fact that His sufferings had to do with sin. But they came on Him, not only because He would not sin, not only because He resisted unto blood, striving victoriously against sin, but because the world had sinned, and in becoming part of the world He stood committed to experience as its Saviour everything in which the divine reaction against sin is brought home to the soul. The cup the Father put into His hand, the cup of trembling from which He shrank in deadly fear—this is the meaning of ἀγωνία—was the cup our sins had mingled. It has to be interpreted, not only through the moral heroism of Jesus triumphing over sin, but through the judgment of God reacting inexorably against sin. The Redeemer on His cross not only vanquished every temptation to sin; He bowed His head in solemn submission to God's sentence upon it, and tasted death for every man. It is in this sense, and not only in a "merely" or "purely" spiritual one, that He bore our sins. No one questions that He bore them on His heart. The New Testament uniformly takes this for granted. But He bore them on His heart supremely in the very act and instant of bearing them in His body on the tree, and it is not in distinguishing these as two truths, and still less by denying either, but in insisting upon their indissoluble interpenetration, that we touch the nerve of Christ's reconciling power. If He had not *died* for us, He would have done nothing at all; for of what use to sinful mortal men would be a Saviour who did not know what sin and death mean when they combine, as they do, to crush poor human nature? And if He had not died for us *in love*, He would have done nothing at all; for it is only love, holding out unimpaired through sin and death, and identifying itself at once with God, who inexorably repels sin and yearns with infinite longing over the sinner, and with man, who is lost in sin and death and yet remains capable of redemption, which is able to win for itself and for the God whom it reveals the faith of creatures sinking beneath the indivisible burden of guilt and mortality. Sin is more concrete than moralists are apt to think, and the reactions against it more deep and far reaching. The Greek fathers were not wholly wrong when they emphasised the idea that Christ by His death delivers us from death: they had some sense of the

RECONCILIATION AS ACHIEVED BY CHRIST

unity of death and sin. They realised that redemption was not merely a triumph for Jesus, but a tragedy, the most awful if also the most glorious moment in the history of man; and if we lose the sense of this, we lose the key to any doctrine of reconciliation which can appeal to the New Testament.

This view, no doubt, assumes what is often contested, and what will seem to many transparently false, that there is a real relation between death and sin.[1] As the New Testament puts it, the wages of sin is death. But before this proposition is denied, it should be understood. It is not understood when it is treated as a piece of primitive mythology, the fanciful explanation given of the origin of death before there was any science in existence to give a real explanation. It is not understood when it is supposed to be refuted by the argument that death is natural, that it is really part of the mechanism of life in the system in which we exist, that it belongs to the constitution of nature as much as life itself does, and that it would have reigned in the world exactly as it has done, even if there had never been any such thing as sin. This argument is doubly unconvincing. In the first place, it is irrelevant, for it treats death as something which does not belong to the moral world at all, but only to the natural, whereas the only death with which we are concerned is that which is the experience of moral beings, and must be brought into the moral system and morally interpreted somehow. In the second place, it is unconvincing, because, like the argument that Christ would have redeemed us even if He had never died, it is an argument about what, when we take all the facts into view, is a hypothetical world, and not an argument providing a rationale of the world as it is. In the world as it is, moral

[1] *Vide supra*, pp. 211 f.

beings die, and it is not saying anything to them to say that they die as natural and not as moral, for to their own consciousness their being does not submit to any such analysis; it is indivisibly one, and whatever befalls it must be interpreted within the unity of its moral consciousness. To put it otherwise, the truth that death is the debt of nature does not exclude the idea that it is the wages of sin; no interpretation of it can possibly be adequate if the natural necessity does not become morally significant. And if a real relation between death and sin is not refuted by arguments like these, just as little is it refuted by showing that in any given case death may be not a defeat or a doom, but a triumph. This is true, and every death for others or for a cause illustrates its truth. But it is a triumph over death itself as a real enemy, and it has already been shown that any such triumph over death is at the same time a triumph over sin; in other words, that it assumes the very connection which it is here adduced to disprove. Fundamentally, the question at issue is an aspect of that which has already been discussed in a more general form: namely, whether there is or is not a divine reaction against sin, not limited to conscience, or to the purely spiritual world, as it is sometimes called, but pervading the world of reality in all its dimensions. We have seen cause to answer this question in the affirmative, and the validity of the answer is here assumed. But the conviction it represents is based on moral experiences, and we can refer to moral experience in Paul as the key to his declaration that the wages of sin is death. "When the commandment came," he writes, "sin sprang to life, and I died" (Rom. vii. 9). The "I" is expressed in Greek, and has the emphasis of some tragic recollection in it. As sin came to life, the sinner tasted death. Here

RECONCILIATION AS ACHIEVED BY CHRIST

also it is a mistake to be analytic, and to say that the death meant can only be moral or spiritual death, because the apostle was physically alive long after the experience referred to. Such distinctions are foreign to his thought, and do not give us the key to his experience. What he felt when he was conscious that sin was alive in him was that this was *fatal*. His doom was sealed. Things like what he had done had no right to be, and those who did them had no right to be either. They knew the just appointment of God, that those who do such things are worthy of death (Rom. i. 32). They did not know it from Gen. iii. or from any Scripture, but by that immediate intuition which assured them that in the world of God such things and such people had no permanent place. God was against them. The inmost nature of things was against them. The sentence might not be executed speedily, but it was irrevocably pronounced: the end of those things was death (Rom. vi. 21).

It is only as part of the whole to which such ideas are native and self-evident that we can take in what the New Testament tells us of the death of Christ as a death for sin. A martyr's death, heroic and inspiring as it may be, is not in this sense a death for sin. It may quite well be a death for righteousness. It may quite well be a death from which others reap spiritual benefits, benefits of which the martyrdom may be called the price. The death of Jesus was of course a martyr's death, and has this heroic and inspiring quality; no doubt also, like every great act of self-sacrifice, it has bought advantages for the race. But this is not only unequal to what the New Testament means, when it says that He bore our sins, or that He suffered for sins once, the just for the unjust, and that He made purgation of sins, or that He put away sin by His sacrifice, or that He is the Lamb of

God which taketh away the sin of the world; it does not even point in the direction of these characteristic New Testament utterances. They all assume, in the death of Jesus, a relation to sin which has no parallel in martyrdom. On the cross the sinless Son of God, in love to man and in obedience to the Father, entered submissively into that tragic experience in which sinful men realise all that sin means. He tasted death for every man. The last and deepest thing we can say about His relation to our sins is that He died for them, that He bore them in His own body on the tree: if we could not say this, we could not say that He knew by experience all that sinful men find to be involved in their sin, nor could we say that He had been made perfect in love.

There are two things which for some time have led to the depreciation of this vital centre of the doctrine of reconciliation. One is the extraordinary tendency in some minds to make light of death. We hear it spoken of as if it were nothing in itself, an insignificant incident, a mere point of transition with no critical importance and no profound or dreadful content. The writer can only say that this is a state of mind which seems incomprehensible to him in anybody who has ever seen death. Of all human experiences it is the most solemn and tremendous, and that from which nature most instinctively recoils. It is the greatest thought of which we are capable, except the thought of God, and it is the extreme opposite of the thought of God. It is neither true humanity nor sound Christianity which ignores this. St. Paul can cry in a moment of rapture, when the mystery of the life to come has been revealed to him, "Where, death, is thy victory? where, death, thy sting?" But he knows also that death is the last enemy that shall be destroyed. He can speak of the body of our humiliation, and of the sowing in corruption, in weakness, in dishonour. In the most happy or the most glorious conditions, the death of a spiritual being has an inevitable indignity and humiliation in it; we feel it is revoltingly out of keeping in a nature akin to God. The sense of this must have been peculiarly profound in those who watched Jesus die on the cross, and it may have been through it that the apostles perceived that the key to the inconceivable indignities and sufferings He endured could only be found in this, that He was bearing the sin of the whole world. All that sin in the last resort meant for men was being experienced and exhausted there. The agony and the shame were intelligible to them in this view, and not otherwise.

The other influence which tends to the depreciation of this central truth of the New Testament comes from the idea that it must have been impossible for Christ to taste what death is to the sinful, because He knew no sin. It is the shadow of the bad conscience cast on what is in itself natural and morally neutral which makes death dreadful to the sinner. But Jesus had no bad conscience, and no black shadow, therefore, can have fallen on death for Him. He must have died as the happy warrior dies in the poem, who,

> "While the mortal mist is gathering, draws
> His breath in confidence of heaven's applause."

But we know that this is not true. Without denying that His death could be described in this key, and celebrated as a triumph over sin, we must repeat that it is presented in the gospels primarily as a tragedy in which He gave Himself up to awful divine necessities. But granting this, it is not for any one to settle beforehand how far it was possible for Him, sinless as He was, to enter by dying into the experiences which death is for sinners, to whom it is in some way one with sin. We may be sure that in His unity of will with the holy God, in whose world and by whose will sin is fatal, and in His unity of nature and of love with sinful men, whose whole life was crushed by this fatality, He realised in a way transcending all our measures the doom which sin had brought upon our race. It is only in going through such an experience that He is perfected in love. It is in view of such an experience that John writes: Herein is love, not that we loved God, but that He loved us, and sent His Son a propitiation for our sins.

Both these conceptions of the death of Christ as the basis of reconciliation—the abstract one, which lays all the emphasis on what it characterises as spiritual in the death; and the concrete, to which the death itself is as essential as any spiritual content which can be distinguished from it—are capable of being perverted, and a glance at the commonest perversions will bring out the significance of each in a new light. The purely spiritual view lends itself readily to those who are disposed to obliterate the distinction between the Redeemer and the redeemed. It is revealed without disguise in an American theologian who tells us that "the difficulty largest in size is our lack of redeemers": we ought all to be, and so few of us are, Redeemers, Saviours, Christs. It is not merely cowardice, or self-indulgent shrinking from the cross, which makes such language repellent. It is hideously out of tune with the New Testament, and there must be something in what leads to it which is inadequate to the New Testament truth. Christ has done something for us which gives Him His place for ever as the only Redeemer of men, and, no matter how thoroughly under His inspiration we are changed into His likeness, we never cease to be the redeemed nor invade His solitary place. The fact that a "purely spiritual" conception of the atonement tends to overbalance itself in this direction is an indication that something is wanting in it.

On the other hand, the concrete view, to which the death itself, as the gospels present it, without any distinction of spiritual or physical elements, is of vital importance, can be perverted in another way. Its self-containedness, its outwardness, its historical character, can be emphasised as though it availed for us simply in itself, unconditionally, without any relation to our attitude to it. Men may say, *There* is the atonement—*there*, outside of us. Christ is our substitute, and there is not another word to be said. He suffered that we might be exempted from suffering. He made Himself a sacrifice for sin, that for us sacrifice might be abolished. He took our responsibilities on Himself that we might have no responsibility more. What His death does is to secure impunity for sin; our punishment is transferred to Him, and the penal consequences of sin need not trouble us further.

It cannot be denied that this perversion of the truth that Christ died for our sins has actually emerged in human experience. The heart is deceitful above all things, and desperately wicked, and it does not stick at corrupting the best into the worst. Even in the apostolic age the thought came to the surface, "Let us continue in sin that grace may abound." But this perversion has not been so common as is sometimes supposed. It has indeed been charged from the beginning against what may be called the evangelical doctrine of atonement, but as an actual or possible result of it in practice, rather than as something to which it led in principle. From Faustus Socinus to the present day the charge has been familiar. In one way it is conspicuously unfair. It allows that the conception of Christ as a substitute operates as a motive, but it assumes that it must always operate as an immoral motive. It represents those who think of Christ on His cross as their substitute as though they were of necessity scoundrels or sneaks, who sought and found nothing in the atonement but a way to continue in sin and escape the consequences. But this is mere unintelligent slander. The conception of Christ as the sinner's substitute may be inadequate to the truth, but it is absurd to say that when it becomes a motive it can only be a motive to vice. In an honest heart it is a motive to gratitude, to love, to devotion, and there have been countless honest hearts among those whose Christian theology has been condensed in this much-censured term. The very fact that it precludes the idea that the Christian himself is to become a Christ or a Redeemer is proof that in it, and in the concrete view of the death of Christ on which it rests, there is something which does greater justice to the New Testament than is done by the purely spiritual view. And if the term itself is objectionable, as admitting of equivocal inferences, it only prompts us to look for better terms which will preclude such inferences, without imperilling the truth which, with whatever drawbacks, the term in question covers.

The matter may be put thus. The concrete view of Christ's death, and the conception of it as in some sense substitutionary, cover the truth that there is something from which Christ's death saves the sinner. It does not save him unconditionally, or apart from any relation he assumes to it; and in the following lecture the conditions on which the Saviour's death avails for salvation will be considered. But it does save the sinner from something. There is some-

RECONCILIATION AS ACHIEVED BY CHRIST

thing from which he is exempted—the due conditions being fulfilled—by the death of Jesus. In other words, Jesus died *for* him, in an irreducible sense of these words; He died for him in a sense and with a potential result which can never be ascribed to any action or experience of his own or of others, but only and for ever to the death of Jesus itself. If the question is put, What, then, is it which we are spared or saved from by the death of Jesus—what is it that we do not experience because He died?—the answer is that He saves us from dying in our sins. But for His death we should have died in our sins; we should have passed into the blackness of darkness with the condemnation of God abiding on us. It is because He died for us, and for no other reason, that the darkness has passed away, and a light shines in which we have peace with God and rejoice in hope of His glory. On the basis of the New Testament, of Christian experience, and of a theistic view of nature to which the separation of physical and spiritual cannot be the final truth, the writer has done what he can to indicate the rationale of this; but imperfect as all such attempts must be, their imperfection does not shake the conviction that they are attempts to deal with a fact, and that fact the one which is vital to Christianity. There are two characteristics of New Testament religion which confirm, as they are only intelligible under this view of the facts. The first is its deep and ever present sense of debt to Christ. This pervades the New Testament throughout, but is most vivid and intense in presence of the cross. It is the inspiration of those doxologies to the Redeemer, which are the very signature of the new religion. And there is no adequate explanation of this feeling which does not recognise that it is thanks to the cross and to what was once for all suffered there, that the doom with which sin threatened our life is lifted, that fear is expelled, and that faith in the love of God fills the heart in its stead. Further, New Testament religion is characterised by a kind of assurance—an *initial* assurance, on which it is sustained from the outset—which cannot be explained at all except on the assumption that the one thing needful for the salvation of sinners was once for all done and endured at the cross. No matter how potent the Passion of Christ may be as a motive to reproduce in us its own characteristic moral qualities, the Christian attitude to it is not that of repeating it; it is that of depending upon it, believing in it, trusting to it to the uttermost. Of course it is a motive of transcendent power, but it is its completeness and finality in itself which make it such a motive, and it is as final and complete in itself that the apostles contemplate it. When we alter the order, the balance, or the proportion of those truths, we are apt to get into an atmosphere which is not that of the New Testament. This is felt even in a book so profoundly spiritual and Christian as Moberly's *Atonement and Personality*. The great word of the New Testament, when the conditions of salvation are concerned, is faith; but faith is a term which hardly figures in Dr. Moberly's exposition at all. He is preoccupied with penitence, with experiences of the soul in relation to sin, not with faith, the experience of the soul in relation to the Saviour. There is no initial assurance in Christianity as he unfolds it, and even a reader who is conscious that faith without penitence is not faith but presumption, cannot get over the feeling that, as compared with that of the New Testament, the Christianity Dr. Moberly expounds has *no pulse*. We lose contact with the New Testament utterly unless we can say from the beginning that because of what Christ suffered for

RECONCILIATION AS ACHIEVED BY CHRIST

us, and on that ground alone, the doom of sin is no longer the doom of those who believe on Him. "Who is he that condemneth? Think of Christ who died!" The Christian life has a beginning as well as a goal, and there is an exultation that belongs to the starting on the race as well as to the finishing of the course. There is not only a rejoicing in God who will perfect that which concerns us, but a rejoicing in God who justifies the ungodly. To depress or extinguish this latter joy is not only to take away all that can be called gospel from sinners, it is to deny its proper meaning and virtue to the Passion of Jesus.[1]

---

[1] It is naturally impossible for any one to write a book on the atonement and not mention faith, and there are one or two explicit references to it in *Atonement and Personality*. Thus on p. 284 we read: "It is not by becoming like Him that men will approach towards incorporation with Him; but by result of incorporation with Him, received in faith as a gift, and in faith adored, *and used,* that they will become like Him." But even this, highly equivocal as it is, stands practically alone. There is nothing which answers to the fact that in the New Testament μετανοεῖν and μετάνοια occur in all 55 times, but πίστις and πιστεύειν 470 times.

CHAPTER VI

RECONCILIATION AS REALISED IN HUMAN LIFE

WHAT has been before us in the previous chapter is reconciliation conceived as the finished work of Christ. It is not a work, so far, which sinners do, nor which is done in them; it is a finished work which is done for them. The legitimacy and necessity of this point of view it is vain to dispute. No one, however, questions that the finished work of Christ must in some way become effective for sinners—must in some way become a power in their lives—if reconciliation is to be realised in their experience. In other words, it must somehow be mediated to them, and this is the subject we have now to consider. We cannot evade it by thinking of the sinner as immediately or unconditionally involved in Christ's work. We cannot evade it, for example, by speaking of Christ's humanity as not individual but inclusive, so that it was not so truly He who achieved the work of reconciliation as the human race in Him; and by then inferring from this assumed metaphysical unity of the sinner with the Saviour all Christian experiences of reconciliation and salvation. To do this is really to abandon the ground of experience at the very point at which it is both necessary and possible to adhere to it most closely. The message of the gospel—the word of reconciliation, as Paul calls it—is not the message of what we have done in Christ, it is the message of what Christ has done for us, and especially of

RECONCILIATION AS REALISED IN HUMAN LIFE

what He has done for us in His death; and the question that remains for our consideration is not one of metaphysics, but of simple fact and experience: How does what Christ did for us, especially on the cross, become a power in our life? A "power" is the New Testament name for it. "I am not ashamed of the gospel, for it is the power of God to salvation to every one who believes" (Rom. i. 16). "The word of the cross is to those who perish folly, but to us who are saved it is the power of God" (1 Cor. i. 18).

It is perhaps necessary to remark that when we speak of a finished work of Christ we do not think of separating the work from Him who achieved it. The New Testament knows only of a living Christ, and all apostolic preaching of the gospel holds up the living Christ to men. But the living Christ is Christ who died, and He is never preached apart from His death and from its reconciling power. It is the living Christ, with the virtue of His reconciling death in Him, who is the burden of the apostolic message, and nothing could be more curiously unlike the New Testament than to use the resurrection to belittle or disparage the death.[1] The task of the evangelist is to preach Christ—of course the living Christ—but in His character as the Crucified; it is to set Him forth in his message, as God has set Him forth already in fact, as "a propitiation, through faith, in His blood." This is the word of reconciliation in the sense of the New Testament, and the Pauline expression just quoted points to the way in which the reconciliation achieved by Christ avails and becomes effective for sinful men. It is through faith. Faith fills the New Testa-

---

[1] As, for example, in Lofthouse, *Ethics and Atonement*, p. 191: "St. Paul never forgets that the resurrection would have been impossible without the death; but the value of the death is that it made possible the resurrection."

ment as completely as Christ does; it is the correlative of Christ wherever Christ really touches the life of men. It is not an arbitrary condition on which forgiveness is granted, or on which the reconciliation achieved by Christ is held to apply to sinners; it is that for which Christ, as the author of the work of reconciliation, by the nature of the case appeals, and when His appeal is met by the response of faith, the faith itself is natural, spontaneous, and in a sense inevitable. It is the right reaction to a new reality brought into the sinner's environment—a new reality so profound and final that the right reaction to it completely transforms him, making him in Scripture language a new creature (2 Cor. v. 17; Gal. vi. 15).

It is important to get rid of the idea that there is anything arbitrary in faith—that it is a condition to which it has pleased God, for reasons best known to Himself, to attach man's salvation, but which, so far as we can see, might just as well have been anything else. It is ideas of this kind which make faith itself a doubtful and uncertain quantity; which raise all sorts of unreal questions as to whether any alleged faith is of the proper kind; which get lost in attempts to distinguish between faith and works, inasmuch as this arbitrarily demanded faith is itself but a kind of work, on which salvation is made legally dependent; and which, worse than all, inevitably leave something artificial in the connection between faith and salvation, an artificiality revealed in all the distinctions between imputed righteousness and infused righteousness, or between the righteousness of faith and that of life, or between justification and sanctification, as things which must indeed both be provided for, but which have no natural, vital, or organic connection with each other. This perplexing and some-

RECONCILIATION AS REALISED IN HUMAN LIFE

times repellent part of the field of theology is cleared and simplified when we see that there is nothing arbitrary in faith, and that it is not so much a condition on which salvation is by the will of God made to depend, as the one natural and inevitable way in which the salvation of God, present in Christ, is and must be accepted by men. When a man has heard the story of Jesus and the gospel interpretation of it—when he takes in the truth that what is before him on the cross is the revelation of a love in God deeper and stronger than sin, entering into all that sin means for him and taking the burden of it, in all its dreadful pressure, upon itself, yet clinging to him through it all, and making to him the final appeal which God can make—what is he to do? What does the situation require of him? Is it legitimate or becoming for him to say that such a revelation of love is unnecessary for him, or irrelevant to his requirements? To say so would be to say that he had no sin, or none with which he did not feel competent to deal without such aid. Is it legitimate for him to say that such a revelation of love is too much, and to attempt negotiations with God on the assumption that further consideration might discover a way of salvation costing less to God, and not so overwhelming to the sinner? Or can he surround the word of reconciliation with conditions of his own, and refuse to take the benefit of God's reconciling love till he has provided moral guarantees that it will not be abused—whether the guarantees are supposed to be given in a sufficient repentance for past sins, or in a sufficient amendment of life for the future? All these suppositions are impossible. If a man with the sense of his sin on him sees what Christ on His cross means, there is only one thing for him to do—one thing which is inevitably demanded in that moral situation: to abandon himself to the sin-bearing love which appeals to Him in Christ, and to do so unreservedly, unconditionally, and for ever. This is what the New Testament means by faith. It is the only thing which is true to the situation in which the sinner finds himself when he is confronted with Christ and the work of reconciliation achieved by Him. To believe in Christ and in the sin-bearing love revealed in Him is to do the one right thing for which the situation calls. When the sinner does thus believe he does the one right thing, and it puts him right with God; in St. Paul's language he is justified by faith. God accepts him as righteous, and he *is* righteous; he has received the reconciliation (Rom. v. 11), and he *is* reconciled. It is quite needless to complicate this simple situation by discussing such questions as whether justification is "forensic," or has some other character, say "real" or "vital," to which "forensic" is more or less of a contrast. Even if Paul envisaged men, as he undoubtedly sometimes did, as standing at God's bar, it does not follow that this situation suggested any such contrasts to his mind. Even in the *fora* of men, the degree to which the "forensic" emerges is very different. There are some in which very abstract and superficial aspects of reality are alone open to consideration, and their verdicts and sentences may be in a high degree "forensic." There may be a wide gulf between the justification—if it should so be—pronounced in such *fora*, and the verdict of God or of conscience upon the case. But in the *forum* of God, at the bar of His tribunal, no occasion can arise for drawing such distinctions. It is nothing superficial or imperfectly real about God which is revealed in the work of reconciliation achieved by Christ; on the contrary, it is the ultimate truth of the divine nature; the deepest thing we can ever know about God is that there is love in Him which bears in all its reality the sin of the world. And there is nothing superficial in what the New Testament calls faith, in its relation to this ultimate truth in God; on the contrary, faith exhausts in itself the being of man in this direction; it is his absolute committal of himself for ever to the sin-bearing love of God for salvation. It is not simply the act of an instant, it is the attitude of a life; it is the one right thing at the moment when a man abandons himself to Christ, and it is the one thing which keeps him right with God for ever. It is just as truly the whole of Christianity subjectively as Christ is the whole of it objectively, and it is no more lawful to supplement or to eke out faith than to supplement or to eke out Christ. Luther is abundantly right in his emphasis on faith alone. It is just the other side of Christ alone. Every Christian experience whatsoever—call it justification, adoption, or sanctification—call it love, or repentance, or regeneration, or the Spirit—lies within faith and is dependent upon it. The virtue of all observances, sacramental or other, is conditioned by it. No doubt, as a term in ordinary use, it is found in the New Testament in narrower meanings and with more restricted applications; but where Christ or the gospel is the object of faith, faith is as comprehensive as Christ or the gospel, and as little raises any questions about what is or is not merely forensic in its issues. It is what the situation demands, and the believer is not one who is reputed to be, but one who in his very being as a believer actually is, right with God. There is no legal fiction in the matter to explain or to overcome; if we think in terms of a *forum*—which we may do if we please—we must remember that the *forum* is that of God, and that the verdict there is always "according to truth."

THE CHRISTIAN DOCTRINE OF RECONCILIATION

When He pronounces the sinner δίκαιος, he *is* δίκαιος. Before he saw Christ and believed in Him he was all wrong with God: God could do nothing but condemn him. Now, in virtue of his faith, he is all right with God, and there is henceforth no condemnation for him. Nor in all this is there anything unreal, anything akin to legal fiction, and needing to be supplemented or transcended by something going beyond faith. Nothing can by any possibility go beyond faith, and the whole promise and potency of Christianity are present in it. The sinner who through faith is right with God is certainly not made perfect in holiness, but the power which alone can make him perfect is already really and vitally operative in him. And it is operative in him only in and through his faith.

Ever since the word of reconciliation was preached by the apostles there have been perplexities and confusions about the relation of the different stages in the Christian life, and especially, to borrow the words in their ordinary Protestant sense, about the relation of justification to sanctification. St. Paul's gospel of justification by faith apart from works of law was construed by some as if it meant a privilege to continue in sin; they saw nothing in justification or forgiveness or faith which essentially or inevitably guaranteed a good life. Those interpreters who find in the sixth, seventh, and eighth chapters of Romans not the explanation of what is implicit in the third, fourth, and fifth, but an addition or supplement to them, in which baptism, or the Spirit, or union with Christ is introduced as a new power to guarantee what is not guaranteed by Christ the propitiation and by faith in Him, virtually take the same position. The "forensic" gospel of justification is for them replaced or eked out by the "ethical" gospel of mystical

RECONCILIATION AS REALISED IN HUMAN LIFE

union with Christ in His death and resurrection; but it is a real case of replacement or eking out; there is no vital or necessary connection between the two things. This is a point of such importance that it is worth while dwelling on it.

The primary interest of it is its bearing on the proper temper of the Christian life, and especially on the place of assurance in it. When we think of the process in which reconciliation works itself out from day to day and year to year, we are face to face with something which is not yet complete; indeed the question forces itself on us whether it can ever be complete on earth. Is not the issue of it, to the last, ambiguous? Can we prevent uncertainty, suspense, and fear hanging over all our life? We are not really and fully right with God; the best we can do is to hope that some day we may be; to hope—and also to fear. In the Church of Rome, and to a considerable extent in the Anglican Church, this temper has predominated. Assurance has been dreaded as lending itself too readily to presumption. It cannot be denied that both the New Testament and human experience speak gravely of the possibilities in this direction. Paul himself practised the severest self-discipline, lest having preached to others he himself should be rejected (1 Cor. ix. 24-27). But neither can it be denied that the temper of timidity, suspense, and uncertainty is not that which predominates in the New Testament. The great awe of the judgment to come does not tell on the believing mind as a power which calls into doubt the reconciling love of God in Christ, or deprives the believer of his joy in it. Rather are we astounded by the assurance with which the apostles speak both of the present and of the future. "Being justified by faith, we have peace with God through our Lord Jesus

Christ, through whom also we have access by faith into this grace wherein we stand, and rejoice in hope of the glory of God" (Rom. v. 1 f.). "It is God that justifieth: who is he that shall condemn?" (Rom. viii. 33). "I am persuaded that neither death, nor life, nor angels, nor principalities, nor powers, nor things present, nor things to come, nor height, nor depth, nor any other creature, shall be able to separate us from the love of God in Christ Jesus our Lord" (Rom. viii. 38 f.). The emotion is not the same, but John also can speak of having "boldness in the day of judgment" (1 John iv. 17), and again of "having boldness and not being ashamed before Him at His coming" (*ib.* ii. 28). The tone and temper of these passages are not characteristic of the historical Churches mentioned, as they are of the New Testament; and the reason seems to be that amid the contingencies and perils of common life they have allowed Christ and faith, in their New Testament dimensions, to fall more into the background than they do in the apostolic writings. They attempt, so to speak, to justify justification too much on the ground of what has been accomplished, or is one day to be accomplished, in the justified, though as yet it can only be seen in germ or promise, and too little on the ground of what Christ has accomplished once for all, and of the faith which His achievement perpetually wins anew from the sinful soul.

If we turn to typical Reformation preachers or theologians, we see the other side of the shield. Luther and those who learned from him were conscious that they were getting a sight of the gospel such as they had never had before, and such as made all things new for them. It gave them what their sinful souls needed and craved for, but what they could never find in any system of ecclesiastical observances, however venerable, nor by any moral efforts of their own, however sincere. It gave them an initial religious assurance, in the strength of which—and only in the strength of which —a new life was possible for them; it filled their souls from the outset with peace, joy, and hope. This initial religious assurance—this assurance of justification, not as God's verdict at the close of a perfect life, but as God's free unmerited mercy to the believing sinner, through which alone he could set out on life, finding the gate of righteousness which he had shut in his own face thrown by redeeming love wide open—this initial religious assurance is the essential mark of Reformation Christianity. The faith in which it is involved is not to be defined by reference to any theological or scholastic standard; it is not any attitude to a creed; it is the whole being and attitude of the soul as determined by the sin-bearing love of God in Christ. That love, and that love alone, evokes it, and on that love and that alone it rests. But just for that reason it keeps that love separate from everything else—separate even from its own consequences in the believing soul. When it believes in it, we may almost say it is for what it is, not for what it does. The soul does not first scrutinise itself, and, when it has discovered in itself sufficient traces of Christ's power to transform it, yield Him thereafter a proportionate faith, or feel entitled to a proportionate assurance; the moment it sees what Christ is and means, that moment it abandons itself passionately and unreservedly to Him, and it is solely on what He is that it rests its assured hope for ever. That it will be like Him one day is guaranteed to faith by what He is.

It is a crude way of putting this, to say that the interest of the Reformation was primarily religious rather than moral. But though it is crude, it is not untrue. No doubt religion must be ethical through and through, and it was through the needs of the moral nature that the eyes of the Reformers were opened to the true import of the gospel. But religion must also in some sense transcend morality, or it has no *raison d'être*. It must deal with moral failure, and have power to renew the moral life when it has been discomfited and driven to despair. This was clearly seen by the Reformers, and it is their glory to have asserted it; but it became the fault of later Protestantism that, in its desire to safeguard the initial religious assurance apart from which the new life cannot be launched—a thoroughly legitimate and essential object if New Testament Christianity was to survive—it lost at least in some quarters the sense that to this initial religious assurance the new life was immediately and vitally related. It thought more about Christ than it did about the new creature, and faith tended to become intellectualised; faith was rather the acceptance of true thoughts about revelation than the sudden and irresistible conquest of the whole being by the Redeemer. This was a Romish rather than a Reformation idea of faith; and when it made way in the Protestant Churches, and overlaid the original Reformation idea, which was also that of the New Testament, it found these Churches less protected than the Romish Church, by their constitution and discipline, against some practical abuses to which it led. Thus it was quite natural, and it seemed a right way of honouring the Saviour, to distinguish that initial justification or acceptance with God, which is as complete in itself as the sin-bearing love on which it rests, from the painfully acquired sanctification which no doubt is conditioned by it, but which is permanently incomplete. It was natural to do this, and to contrast the

RECONCILIATION AS REALISED IN HUMAN LIFE

perfect work of Christ, and our absolute dependence on it, with the imperfect work which in a sense is our achievement as well as His. But though this was natural, there was something in it radically unsound. The only justification of which the New Testament speaks is justification of *life* (Rom. v. 18); what Paul does with his faith is to *live* by it (Gal. ii. 20). There is no religious assurance contemplated by the apostles which is not *ipso facto* a new moral power. Protestantism has had its saints, whatever the ignorant may say, but the candid student of theological history will admit, what great and simple souls like Chalmers have avowed, that it has suffered from the tendency to dwell on the initial religious assurance—on faith and justification—too abstractly, and with too little regard to its spontaneous and inevitable outcome in the new life. It has exhausted itself in attempts to distinguish justification from sanctification, partly to give Christ all the glory which is His due as the sin-bearer, partly to safeguard for the sinner an assurance of mercy not dependent on his own achievements; and in these quite intelligible and legitimate interests it has sometimes forgotten that the great matter is not the distinction of justification and sanctification, but their connection, and that justification or reconciliation is a delusion unless the life of the reconciled and justified is inevitably and naturally a holy life.

In the Romish Church, when the Reformation brought on a crisis in its history, the interest was different. Those who in the sixteenth century adhered to the existing order, did not, like Luther, and those who learned from him, get a new vision of Christ, which made all things new, and brought an infinite emancipation and joy to the sinful soul. It was their task to guard with anxious care a vast institution

THE CHRISTIAN DOCTRINE OF RECONCILIATION

with which, as they might assert, the moral wellbeing of humanity was bound up; and from this point of view it might be said that the interest of the Romish Church was in morality rather than religion. It is indeed paradoxical to say this of a Church which owed so much to two of the most infamous institutions in the moral history of mankind, the Spanish Inquisition and the Society of Jesus; but it will not be misunderstood by any one who studies the Canons and Decrees of the Council of Trent on the subject of justification. In the seventh chapter of the sixth session of the Council there is an elaborate statement of what justification is which may be cited in illustration. Barring the sacramental part of it, it has often appealed even to Protestants as at once comprehensive and cautious, doing justice to some things which in the exuberant utterance of revival-preachers, like Paul and Luther, were perhaps not explicitly enough regarded, and shutting up beforehand a variety of bypaths down which heedless souls might be tempted by the flesh or the devil. Justification itself—which is here assumed to be the state of the man reconciled to God through faith in Christ—is defined as "not remission of sins merely, but also the sanctification and renewal of the inward man through the voluntary reception of the graces and gifts whereby man of unjust becomes just, and of an enemy a friend, that so he may be *an heir according to the hope of life everlasting*. Of this justification the causes are these: the final cause indeed is the glory of God and of Jesus Christ, and life everlasting; while the efficient cause is a merciful God who washes and sanctifies gratuitously, sealing and anointing with the Holy *Spirit of promise, who is the pledge of our inheritance;* the meritorious cause is His most beloved only begotten, our Lord Jesus Christ, who when we were sinners,

RECONCILIATION AS REALISED IN HUMAN LIFE

for the exceeding charity with which He loved us, merited justification for us by His most holy Passion on the wood of the cross, and made satisfaction for us unto God the Father; the instrumental cause is the sacrament of baptism, which is the sacrament of faith, without which [faith] no man was ever justified; lastly, the alone formal cause is the justice of God, not that whereby He Himself is just, but that whereby He maketh us just, that, to wit, with which *we*, being endowed by Him, *are renewed in the spirit of our mind*, and are not only reputed but are truly called and are just, receiving justice within us, each one according to his own measure, *which the Holy Ghost distributes to every one as He wills*, and according to each man's disposition and co-operation. For although no one can be just, but he to whom the merits of our Lord Jesus Christ are communicated, yet is this done in the said justification of the impious when, by the merit of that same holy Passion, *the charity of God is poured forth* by the Holy Spirit *in the hearts* of those that are justified, and is inherent therein: whence man, through Jesus Christ, in whom he is ingrafted, receives in the said justification, together with the remission of sins, all these [gifts] infused at once, faith, hope, and charity. For faith, unless hope and charity be added thereto, neither unites man perfectly with Christ, nor makes him a living member of His body. For which reason it is most truly said, that *Faith without works is dead* and profitless; and, *In Christ Jesus neither circumcision availeth anything nor uncircumcision, but faith which worketh by charity.* This faith catechumens beg of the Church —agreeably to a tradition of the apostles—previously to the sacrament of baptism; when they beg for the faith which bestows life everlasting, which without hope and charity faith cannot bestow; whence also do they immediately hear that word of Christ: *If thou wilt enter into life, keep the commandments.*" [1]

This exhaustive analysis and definition, in which all the "causes" of justification are precisely distinguished—final, efficient, meritorious, instrumental, and formal—may be said to aim at doing justice to every aspect of the truth, religious and ethical alike; but its controversial purpose is unquestionable. It is aimed at the Protestant conception of justification, which was regarded as failing to safeguard moral interests, and as maintaining a faith or a religion in which ethical distinctions ceased to count. In this sense it may be said that the interest emphasised here is the moral one which the Reformation was charged with neglecting. Justification is defined not as remission of sins merely—this was assumed to be the Lutheran definition—but as the sanctification and renewal of the inward man, through the voluntary reception of the graces and gifts whereby man of unjust became just, and so on. But legitimate as the interest in the new life is—and legitimate also as is the resolve to connect it immediately and vitally with justification—it cannot be admitted that the way in which this legitimate interest and resolve are here satisfied has any analogy in the New Testament. The faith which is here spoken of—a faith which catechumens seek from the Church before baptism *ex apostolorum traditione*, and to which hope and charity have somehow to be added—has no definable relation to the faith which in St. Paul (and in Reformation religion) is the sum total of Christian life, the indivisible and all-inclusive response of the soul to Christ. In spite

---

[1] The translation is borrowed, with the single change of *signing* into *sealing* (for *signans*), from Schaff, *The Creeds of the Greek and Latin Churches*, pp. 94 ff.

RECONCILIATION AS REALISED IN HUMAN LIFE

of the mention of our Lord Jesus Christ and of the exceeding charity with which He loved us, it is not recognised that the soul's response to that love, its abandonment to it as the last reality in God—which the New Testament calls faith—must have love as of its very essence. To speak of love as some kind of *plus* to faith is to depart at once from the facts and the language of the New Testament. But the fundamental objection to the way in which the new life is safeguarded in the Tridentine definition is that with its references to graces and gifts, such as love and hope, which must be added to faith to make the new life secure, it is operating with categories which are inadequate to the personal relations of the soul and Christ in which alone that life is realised. Grace is not a thing which can be infused, nor is there any meaning in such an expression as that love is inherent in the heart; there are no gifts of grace which, so to speak, can be lodged bodily in the soul. Grace is the attitude of God to man which is revealed and made sure in Christ, and the only way in which it becomes effective in us for new life is when it wins for us the response of faith. And just as grace is the whole attitude of God in Christ to sinful men, so faith is the whole attitude of the sinful soul as it surrenders itself to that grace. Whether we call it the life of the justified, or the life of the reconciled, or the life of the regenerate, or the life of grace or of love, the new life is the life of faith and nothing else. To maintain the original attitude of welcoming God's love as it is revealed in Christ bearing our sins—not only to trust it, but to go on trusting—not merely to believe in it as a mode of transition from the old to the new, but to keep on believing—to say with every breath we draw, "Thou, O Christ, art all I want; more than all in Thee I find"—is not a part of the

Christian life but the whole of it. It does not need to be, and cannot be, supplemented or eked out by "gifts" and "graces." All gifts and graces are where Christ is, and faith is the indivisible acceptance of them all in Him. Everything is present in faith—not indeed as something begged from the Church *ex apostolorum traditione*, but as that which is evoked in the soul by the love of Jesus. Everything is present in it—contrition, love, the impulse to self-sacrifice, the whole manifestation of Christianity in life and act. "The life that I now live in the flesh I live by faith, faith in the Son of God who loved me and gave Himself up for me" (Gal. ii. 20).

Faith of this scope and intensity is easily misunderstood, and it is often set in some kind of contrast to Christian experiences which are really dependent upon it. This makes it desirable to show in more detail how fundamental faith is to every experience in which reconciliation is realised in the life of sinful men.

A favourite Pauline description of the Christian life is that it is a life "in Christ." The Christian is conceived as one who lives and moves and has his being in Christ; to say, "I knew a man in Christ" is the same thing as to say, "I knew a Christian man." This being in Christ is specially represented as being one with Him in the great experiences in which the gospel is concentrated, His death and His resurrection. It means that the Christian dies with his Lord and rises with Him. It finds passionate and classical expression in the Epistle to the Galatians (ii. 20): "I have been crucified with Christ, and it is no more I that live, but Christ that liveth in me." On the basis of such expressions as these the doctrine of a union—sometimes it is called a mystical union—of Christ and the Christian has been supported;

RECONCILIATION AS REALISED IN HUMAN LIFE

and either justification or reconciliation itself, or the life of the justified and reconciled, is explained by reference to this union. The objective atonement, the finished work of Christ on the cross, is viewed with impatience if it is not denied, and union with Christ, participation in His death and resurrection, is regarded as something far higher and finer, and containing far surer guarantees for a new and holy life, than mere trust in one who died for our sins.

Such a mode of thought, however, involves a complete departure from New Testament lines. Certainly the New Testament is full of the idea that the Christian is united to Christ, that in a real sense he is one with his Lord. But he is one with Him simply and solely through faith. It is not indeed faith in the sense of the Council of Trent, faith as a creed which has been transmitted by the apostles and is taught by the Church for the acceptance of its children; such faith unites no one to Christ. It is faith as a passion in which the whole being of man is caught up and abandoned unconditionally to the love revealed in the Saviour; faith to which love is integral, because it is itself a response to a love which passes knowledge. But the one thing in the universe which evokes such faith—the one thing therefore which brings any one into union with Christ in the sense of the New Testament—is the love of Christ in which He bears our sins in His own body on the tree. What enabled Paul to say, "I am crucified with Christ, and it is no more I that live but Christ that liveth in me," was his faith in the Son of God, who loved him and gave Himself up for him. It is not permissible to speak of union with Christ except in this atmosphere, and with this intensity of feeling. It is true when it is the expression of apostolic passion; when it is the expression of commonplace orthodox formal piety it is not only false but repulsive.

Faith in Christ who died for us is a power so strong that through it we are, so to speak, lost in Him. The feeble stream of our life, with all its aimless eddies and wanderings, is caught up and carried forward in the mighty stream of His eternal life. To say that through faith we die with Him and live with Him is to give a vivid and pictorial statement of the truth, conditioned by the fact that the death and resurrection of Jesus were the great *momenta* of His reconciling work as it is exhibited in the gospel. But to die with Him and to live with Him are themselves expressions which need interpretation. As applied to Jesus they have a historical, it might even be said a physical sense, in which they do not apply to us. We do not, even in virtue of our union with Him through faith, die as He died on Calvary, and rise into newness of life as He rose from Joseph's grave. There may be a continuity between this and our present experience in union with Him, but this is not our present experience. Our dying with Him, even if we call it, as Paul does, our crucifixion with Him, is a present and an ethical experience; it is a dying to sin, a being or rather a becoming insensible to its appeals and its power; our living with Him is a being alive to God, a new sensibility to His claim upon our life. In other words, our union with Christ is not metaphysical or mystical, but moral; it is not a basis for a new life such as faith could not give, or such as includes a security for the new life beyond what faith could bestow; it is something achieved by faith in the very measure in which faith makes Christ's attitude to sin and to God its own. It is this which gives importance to all that was said in the last chapter of the ethical content of the Passion of Jesus. When we believe in Him, we believe in this. All His thoughts and feelings in relation to sin as disclosed in His Passion—all His submission to the Father who condemns sin and reacts inexorably against it—all His obedience in the spirit of sonship—in their measure become ours through faith. This itself, and nothing else, is our union to Christ. It is something which is accomplished through faith and the experiences to which faith leads, not something which has an antecedent existence and value of its own on which faith can presume. Faith freely and passionately identifies the sinner with the sin-bearer, absorbing into itself all His attitude in relation to sin: this is the only union with Christ of which experience has a word to say.

Sometimes, however, this subject is approached from the other side, and emphasis is laid not on our union with Christ, but on His union with us. This is apparently what is in view in the doctrine that Christ's humanity is not individual, but inclusive, and that therefore all that He did and suffered was somehow done and suffered by us. It was humanity which in Him made atonement for sin and rose again from the dead. His acts and experiences, including His Passion and resurrection, were racial acts and experiences; they were ours in Him; we might almost say they were ours as well as His. Even if we allow that this is intelligible, it is difficult to see where its interest or its moral power lies. St. Paul does indeed represent Christ as the head of a new humanity, as a typical or representative person, whose action, like that of Adam, has universal significance, and with whom all men can identify themselves; but the mere existence of Christ does not constitute the new humanity. It is only constituted as men in faith freely identify themselves with Him. And it ought to be clearly understood that the power in Christ which wins from men the faith in which they freely identify themselves with Him does not lie in any metaphysical fact, like His inclusive humanity—if such a thing there be—but in the moral fact that the Son of God freely and in love identified Himself with us. He looked not on His own things only, but on our low and lost life. When He was rich, for our sakes He became poor. He was not ashamed to call us brethren. He bore our sins. It is not His being essentially and metaphysically one with us which counts in the gospel—to such words most people who need salvation have difficulty in attaching any meaning; it is His free self-identification with us as condemned and unsheltered men in which His whole power to save lies. Christ's union with us is a union in love, and our union with Him is a union in the faith evoked by this love. As long as we occupy this ground we know that we are in the real moral world; we have fact and experience to stand upon. That there is anything to be gained by venturing beyond it into the regions of mysticism and metaphysics is at best problematical. It is certainly no gain, but a serious if not a fatal loss, to foster the impression that the New Testament can be understood at a lower moral temperature than that at which it was written, and to extract from the loftiest outbursts of apostolic passion nothing better than support for a pretentious and not very intelligible idea of Christ's metaphysical relation to mankind.

It hardly needs to be said that no union of Christ with men or of men with Christ is contemplated in the New Testament which would destroy the personality or individuality of the sinner. There are some things which it is hardly possible for a man to utter, and the passion which leaps up

RECONCILIATION AS REALISED IN HUMAN LIFE

to express them may at times overleap itself. When Paul exclaimed, "It is no more I that live but Christ liveth in me," he was throwing out words at one of these permanently inexpressible things, and it is beside the mark to reduce them to cold prose and read them as if they had been dictated in a psychologist's laboratory; they do not mean that Christ or the Spirit of Christ had become the "constituting reality"[1] of Paul himself, so that Paul virtually ceased to be, his old personality vanishing, and that of Christ appearing in its place. Paul never ceased to be; if he had, he would not have been saved in Christ, but lost in God. Whatever union with Christ does, it enables a man to become himself, the true self with all the individuality for which God created Him; when Paul says, "I live no longer, but Christ liveth in me," he is not declaring his pure passivity or abnegation of striving henceforth, but the completeness with which Christ is taking his personality into His service.

This leads one naturally to speak of another mode in which the life of the reconciled is represented in the New Testament —that which explains it not as life in union with Christ, but as life in the Spirit. Of all New Testament subjects on which much has been written, one may venture to think the doctrine of the Spirit the most unfortunate. It has become popular in circles in which the conditions are wanting for the proper appreciation of the New Testament facts, and there are coteries of Christians, not without influence, whose very badge is a way of thinking, or at least of speaking, about the Spirit, which to many of their fellow Christians seems eccentric and unreal. Unquestionably the New Testament justifies the amplest attention to the place of the Spirit in the life of reconciliation, but it is not so easy to do justice

[1] Moberly, *Atonement and Personality*, p. 151.

to the New Testament facts as some of those who speak most of the Spirit appear to think.

It will not be disputed that in the New Testament the Spirit is only given to believers. By believers is meant, of course, believers in Jesus, believers in Christ as the apostolic gospel exhibits Him appealing for faith. In spite of the creeds, there is no such expression in the New Testament as believing in the Holy Ghost. The Spirit is not an object of faith like Christ or God, it is an experience which comes to people through faith. Whether we judge from the accounts in the Book of Acts or in the Epistles of Paul, it was a vivid emotional experience. The figures employed in the story of Pentecost—the sound as of a rushing mighty wind, tongues like as of fire—are fundamentally true and of permanent importance. The Spirit was an experience in which believers were the subjects of a divine excitement in which their life was raised to a new power. In the Acts of the Apostles the manifestations of this excitement specified are speaking with tongues and prophecy. Speaking with tongues was an unintelligible and almost inarticulate ecstasy of praise, a rapture of joy in which believers declared the mighty works of God (Acts ii. 11), or gave thanks for what He had done (1 Cor. xiv. 16); prophecy was a more conscious and controlled utterance, yet one in which the soul of the speaker was on fire. There are three ideas mainly which are connected with the Spirit everywhere, in addition to the general idea—that in the Spirit it is God who is acting upon and in men. These are the ideas of power, of life, and of joy. The first is omnipresent in the New Testament. God anointed Jesus of Nazareth with Holy Spirit and power: the two are one. Paul preached at Thessalonica in power and in the Holy Spirit: again the two are one. Life is not essentially distinct from power, and it is in the experience of the Spirit strengthening them that believers are conscious of it as a quickening or life-giving Spirit. Possibly the most characteristic of the three terms is joy. The emotional excitement which was characteristic of primitive Christianity was a glad excitement. It breathes upon us still from the early pages of Acts. It is declared in Paul when he tells us that the fruit of the Spirit is love, joy, peace, or that the Thessalonians received the gospel in much affliction with joy of the Holy Spirit; indeed this combination —much affliction and joy of the Spirit—is more than anything else the seal of apostolic Christianity. It is as an experience of power, life, and joy—an exciting and overwhelming experience due to God Himself—that the Spirit can be spoken of as the key to the life of reconciliation.

It has become a commonplace of New Testament theology to show how St. Paul modified and developed this primitive conception of the Spirit till Spirit was no longer the name for unusual or exciting religious experiences, but for the principle of all religious experience whatsoever. But Paul never lost contact with the primitive conception, nor with its essential characteristics. All he has to say about the Spirit might be condensed in the striking words of Rom. v. 5: "The Christian hope puts no man to shame, for the love of God is poured out in our hearts through the Holy Spirit given to us." This is what the Holy Spirit does: it fills the Christian heart with an exultant assurance of the love of God. The man who has such an assurance—the man whose heart is full to overflowing with the sense of that love which God demonstrated to men when He gave His Son to die for sinners—is full of the Holy Ghost. In the words of the Old Testament, the joy of the Lord is his strength. It is the inspiration of everything in his Christian life. It is the motive and the power of all his service of God and man. It enables him to subdue the flesh, to rejoice in tribulation, to exult in hope of the glory of God. It is best understood by the man who has had experience of a real religious revival and who has shared the emotion of the hymn, "I feel like singing all the time." Such emotion is to a great extent social or contagious, but it only represents more truly in that respect the experience of the Spirit in primitive Christianity. The Spirit fell as a rule on groups or bodies of men united in a common faith or expectation, or subject in common to some strong religious impression. They were all filled with it, and uplifted accordingly in a new power, life, and joy, which they recognised as divine.

This may appear to some extremely vague, and lacking in definitely Christian character. It will be charged with ignoring the personality of the Holy Spirit, and reducing the Third Person of the Trinity to an emotional disturbance of human nature, as likely to delude as to promote sanctification. Perhaps the best answer to such criticisms is to point out that even in the apostolic age the inconveniences of the doctrine of the Spirit were already felt, and various attempts made to remedy or to guard against them. Substantially these attempts came to this: the Spirit had to be more precisely connected with Christ, and with His work and purposes for men. In itself Spirit is a very vague term. The gospels explain morbid phenomena of various kinds, intellectual or moral, by describing the subject of them as "in an unclean spirit." The mood of sullenness or frenzy or despair in which the man lived was due to a power not simply himself, and not God either. It was due to a spirit which the Spirit of God in Jesus could vanquish. It is quite clear from 1 Cor. xii. 1-3, and other passages that there were ambiguous "spiritual" phenomena in the Pauline Churches, and that the apostle found it necessary to state a criterion by which the true could be distinguished from the false. Here, apparently, it is a dogmatic criterion: the spirit is genuinely Christian if its utterance is one which exalts Jesus, calling Him Lord. But in other places Paul seems to find it necessary to connect Jesus and the Spirit still more closely. Thus, as has often been pointed out, in Rom. viii. 9-11, the Spirit of God, the Spirit of Christ, and Christ Himself are practically indistinguishable. It is all one if we can say of people that the Spirit of God dwells in them, or that they have the Spirit of Christ, or that Christ is in them. All these are ways in which we can describe the life of reconciliation as it is realised in men. They make it plain that the explanation of that life is divine, and they prevent any misapprehension about the divine Spirit by frankly identifying the indwelling of the Spirit in the Christian sense with the spiritual indwelling of Christ Himself. But there is no justification in this for representing the Spirit as a third person in the same sense as God and Christ. Paul never knew Christ except as Spirit—except as a being who could enter into and tell upon his life as God Himself entered; and his whole concern in this passage is not to distinguish Christ and the Spirit, but to show that nothing is entitled to be recognised as really Spirit among Christians if it is distinguishable from Christ and from the divine power with which He acts in the souls and in the life of men.

This brings us back inevitably to Christ Himself, and to the faith by which a saving connection is established between Christ and the soul. When faith is taken in its full New Testament sense—when it is the unreserved and passionate

THE CHRISTIAN DOCTRINE OF RECONCILIATION

abandonment of the sinner to the sin-bearing love of God in Christ—it is related to the Spirit as immediately as to Christ Himself. To be a believer in Christ and to have the Spirit are identically the same. No man has the Spirit who is not a believer in Christ, and no man who is a believer in Christ has not the Spirit. Faith and the Spirit, in short, as has been pointed out above, are correlative terms. They describe the very same Christian experience from complementary points of view, the human and the divine. There is no genuine Christian experience of which you cannot say at one and the same time that it is the experience of a believer and an experience in the Spirit; it is conditioned by faith and its causality is divine. But the faith of which we are speaking is faith in Christ as He is proclaimed in the gospel, and the divine causality is one which operates solely through this Christ and the appeal He makes to the sinful soul. The doctrine of the Holy Spirit, as an element in the ecclesiastical doctrine of the Trinity, goes far beyond this, and far beyond anything which the New Testament defines. Accordingly, while we may admit that a view like that of Moberly is substantially correct in asserting that men are saved through the production or reproduction in them of the mind of Christ in relation to sin, we can only decline as an incredible artificiality his conception of the process by which this production or reproduction is achieved. We can think of no presence of the Spirit except the spiritual presence of Christ Himself. We can think of no condition which secures this presence except the condition of faith in Christ. Nor can we, in consistency with the gospel, think of any faith in Christ by which this presence is not secured. In experience, faith and the Spirit are the same thing; in both alike we are reconciled to God and enabled to live the life of reconciliation.

RECONCILIATION AS REALISED IN HUMAN LIFE

The same truth comes out in another way if we look to the moral features of the life of faith. Faith, as has already been shown, involves the self-identification of the soul with Christ in a passion of trust and love, and through such self-identification the mind of Christ in relation to sin is spontaneously produced in the believing sinner. This has been described in two different ways. Sometimes it is spoken of as repentance, sometimes as regeneration or the new creature. Calvin identified the two when he said *poenitentiam interpretor regenerationem.* But it is interesting to notice the different relations which explain the different names of the same thing. It is called repentance when we think of it from the side of the sinner, and of his responsibility and initiative in it; it is called regeneration when we think of it from the side of God, as something in which a gracious initiative belongs to Him. Both ways of conceiving it are equally just, and indeed equally necessary. But what invites our attention here is the analogy they present to what has just been said of faith and the Spirit. We come perpetually, in the relations of God and man, to a point at which the same thing has to be described as at once divine and human—as present in virtue of a divine causality and a human condition, neither of which exists except as calling for, or called for by, the other. It is a curious confirmation of this, in the case with which we are now dealing, that in the synoptic gospels, in which human responsibility is certainly emphasised as nowhere else in the New Testament, repentance is frequently spoken of, but regeneration never; whereas in the fourth gospel, with its dominantly theological outlook, regeneration is conspicuous, and repentance is never mentioned. Nevertheless, they are one thing, and it is a thing unintelligible except through God on the one side and faith on the other.

THE CHRISTIAN DOCTRINE OF RECONCILIATION

A further complication has been introduced into the life of reconciliation by the place which in some Churches is given to the sacraments, and especially to baptism as the sacrament of initiation or of regeneration. The Council of Trent, as quoted above, speaks of the sacrament of baptism as the instrumental cause of justification; it is by baptism as a sacrament, effective *ex opere operato*, that the sinner is united to Christ and at once purged from his sins and initiated into the new, supernatural, and divine life. Views akin to this, though not perhaps very authoritatively defined, are certainly current also in other Churches which affect the Catholic character. It is not easy for one who does not accept them to be sure that he knows what they mean, but they make it desirable that the contrary view should be stated as explicitly as possible.

The basis in the New Testament for the doctrine that connects the life of reconciliation with baptism is the passage in Rom. vi. 1-11, in which Paul appeals to baptism in his argument against the idea that we may continue in sin that grace may abound. It is taken for granted that all Christians are baptized, and that there is something in baptism quite inconsistent with the idea in question. Now what is this something? What is it in baptism which precludes the idea that the Christian may live on in sin? Baptism is a rite with a meaning, of course, but the meaning may be more or less distinctly made out; it is a symbol—every one admits this at least, however far he may go beyond it—but a symbol which may be more superficially or more profoundly understood. The most obvious interpretation of it is that it is a washing, or if regard is paid to immersion, a bath, and that is what we sometimes find in the New Testament. When Paul himself was baptized, Ananias said to

RECONCILIATION AS REALISED IN HUMAN LIFE

him, "Arise, have thyself baptized, and wash away thy sins, calling upon His name" (Acts xxii. 16). So also in 1 Cor. vi. 11, referring to the same crisis in the spiritual history of the Corinthians: "Ye were washed, ye were sanctified"—that is, consecrated to God, made His people—"ye were justified in the name of the Lord Jesus Christ and in the Spirit of our God." But this symbolism of washing or cleansing is not the one of which Paul makes use in Romans vi. What he speaks of is being baptized into Christ, and therefore, by consequence, into His death and resurrection. The immersion represents death with Christ, or, to put it as strongly and vividly as possible, death and burial with Him; the emersion represents resurrection with Christ, rising from the dead with Him to walk in newness of life. It is because this is what baptism means, and because all Christians have been baptized, that to live on deliberately in sin is for the Christian an inconceivable, self-contradictory, and impossible course.

There are two questions to ask about this argument. The first is, How did Paul light upon it? How did it occur to him to ignore the simple idea of baptism as a washing with water, and to replace it by this striking and original idea of a union with Christ in His death and resurrection, which—although, as has already been noticed, the death and resurrection were historical or natural events—is supposed to carry with it of necessity ethical or spiritual consequences? Reference has been made to the Hellenistic mystery religions and their influence on the thought of the Church, but, so far as the writer knows, there is no evidence whatever that in any of these religions the idea can be found of a "mystical" union of the initiate, by a lustral or any other rite, with his dying and rising God. Sound or unsound, the idea belongs to the sixth chapter of Romans alone. It is forcing the language of verse 6—"*knowing this*, that our old man was crucified with Him"—to argue from it, as Lagrange does in his commentary on the passage, that this whole conception of baptism was familiar to the Romans independently of Paul, and was in fact current in the Church and simply inherited by him. The whole difficulty of understanding the passage has arisen from the fact that baptism has been taken in it as if it were a thing in itself, whereas the only baptism known to the apostolic Church, and therefore the baptism here spoken of, was that of believers solemnly and publicly declaring their faith in Christ. The death and the resurrection with Christ are not in the rite of baptism, apart from faith, and with a view to the experience of them by faith; they are in the gospel, to begin with, and in the rite only through the faith which accepts the gospel. Essentially there is nothing in Paul's gospel but Christ and faith, and faith, it cannot be said too often, is the unreserved abandonment of the sinful soul to Christ, its unreserved identification of itself with Him in trust and love; when it is unfolded with any detail, it is the soul's self-identification with Christ in His death and resurrection, the two great events in which His saving significance is summed up. It is through faith, as that which establishes our fundamental relation to Christ, that all this can be read into the rite of baptism, and actually is read into it by Paul. Baptism is for him a picture of what faith really is. It is not baptism as a sacrament *ex opere operato* that involves death and resurrection with Christ, and is therefore inconsistent with a continued life in sin; it is the baptism of believers who have in faith identified themselves with the Lord who died for them and rose again.

The further question suggested by Romans vi. is one as

to the soundness of the argument itself. Setting aside as impossible for our minds the idea that this death and rising again with Christ was the supernaturally revealed significance of baptism, and that, therefore, however mysterious or incomprehensible it is it must be true, we are compelled to ask whether it is logically coherent, and whether it is supported by appeal to experience. In both respects it has seemed to many to leave something to be desired. The death and resurrection of Christ have one meaning in the premises and another in the conclusion—one meaning in Him, and another in application to us. Paul does indeed say that Christ died to sin once for all, but there is not a word in the New Testament more hard to understand or to explain than this; nor is it any easier to understand or to explain, whatever be its sense, how a "mystical" union with Him, effected in baptism, reproduces His death to sin in us.[1] Similarly Paul says that Christ was raised from the dead by the glory of the Father, and that we accordingly must walk in newness of life. But there is no real connection of thought in this. Christ was not more holy after the resurrection than before, and there is no more security for a good life in being united to Him in one mode of being than in another. As for the appeal to experience, it is frankly given up by the apostle himself when, at the close of this ingenious but perplexed digression, he says to his readers: "*Reckon yourselves* dead to sin, but alive to God in Christ Jesus." Apart from this self-reckoning, which when real is simply the renewal of faith's identification of itself with the Saviour, all this about union with the death and resurrection of Christ in baptism is meaningless.

It may occur to some readers that justice is not done in

[1] See pp. 246 f., *supra*.

this to those passages in the New Testament in which the gift of the Spirit is associated with baptism. When Christ Himself was baptized, the Spirit descended on Him in the form of a dove, and this became the type of Christian baptism. The forerunner had contrasted baptism with water and baptism with the Spirit, but in the Church they were normally coincident. "Repent, and be baptized every one of you in the name of Jesus Christ for the remission of your sins, and ye shall receive the gift of the Holy Ghost" (Acts ii. 38). "Except a man be born of water and of the Spirit he cannot enter into the Kingdom of God" (John iii. 5). "He saved us through the laver of regeneration and renewing of the Holy Spirit, which He poured out on us richly, through Jesus Christ our Saviour" (Titus iii. 5). These passages belong, indeed, to the latest in the New Testament, and in the form of them there is as much which is due to nascent Catholicism as to the experience of the first days, but there is nothing in them which is not easily enough understood. The prime necessity is to remember that the baptism of those days was the baptism of believers, and that the occasion on which the believer made public and solemn confession of his faith in baptism, calling upon the name of the Lord, and renouncing the life in which he had hitherto lived, was normally an occasion of high and serious emotion—an occasion of precisely such experiences as were then explained by reference to the Spirit. Where baptism took place with no such experience, it was recognised that something which ought to have been there was absent (Acts viii. 14 f.; xix. 2 ff.), and special efforts were made to remedy the defect. This is what we see in Acts viii. 14 f. and Acts xix. 2 ff. In spite of these two passages, however, in which we are told how Peter and John at Samaria, and Paul at Ephesus, obtained the Spirit

RECONCILIATION AS REALISED IN HUMAN LIFE

by prayer and laying on of hands for baptized persons who had not received the gift, there is no suggestion anywhere in the New Testament that it was not normally connected with faith and baptism, but only came when these were confirmed by the imposition of apostolic (or episcopal) hands. The cases in question are both marked as abnormal, and unusual efforts were made to secure in them the normal accompaniments of the rite. In both cases, too, these efforts were successful. There was an outburst of the emotion which was regarded in those days as the work of the Spirit. "They spake with tongues and prophesied." The general practice of infant baptism has made it difficult to apply this circle of ideas in the modern Church. When believing men, confessing their faith in baptism, were said in the apostolic age to receive the Holy Spirit, it meant that they had religious experiences of a powerful and moving character, due to Jesus and to their faith in Him, and to the whole circumstances in which it was declared. But no part of this has any application whatever to the baptism of unconscious infants, and to speak of *their* regeneration by the Spirit in baptism is to use language which has no relation to the New Testament facts, language which neither has nor ever can have any intelligible meaning. There may be justification for infant baptism, but not along this line. The love of God which is declared in the name in which baptism is administered is the one power by which a human soul is ever raised from death to life, and in that sense the grace of baptism—to use an ambiguous and misleading expression—is the grace which saves; but to say that baptism *ex opere operato* regenerates, or confers the gift of the Spirit, or unites us to Christ, or implants in us the seed of the new life, is not to help but only to bewilder or rather to extinguish the mind. Baptism enters into the process of salvation only when it coincides with the act of faith in which the soul, under solemn and moving conditions, consciously and irrevocably commits itself to Christ, identifying itself, in spiritual passion, with Him who died for it and rose again.

The same considerations would apply to the Lord's Supper, on which also stress has been laid as the support of the new reconciled life. It is obvious from the tenth chapter of First Corinthians, that at a very early date superstitious ideas began to be associated with this rite as well as with baptism. There were people in the Church at Corinth who thought that to be baptized and to eat and drink at the Lord's table gave them a moral security which enabled them to ignore or despise temptation, and to relax self-discipline; they were secure of a blessed immortality no matter what they did or what happened to them in this world. Such ideas were undoubtedly common in connection with the rites of the pagan mystery religions, and the apostle sets himself vigorously to purge out this immoral leaven from the Christian society. He bids the Corinthians look at the Old Testament history and learn its lessons. The Israelites had sacraments as well as we; they were baptized into Moses in the cloud and the sea; they had spiritual—or supernatural—food and drink, the manna from heaven and the water from the rock; nay, it was the very same food and drink which we have at the Lord's table, for the spiritual rock which followed him was the Christ. But their privileges did not guarantee their moral security; their carcasses fell in the wilderness; they never saw the promised land. When we speak of eating the flesh of the Son of Man and drinking His blood, we are bound to remember that the words can only be understood in the moral and spiritual world. There

RECONCILIATION AS REALISED IN HUMAN LIFE

is no intelligible meaning in saying that Christ is present in the bread and wine, or in, with, and under the bread and wine, or, what is the poorest of all evasions of intelligence, in "sacramental union" with the bread and wine; the presence of Christ neither has nor can have any metaphysical relation whatever to the sacramental elements. Christ is present when the supper is celebrated, and present in the sense of these elements; He is present to be our meat and drink; He is present as the Lord whose body was broken and whose blood was shed for us, as He who once gave Himself for us, and perpetually offers Himself to us; He is personally present that in faith we may open our being to Him and receive Him in that significance in which He is declared by the symbols. But He is always present so; always, and not only in the celebration of the sacraments. The sacraments are pictures which enable us to see better what Christ is to sinners; as Robert Bruce put it, we get a better grip of Him in the sacrament; but Christ is a person, and though we see better in the sacrament what kind of person He is, the personal relation to Him in which salvation consists can never depend on what is sometimes spoken of as sacramental grace. No sacrament can do anything but interpret the grace which is in Him. And this grace is not a thing, which can be absorbed as food or medicine is absorbed; it is the redeeming love of Christ; it is His attitude of mercy, as the sin-bearing Saviour, to men lost in sin; and it tells on us simply and solely as it wins from us the unreserved response of faith. When we celebrate the Lord's supper we declare that we live by faith in the Son of God, who loved us and died for us, but we do not mean that the celebration is the act or the process in which the life of faith is realised, or in which it has its essential support, or even its supreme manifestation. Still less do we mean that the bread and the wine, consecrated or unconsecrated—expressions totally destitute of New Testament authority—have anything to do with it. Christ and faith are the supreme realities in Christianity, the supreme categories under which everything Christian, not excepting the sacraments, has to be reduced; and however the believing soul may be helped in its relation to Christ by rites like baptism and the supper, it is the negation not only of Christian experience, but of human intelligence, to say that the new life is essentially or vitally related to the water, or to the bread and the wine.

The primacy of Christ and faith must determine also our judgment as to the place of the Church in the life of reconciliation. Of all terms in the vocabulary of religion, "Church" is probably the most ambiguous, and it is therefore very difficult to tell what is meant by it in any given case. There is a sense, no doubt, in which the life of reconciliation can only be lived in the Church. The faith which unites men to Christ is a common faith, and in uniting them to Him it unites them to one another. It constitutes them members of a society, of a new humanity living with a new life, the life of faith in Jesus. It is as a member of this new humanity that the believer in Jesus realises his new life. But no corporation or aggregate of corporations on earth—whether it be the Church of Rome, or the Greek Church, or the Church of England, or all of them together—can take the place of the new humanity, and say that the life of reconciliation can only be lived within its fellowship, and indeed can only be produced by a sacramental initiation into it as the body of Christ. No one who knows the meaning of Christ and of faith can ever assent to any such doctrine. On the other

RECONCILIATION AS REALISED IN HUMAN LIFE

hand, while asserting in principle the primacy of Christ and of faith, and the dependence of the Church, for its very existence, upon these as the final realities in Christianity, it can be frankly admitted that in Christian as in all history the society is of immense consequence to the individual. It was individual believers in Christ who first constituted the Church, but the historical Church is prior to the individual believer to-day. In most cases he has been brought up in it, and has known instinctively, from the very beginning, what the Christian attitude of the soul to Christ is; in other words, he has known what faith is. He has had the benefit of an atmosphere. Faith is the faith of the society in which he has been born and bred; it is social faith, and he has been unconsciously impregnated with it. But it is a quite misleading way to put this truth if we say that it is the Church which is the guardian of grace, or the Spirit-filled body of Christ, or the object of justification, and that it is only through membership in the Church that grace, or the Spirit, or justification, or reconciliation, can be assured to the individual. In history all things are historically mediated, and the debt of any given believer to-day to the new humanity which has been growing through nineteen centuries is immeasurable; but he does not owe to it—and still less to any corporation in which some part of it has found self-expression—his definitive relation to God as a sinner reconciled, and living the life of reconciliation. This he owes to Christ alone, and to faith in Him; and the supremacy of Christ and faith gives him, as a member of the new humanity, the freedom of a final responsibility to Christ. He is not and dare not be the slave of men (1 Cor. vii. 23), even though the men who claim his subjection may call themselves the Church. He must give account of himself to God, and no

THE CHRISTIAN DOCTRINE OF RECONCILIATION

definitions of doctrine, no claims of orders, no clerical constitution, no judgments passed by other men's consciences, are *ipso facto* valid for him. He lives the common life of Christians, but he is free to react against any manifestation of it, intellectual or moral, in the strength of that faith in Christ which for him is the first and last of realities. He judges all things through it—not excepting the creeds and constitutions which men in the course of history have framed for the Church; he judges all things, and does not submit to be judged by any (1 Cor. ii. 15).

Assuming, then, that the life of reconciliation is simply the life of faith in Christ, and that faith in Christ is what we have maintained it to be—the passionate identification of the sinner with Him in trust and love, his self-abandonment to the sin-bearing love of God revealed in Christ—in what way will the life of reconciliation manifest itself in men?

In the first place, it will appear as reconciliation to the mind of God about sin, as that has been declared in Christ, and especially in His cross and passion. The tendency in human nature to excuse sin, to put forward pleas in extenuation and defence, to provide in the constitution or education or environment of the sinner explanations which neutralise his guilt, is instinctive and almost ineradicable. Few sayings are more popular with the morally feeble, than that to understand everything is to pardon everything. To be reconciled to God through faith in Christ, who died bearing our sins, is death to this tendency. It means that we enter into the mind of Christ in relation to sin, that we see it in its truth as He saw it, that we sorrow over it as He sorrowed, that we repel it henceforth as He repelled it; all of which is part at least of what is meant by repentance. There is no salvation except in and through the truth, and to take

RECONCILIATION AS REALISED IN HUMAN LIFE

our sin as what it truly is—as what in the Passion of Jesus it has been revealed really to be—is to enter into the truth through which salvation is realised. Repentance in this sense is not a condition preliminary to salvation; it is part of the experience of being saved. It is not something which we produce out of our own resources, and bring to God, in the assurance that now of course He will forgive us; it is something which is only produced in us by the sense that there is already forgiveness with Him; it is a saving grace begotten in our hearts by that Passion of love in which Jesus made our sins His own. It is not a substitute for the atonement, or something which makes it unnecessary; it is the fruit of the atonement, and of nothing else.

Perhaps in evangelical theology the scope of repentance has been in one respect unduly narrowed. There has been a quite proper emphasis on the absolute removal of condemnation, on the joyful assurance of God's love, on the certainty of a consummation where sin will leave no trace of itself except in the doxologies which celebrate complete redemption from it. But earth is not heaven, and the acceptance of God's verdict upon sin, even while He forgives it, is more painful than has sometimes been allowed. It involves what is called in the book of Leviticus (xxvi. 41) "accepting the punishment of our iniquities." The divine reaction against sin does not cease with faith. It goes on in the constitution and course of nature, and to be reconciled to God in Christ means that we acknowledge the justice of God in it, and submit to His holy will as expressed in this reaction without resentment, bitterness, querulousness, or discontent. When we have sinned, and especially if we have sinned habitually, the reaction will be felt inevitably, painfully—and indispensably. It is a discipline which even the sinner, who now identifies himself with Christ by faith, cannot do without. But as part of the treatment of a reconciled sinner by the God to whom he is reconciled—in other words, as part of the treatment of a child by the Father—discipline is the proper name for it. It is indeed retributive, or it would have no disciplinary value. But the sternness in it is that of love; it is a severity of God which is not distinct from, but an element in, His goodness. To submit to it without repining is part of the life of reconciliation as that life is inspired and sustained by self-identification with Jesus in faith. For He lived under the same inexorable moral order as we, and, though He knew not sin, He bore without murmuring the whole conditions of our human lot in which the divine reaction against sin speaks perpetually to a sensitive conscience.

But there is another and more positive side to the life of reconciliation. The man who is reconciled to God through Christ and His Passion is reconciled to love as the law of life. God is love, and there is no reconciliation to Him which does not involve the acceptance of love as the law of our own conduct as it is the law of His. As John puts it, Christ laid down His life for us, "and we ought to lay down our lives for the brethren" (1 John iii. 16). Many have fought shy of this saying, and of what corresponds to it in Paul: "I now rejoice in my sufferings for you, and fill up that which is lacking of the afflictions of Christ in my flesh for His body's sake, which is the Church" (Col. i. 24). Perhaps the motive for this was good. Men were unwilling to intrude, as it were, upon the sphere of Christ, to say anything which seemed to question the solitariness or the completeness of His work of reconciliation. But the apostles do not seem to have been apprehensive on this score. For them the

RECONCILIATION AS REALISED IN HUMAN LIFE

solitariness and completeness of Christ's work are beyond question. He, says John, is the propitiation for the whole world. "In Him," says Paul, "it pleased the Father that all fulness should dwell, and through Him to reconcile all things to Himself, having made peace by the blood of His cross, whether they be things on earth or things in the heavens." They are careful to make it plain that neither in earth nor heaven—that is, nowhere in the universe—is there such a thing as reconciliation that is not due to Him. But without ascribing the work of reconciliation to men, any more than they would have ascribed sin to Christ, they perceive that reconciliation to God through Christ means that the law and the spirit of Christ's life become the law and the spirit of life in those who are reconciled. By faith in Him we are really united to Him, not metaphysically but in the passion of love and trust. He brings us into an ethical fellowship with Himself, in which the inspiration of His life becomes the inspiration of ours; the love which moved and controlled Him moves and controls us also. When this is not realised, the most dreadful of all dangers overhangs the soul. It thinks of itself as reconciled to God, but in truth it is keeping God out of its life; for God is love. Instead of being reconciled to God it is being reconciled to its sin. It is acquiescing in a life remote from the life of God. We do not need to be afraid that the love we learn from Christ and exercise in union with Him will invade His prerogative or prompt us to think that we too are making atonement either for our own sins or for the sins of others. But if we have not learned from Him to look not on our own things only, but on the things of others also—to bear each other's burdens, even the burden of each other's sins, so as to fulfil His law —if we are not willing to do and to suffer for the good of others as He did and suffered for the good of all—then we must ask ourselves what we mean, or whether we mean anything, when we speak of being reconciled to God through Him. Are we really reconciled when we stand outside of that love which is His life? Does not reconciliation to God imply acceptance of love as the law of life? Does it not mean that we acknowledge the obligation to lay down our lives for the brethren, and to fill up what is lacking in the measure of toil and suffering through which alone the kingdom of God can be established on earth? The love of God can only redeem those whom it inspires; to be inspired by it is to have the experience of redemption and reconciliation. If we question this, is it not as much as to say that we claim to be reconciled to God while we are alienated from the life of God through an ignorance that is in us owing to the hardening of our hearts? This would be the most melancholy of all perversions of the gospel—the turning against itself of the very power from which redemption and reconciliation proceed. Salvation does not mean that we are exempted from living Christ's life; it means that we are enabled to share in that life, to know the fellowship of His sufferings, even to be conformed to His death.

Acceptance of the mind of God with regard to sin, as something which wounds His holy love, to which He is finally and inexorably opposed—in other words, repentance and submission to all the divine reaction against evil; acceptance of love as the divine law of life—in other words, self-renunciation and sacrifice for the good of others: these are the main characteristics of the life of reconciliation as a life in which the soul identifies itself with Christ through faith. Each of them may grow continuously in depth and intensity. Repentance is not the act of an instant, in which the sinner

RECONCILIATION AS REALISED IN HUMAN LIFE

passes from death to life, it is the habit of a lifetime, in which he assimilates ever more perfectly the mind of Christ in relation to sin—his sorrow, his confession of God's righteousness in judging it as He does, his unreserved submission to everything in which God's reaction against it comes home to him. Similarly the acceptance of love as the law of life grows perpetually more complete and profound. Under the inspiration of Jesus the reconciled soul sees opportunities for self-denial, calls for sacrifice, appeals for love, to which it would once have been insensible, or to which it would have been too selfish or too cowardly to respond. And it is in responding without reserve to such appeals, and entering without reserve into the mind of Christ in relation to sin, that the life of reconciliation to God is realised in sinners through faith in Christ.

One thing further follows from this. The life of reconciliation is a life which itself exercises a reconciling power. It is the ultimate witness to that in God which overcomes all that separates man from himself and men from each other. Hence it is indispensable to all who work for peace and good will among men. Not only the alienation of men from God, but their alienation from one another—the estrangement of classes within the same society, the estrangement of nations and races within the great family of humanity—yield in the last resort to love alone. Impartial justice, arbitrating from without, can do little for them. But a spirit delivered from pride and made truly humble by repentance, a spirit purged from selfishness and able in the power of Christ's love to see its neighbour's interest as its own, will prove victorious alike in the class rivalries of capital and labour, and in the international rivalries that are now devastating the world. It is in its all-reconciling power that Paul sees most clearly the absoluteness and finality of the Christian religion. Where all the differences have been transcended which cause painful tension among men, where there is neither Greek nor Jew, male nor female, bond nor free, there the perfect revelation of God has been made. But these differences are transcended only as men find themselves in spite of them all one in Christ, and reconciled to God through Him. It is in this central oneness that the power lies hidden which will subdue all the differences to itself. The evangelist is the only pacificator whose specific goes to the root of the matter, and it is in Christ only, the one Reconciler of God and man, that it has pleased the Father to gather together all things in one.

The centrality and absoluteness of the reconciliation achieved by Christ and realised in man through faith make it in the New Testament the basis of far-reaching inferences of every kind. Whenever Paul speaks of God as having reconciled us to Himself, he can argue from this to any conclusion as from the greater to the less. It is on this he bases his assurance of God's ever present good will through all the chance and change of mortal life. "He that spared not His own Son, but delivered Him up for us all, how shall He not also with Him freely give us all things?" "All things are yours . . . the world, or life, or death." "We know that to them that love God all things work together for good." Who know this? Christians know it who have been reconciled to God by the death of His Son, and who know that the last reality in the world is the love which has borne their sins and will not suffer anything to frustrate its gracious purpose. The Christian faith in providence is an immediate inference from the Christian experience of redemption, and it is an inference as vast and unqualified as the redeeming

RECONCILIATION AS REALISED IN HUMAN LIFE

love on which it rests. "Who shall separate us from the love of Christ? Shall tribulation, or distress, or persecution, or famine, or nakedness, or peril, or sword? . . . Nay, in all these things we are more than conquerors through Him who loved us."

In Paul, in particular, this inference reaches out into the unseen and sustains the hope of immortality. Probably we underrate, as a rule, the immense place of this hope throughout the New Testament, and especially in Paul. It is true that to understand him we must begin at the centre, with the sinner's reconciliation to God through the sin-bearing love of Christ, but we should only make a beginning of understanding him if this experience had not in our minds the inspiring power which it had in his. For him, sin and death were one, and the victory over sin was a victory over death also. There is no more comprehensive and concentrated utterance of his whole Christian convictions than "We have worn the image of the earthy, and we shall wear the image of the heavenly"; that is, we have lived as Adam did in a body burdened with sin, dishonour, and mortality; and we shall live as Christ lives, in a spiritual body radiant with holiness and with life, over which death has no more dominion. There are various more or less specific ways in which this connection of truths appears in the apostle's mind. Sometimes it is Christ in us who is the hope of glory, sometimes the Spirit which is the earnest of our inheritance, sometimes God Himself who raises the dead, who is the object of our hope. But always, at bottom, it is redeeming and reconciling love, apprehended by faith—that is, in spiritual experience—which sustains this outlook into the future. And in this the Old Testament and the New are at one. In the sublimest words of the Psalter, immortality is involved in

THE CHRISTIAN DOCTRINE OF RECONCILIATION

the experience of God's gracious and faithful providence on earth. "Nevertheless, I am continually with Thee; Thou hast holden my right hand. Thou shalt guide me with Thy counsel, and afterwards receive me to glory." In the sublimest words of the apostle it is made to rest on the specifically Christian knowledge of God, but the soul's attitude is the same, and so is the inspiration out of which it speaks. "I am persuaded that neither death, nor life, nor angels, nor principalities, nor powers, nor things present, nor things to come, nor height, nor depth, nor any other creature, shall be able to separate us from the love of God, which is in Christ Jesus our Lord."

The Christian's faith in reconciliation does not find its full expression till it finds it here.

INDEX

(1) SUBJECTS AND AUTHORS

ABALARD, 78-82.
Adam, the sin of, 43, 201, 210 f.
ἀγωνία, 274.
American Puritanism, 95 f.
Anselm, 28; merits and defects of his theory, 64-79; and Luther, 92; on fallen angels, 230.
ἀπάθεια, 4-5.
Aquinas, on the atonement, 84 f.
ἀρχηγός, 249 f.
Articles of faith, 92, 109.
Assurance, place of religious, 284, 293 f.
ἀταραξία, 4-5.
Athanasius, on incarnation and atonement, 36 f., 44; on Christ's victory over death, 244.
Atonement, need for an objective, 30, 33, 90, 108 f., 235 f., 239, 260; extent of, 67, 84, 119; and the incarnation, 181 f., 240, 268 f.; subjective theories of, 80-81, 260.
Attributes, the divine, 104.
Augsburg, the Confession of, on the satisfaction of Christ, 92-93, 108.
Augustine, 44; on Christ's salvation, 51 f.; on sin, 196-198.
Authority of Bible, 122.

BAPTISM, 91, 216 f., 314 f.
Baur, F. C., 28, 79, 81.
Beatitudes, the, 11 f.
Bernard of Clairvaux, 78, 165.
Bruce, Robert, quoted, 321.
Bushnell, Horace, on vicariousness, 118, 255 f.; on the power of Christ, 250.

CALVIN, on the *descensus ad inferos*, 49, 263; on Christ's intercession, 96; on the grace of God, 100 f.; on the sufferings of Christ, 263; on regeneration, 313.
Chalmers quoted, 106, 180, 297.
Christ, essential to reconciliation, 8 f.; God's gift, 30-31, 102-103; His satisfaction for sin, 49 f.; His sacrifice, 55 f.; an illustration of God's grace, 63, 74, 81, 102; death of, 75 f., 277 f.; His work determined by sin, 235 f., 273; bearing our sins, 253 f.; union with, 304 f.
Church (the), place of, in reconciliation, 47 f., 51, 58 f., 88 f., 116, 322 f.
Conscience, a bad, 189 f., 204 f., 214 f.
Consequences, moral, 145 f.; of sin, 24 f., 224 f.
Cost of reconciliation, 21-22, 32 f., 102-103, 133, 135.
"Covenant blood," 140-141.
Cremer, 76.
Cross of Jesus, the, 268 f.
Cyprian, 47.

Damnosa haereditas, 216 f.
Death, religious problem of, 39 f., 244; the experience of, 211 f., 229, 276, 278; in relation to sin, 156 f., 209 f., 229 f., 244 f., 275 f.; significance for Jesus Christ, 40 f., 75, 269 f., 273 f., 280.
Declaratory Act, the, 199.
Deissmann on ἱλαστήριον, 153 f.; on πίστις Ἰησοῦ Χριστοῦ, 155.
Deliverance from sin, man's yearning for, 218 f.
Depravity, human, 199.
Devil, redemption from the, 31 f., 83 f.; salvation of the, 83.
δικαιοσύνη Θεοῦ, 142 f., 151.

THE CHRISTIAN DOCTRINE OF RECONCILIATION

Dogma of reconciliation, no, 27 f.
Doxologies of New Testament, 133, 283.
Du Bose, 245-246.
Duns Scotus, 90.

EASTERN CHURCH, characteristics of its theology, 33 f., 44, 52, 244, 274.
Edwards, Jonathan, quoted, 118.
Erskine of Linlathen, quoted, 145.
Evolution in relation to sin, 73 f., 196 f., 210.
Example, Christ as our, 245 f.
Experience and reconciliation, 7 f., 24-25, 199 f.; and doctrine, 43, 109 f., 115 f., 148.

FAITH, in theology of Athanasius, 43; in the New Testament, 284-285, 287 f., 303 f., 316; in Pauline theology, 162 f., 287 f.; in Reformation preaching, 91, 92, 294 f.; in Roman Catholic theology, 297 f.; evoked by Christ, 304 f.; moral features of, 313 f.; and love, 164, 295, 301; and penitence, 284-285; and the Spirit, 311 f.
Fides informis, 164.
Flesh, New Testament doctrine of, 147 f.
"Forensic" justification, 290 f.
Forgiveness and reconciliation, 6; free and divine, 15-16, 97 f., 102 f., 132; in Jesus, 103; not "a fiction," 137 f., 291 f.; human, 133 f.; New Testament doctrine of, 284 f., 287 f.; regenerating power of, 6, 137 f.; limits of, 218 f.
Future, religious significance of the, 168 f.

GERMANIC Law, 70 f., 76.
God, Grotius' idea of, 111 f.; relation to man, 187 f.; reconciled to man, 100, 236 f.; in what sense He hates sin, 60 f., 215; His mercy, 22; His honour, 67 f., 74; His omnipotence, 84-85.
Goethe, on unity of man and nature, 3 f.; on sense of evil, 114 f.
Goodness of Jesus, the, 252 f.
Gospels, are there two in the New Testament? 126 f.; are there two in Paul? 165 f.
Gottschick, 54 f.
Grace, in early Christian theology, 45 f., 52 f.; in the mediæval Church, 74, 91 f.; meaning of, 261, 301; in the sacraments, 321; Christ an illustration of, 63 f., 74, 81, 102; in relation to merits of Christ, 97 f.
Greek Fathers, the (*see* Eastern Church), speculative note in, 34, 35, 42 f.; on Christ's victory over death, 274 f.
Gregory of Nyssa, 32.
Grotius, his criticisms of Socinianism, 110 f.; quoted, 30, 131.

HALYBURTON, quoted, 168.
Harnack, on the two gospels in the New Testament, 126 f.
Hatred, the divine, 60 f., 215.
Haupt, 146.
Hebrews, theology of epistle to the, 172-174.
Hegel, quoted, 168.
Historical Christ, the, 9, 129 f.
Höffding, quoted, 207.
Holtzmann, 160, 246.
Honour, the divine, 67 f., 74.
Hooker, quoted, 106.
Hope, in Christianity, 169.
Hopkins, quoted, 95-96, 108.
Humility, Christ's, 61 f., 84.
Hypostatic union, the, 240 f.

IDENTIFICATION of Christ with sinful men, 58, 118 f., 173, 249 f., 263, 274, 306.
Ignorance, sins of, 222 f.
ἱλασμός, 175-176, 234.
ἱλαστήριον, 152 f., 157-159, 175, 234.
Immortality, 226, 331 f.
Imputation, doctrine of, 119, 178.
Incarnation, the, in the theology of Athanasius, 36 f.; motives of, 59 f.; to be interpreted through the atonement, 65 f., 71, 181 f., 240 f.; real meaning of, 183-184, 242.
"In Christ," meaning of, 302 f.
Infants, baptism of, 216 f., 321; salvation of, 217 f.
Irenaeus, 34-35.

INDEX

JESUS (*see under* Christ), reconciling power of, 9-10, 12 f.; decisive nature of His death, 17 f., 75, 271 f.; significance of His life, 38, 94 f., 242 f., 255 f.; obedience of, 94 f.; humility of, 61 f.; sufferings of, 112; personality of, 119 f.; receiving sinners, 131 f., 252 f.; dying to sin, 246 f.; an example of faith, 127, 245 f.; sinlessness of, 243 f.; baptism of, 251 f.; bearing sins, 254 f., 274 f.; sympathy of, 17, 258 f.; our indebtedness to, 99, 163, 283; unique position of, 280-281; surrender to, 163, 291, 295 f.
Job, the book of, 213.
Johannine theology, the, 174 f., 272.
John of Damascus, 32.
Joy of reconciliation, the, 285, 293, 295, 309 f.
Judgment according to works, 170.
Justice, never opposed to mercy, 22, 103 f., 231 f.
Justification, and sanctification, 105 f., 288 f., 297; "forensic," 290 f.

KANT, on need for reconciliation, 3 f.; on radical evil, 113 f.
καταλλαγή, 239.
Kingdom of God, 113, 138 f., 230.

LAGRANGE, 316.
Latin theology, 44, 51 f.
Law, Pauline doctrine of the, 166 f.; in relations of God and man, 187 f.; the law of God, 223.
Life, reconciliation to conditions of, 1 f., 11, 171; the new, 104 f., 313 f.
Lightfoot quoted, 152, 158.
Lofthouse quoted, 287.
Logos, theology of the, 33 f.
Loofs, 78, 92.
Love, God's, the supreme reality, 20; revealed by death of Christ, 18, 60 f., 79; undervalued in Anselm, 75; ethical seriousness of, 228, 231 f., 234 f.; the origin and essence of reconciliation, 59 f., 90 f., 255 f., 295; the inspiration and law for human life, 326 f.
Lucretius quoted, 2.
Luther, 49, 92 f.; on the merits of Christ, 96; on the sufferings of Christ, 263; on faith, 291, 294.
Lyman, quoted, 26.

McLEOD CAMPBELL, 51, 90, 239; on Christ acknowledging God's condemnation of sin, 117 f.; on the love of Christ, 255 f.; on the death of Christ, 266 f.
Mediator, Christ as, 54 f., 60.
Melanchthon, on sacraments, 91; on the divine satisfaction, 94.
Menken, 245-246.
Mercy, not opposed to justice, 22, 103 f., 231.
Merit(s) of Christ, meaning of, 23-24, 96; in Anselm, 77 f.; in Aquinas, 86-87.
Moberly, R. C., criticisms of, 44, 51, 284-285, 307.
Moffatt, 131, 249.
Montaigne, 5.
Mysticism, in Osiander, 106; Schleiermacher and Ritschl, 116; Johannine, 176; Pauline, 302 f.

NATURE, and the spiritual world, 3, 201 f., 225 f.
Necessity, and freedom in God, 7, 84-85, 230 f.
Neoplatonism, in Augustine, 51-53, 60.
Newman, on justification, 107-108.

OBEDIENCE, of Jesus, 95 f., 233.
Omnipotence of God, 84-85.
ὀργὴ Θεοῦ, 149.
Origen, 34-35.
Orthodoxy, danger of, 105, 109 f., 184, 263.
Osiander, 106-107.
Owen, John, quoted, 49.

PARABLES, of Jesus: the prodigal son, 13, 132, 135, 170; the two debtors, 13, 132; the unmerciful servant, 136; the rock and the sand, 170.
πάρεσις, 158.
Passion of Jesus, the, 85 f., 129 f.; misinterpretations of, 262 f.
Paul, on the Old Testament, 124 f.; a preacher of reconciliation, 141 f.; permanent message of, 179 f.; on the flesh, 147 f.; on the law, 166 f.;

# THE CHRISTIAN DOCTRINE OF RECONCILIATION

on justification, 292 f.; on union with Christ, 302 f.; on the Spirit, 309 f.; on baptism, 314 f.; on the Lord's Supper, 320 f.; on immortality, 331 f.
Peace, human instinct for harmony and, 1, 3-4; Jesus our, 10, 25.
Pelagianism, 114, 196.
Penal character of Christ's sufferings, 48 f., 110 f.; of human suffering, 214 f.
Penitence, mediæval idea of, 46 f., 89 f.; and faith, 284-285.
Peter the Lombard, 82 f., 90, 102.
πίστις Ἰησοῦ Χριστοῦ, 155.
Predestination, 64, 108.
Propitiation, New Testament doctrine of, 152 f.; essential, 161 f., 176, 236.
Providence, belief in, 179, 330-333.
Punishment, and satisfaction, 48, 87 f.; endured by Christ, 57 f., 101 f., 262 f.; in relation to sin, 69 f., 203 f.; object of, 112; ethics of, 207 f.; and retribution, 209; human and divine, 209 f.; not confined to conscience, 214 f., 276; and chastisement, 227, 325-326; of innocent, 2.

RANSOM, religious category of, 31 f.
Reconciliation, scope of, 2 f., 12, 171, 177 f.; not confined to sphere of conscience, 212 f.; between man and man, 176 f., 329 f.; determined by fact of sin, 12 f.; absoluteness of, 21, 168 f.; cost of, 21-22, 102-103, 135 f.; a moral process, 22 f., 56; the work of Jesus, 129 f., 261 f.; in relation to experience, 24 f., 293 f.; subjective and objective, 109; the preparation for, 135 f.; man's need of, 187 f.; effected by God's love, 82, 218; alleged contradiction in, 109 f.; how far a divine necessity, 230 f., 236 f.; power of, 287 f.; obligations of, 326 f.; main features of, 328.
Redemptiones, in mediæval theology, 50 f., 76.
Reformation, the sixteenth century, an epoch in theology, 28; attitude towards Christ, 91 f., 119 f.; religious vitality of, 294 f.
Regeneration, 313 f.

Repentance, evoked by Jesus, 16, 254; characterised, 313, 324 f.
Responsibility, individual and corporate, 191 f., 323 f.
Retribution, essential to punishment, 208 f., 326.
Righteousness, the divine, in Osiander's theology, 106 f.; in Paulinism, 142 f.
Ritschl, on reconciliation, 2, 6-7, 28, 115 f.; his definition of love, 61; on the presupposition of reconciliation, 186; on sins of ignorance, 222; on the Kingdom of God, 230.
Rivière, Abbé, 28; on Origen, 34; on the hypostatic union, 240 f.; on the sufferings of Christ, 49, 263 f.

SACRAMENTS, mediæval idea of, 91, 108; in relation to reconciliation, 314 f.
Sacrifice, religious category of, 29 f., 55 f.; as applied to death of Christ, 160 f.
Sanctification. *See* under Justification.
Sanday and Headlam, quoted, 137, 151, 153.
Satan. *See under* Devil.
Satisfaction, as employed by Tertullian, 46 f., 67; by Augustine, 58; by Anselm, 69 f., 76 f.; by Aquinas, 87 f., 89 f.; by Protestant theology, 93 f.; by Grotius, 110 f.; meaning of term, 48; ambiguity of term, 48, 76 f.; and punishment, 87, 94; made by Christ to God, 102 f., 161 f.
Saviour, Grotius' conception of Christ as, 98; Christ as, 116.
Schleiermacher, on the church, 116 f.; on the preparation for Christianity, 125; on the incarnation, 183.
Seneca, quoted, 30.
Servant, the suffering, 139.
Shakespeare, quoted, 205.
Sin, twofold effect of, 52; the problem of, 67 f., 159; seriousness of, 73 f.; in relation to human nature, 147 f.; sense of, 189 f., 324 f.; responsibility for, 191 f.; divine reaction against, 203 f.; Biblical doctrine of, 210 f.; followed by death, 209,

INDEX

229 f., 275 f.; not inevitable, 248 f.; divine condemnation of, 248 f., 270 f.; pardonable and unpardonable, 218 f.; definition of, 223; attitude of Jesus to, 258 f.; consequences of, 224 f., 325 f.
Socinus, theology of, 97 f., 108.
Son of Man, 138 f.
Spinoza, 3, 183.
Spirit, doctrine of the Holy, 166, 169, 307 f.
Stade, quoted, 122.
Strauss, 104.
Substitute, Christ as our, 106, 118, 282.
Suffering, in relation to sin, 212 f.; of Christ, 112.
Supper, the Lord's, 140, 320 f.
Supplicium, 78.

TERTULLIAN, on atonement, 44 f., 51, 58.
Testament, the New, value of, 8-9, 26 f.; religious ideas of, 121 f., 283 f., 287; unity of, 122 f.
Testament, the Old, 122 f.
Theology, irrelevant speculations of Catholic, 241 f., 264-266, 297 f.; defects of Protestant, 92, 109 f., 296 f.
Thomasius, 44, 90.
Time and eternity, 168-169.
Tradition, function of Christian, 18-20, 323.
Trent, the Council of, on the sacraments, 91, 217; on justification, 93 f., 96, 298.
Tröltsch, quoted, 8.

UNION, of Christ and His people, 52 f., 88 f., 119, 173, 305; of Christians and Christ, 304 f.

VICARIOUSNESS, 90, 118.
Virgil, quoted, 2.

WESTMINSTER CONFESSION, on free grace, 101; on human depravity, 199; on salvation of infants, 217.
White, Douglas, quoted, 16.
Wordsworth quoted, 202 f., 205 f., 279.
Wrath of God, real and objective, 142 f.; how far eschatological, 146 f., 227 f.

ZACCHÆUS, 14 f.

· (2) TEXTS

(Those specially discussed are marked with an asterisk)

	PAGE
Genesis	
iii. 1 f.,	41, 210-211
Leviticus	
xxvi. 41,	227, 325
Numbers	
xv. 22 f.,	220
1 Samuel	
iii. 14,	219
Nehemiah	
viii. 10,	309
Psalms	
lxxiii. 23-24,	331-332
ciii. 10,	225
cxxxix. 1 f.,	188*
Isaiah	
xxii. 12 f.,	219-220
liii. 12,	139
Jeremiah	
xviii.-xix.,	219
xxiii. 6,	107
xxxi. 31 f.,	140
Joel	
ii. 25,	225
Micah	
vii. 18,	22
Wisdom of Solomon	
xvi. 24,	212
Matthew	
vi. 12,	133*
viii. 17,	255*
xi. 27 f.,	10, 138
xii. 41,	249
xviii. 15 f.,	134 f.
xviii. 23 f.,	136 f.*
xxvi. 28,	140*

THE CHRISTIAN DOCTRINE OF RECONCILIATION

	PAGE
Mark	
ii. 5, 11,	225
ii. 17,	253 f.
iii. 28-30,	221
x. 45,	141, 254
xv. 34,	58
Luke	
vii. 36-50,	13-14,* 132
vii. 41 f.,	132 f.
xv. 10 f.,	135
xix. 1-10,	14-15,* 254
xxiii. 28,	18, 130
xxiii. 34,	18, 130, 220
xxiii. 43,	18, 130
John	
i. 29,	175 f., 130
iii. 5,	318
iv. 6,	17
v. 14,	213
ix. 2,	213*
xv. 13,	79
xviii. 8,	18
Acts	
ii. 11,	308
ii. 38,	318
iii. 15,	249*
iii 17,	220
v. 31,	249
viii. 14 f.,	318
xix. 2 f.,	318
xxii. 16,	315
Romans	
i. 16 f.,	142 f.,* 287
i. 28,	144, 190
i. 32,	144, 146, 277
iii. 5,	146
iii. 19,	147
iii. 21 f.,	149 f.,* 152 f.,* 165, 287
v. 1 f.,	124, 168, 294
v. 3,	178
v. 5,	309
v. 9,	227
v. 11,	141, 239, 290
v. 12 f.,	200, 210
v. 18,	297
vi. 1 f.,	246, 281, 314 f.*
vi. 6,	316
vi. 10,	246-247*
vi. 11,	317
vi. 21,	277
vi. 23,	202
vii. 9,	276*
vii. 24,	124, 148, 196
viii. 1,	168

	PAGE
Romans	
viii. 3 f.,	247 f.*
viii. 9-11,	311
viii. 28,	177
viii. 32,	179
viii. 33 f.,	285, 294, 330
viii. 38 f.,	178, 294, 330 f.
1 Corinthians	
i. 18,	287
ii. 15,	324
iii. 21,	177
vi. 11,	315
vii. 23,	323
ix. 24-27,	293
x. 1 f.,	320*
xii 1-3,	311
xiv. 16,	308
xv. 3 f.,	122 f, 171
xv. 44-49,	200
xv. 49,	331*
xv. 53,	43
2 Corinthians	
v. 17,	288
v. 18-20,	141
v. 20,	239
v. 21,	243
Galatians	
ii. 20,	99, 166, 297, 302 f., 307
iii. 1,	18
iii. 13,	167
v. 5,	169*
vi. 7,	225
vi. 15,	288
Ephesians	
ii. 14 f.,	177
Philippians	
iv. 11,	178
Colossians	
i. 16,	182
i. 20,	177
i. 20-22,	141 f., 327
i. 24,	326
1 Thessalonians	
i. 1,	176
i. 6,	309
i. 10,	227
1 Timothy	
ii. 5,	55
vi. 19,	187
Titus	
iii. 5,	318
Hebrews	
i. 1,	27

INDEX

	PAGE
Hebrews	
ii. 10,	249
ii. 11,	71
ii. 14,	173*
vi. 4-6,	221
x. 28 f.,	222
xii. 2,	249
1 Peter	
iii. 17 f.,	171 f*
2 Peter	
iii. 9,	228

	PAGE
1 John	
ii. 2,	175
ii. 28,	294
iii. 1,	231
iii. 16,	326
iv. 10,	175, 280
iv. 17,	294
v. 16 f.,	222*
Revelation	
i. 5-6,	133